Karoline Bauer

Memoirs of Karoline Bauer

from the German, Vol. 4

Karoline Bauer

Memoirs of Karoline Bauer
from the German, Vol. 4

ISBN/EAN: 9783744648370

Printed in Europe, USA, Canada, Australia, Japan

Cover: Foto ©ninafisch / pixelio.de

More available books at **www.hansebooks.com**

MEMOIRS

OF

KAROLINE BAUER

From the German.

IN FOUR VOLUMES.

VOL. IV.

———

London:
REMINGTON AND CO., PUBLISHERS,
HENRIETTA STREET, COVENT GARDEN.
1885.
[*All Rights Reserved.*]

CHAPTER I.

VIENNA.

Preparations for Performances at the Burg Theatre—Karoline Müller—Frau von Weiszenthurn the Authoress—Qualified Success—Pauli—The Power of Dress and of Coquetry—To Hungary—Pressburg—Linz—Brünn—Prague—Dresden—Devrient—Julie Rettich—Hofrath Böttger—Tieck—Hofrath Winkler—Baron Sternberg—Baron Gotthilf August von Maltitz—Tiedge—Cagliostro—A Sad Spring-scented Memorial.

So the time went on till one day we found ourselves once more re-installed, hale and hearty, in the neat "Erzherzog Karl," in Vienna; now the preparations for my starring engagement could begin. In the first place I called on the artistes of the Burg Theatre.

I was received very kindly by all, even by Karoline Müller, with whom I had had an encounter at the Königstadt Theatre nine years ago, which had cost me many tears. Now we laughed heartily at these old rival-skirmishes, on account of my beloved Countess Elsbeth in the "Tournier von Kronstadt," and her still more beloved blind theatrical grey horse.

"Now," she said, "you yourself will allow that I could not let you have the beloved grey horse, won't you? Self-preservation is the first duty of an artiste!"

I purposed to *début* as "Suschen," because I had achieved in this very *rôle* the most brilliant successes, even upon the desolate drill-ground of the Pesth Theatre.

"Not brilliant enough for Vienna—no toilet-effects!" Karoline Müller said doubtfully.

I had reason afterwards to rue not having followed the advice of her who had such experience of the world, and in particular of Vienna.

From a visit I paid to Frau von Weiszenthurn, to whose very pretty pieces, such as Pauline, Baroness Waldbüll, Julie in "Beschämte Eifersucht," &c., &c., I owed so many handsome successes, I promised myself some pleasure. She lived in a charming villa in one of the suburbs of Vienna, in very comfortable circumstances. As the child of a Koblenz actor, Veronika Grünberg had played, together with her brothers and sisters as far back as the seventh and eight decade of last century, the juvenile comedies from Weisze's "Kinderfreund" (Children's Friend), now long forgotten. From the Court Theatre in München she came to the Burg Theatre in Vienna in the year 1790, married Herr von Weiszenthurn, and played for many years—a naughty world even said for too many years—the parts of first lovers. Even now, despite her successes as a comedy-writer, and in spite of her 61 years, she still acted elderly character-*rôles*.

Frau von Weiszenthurn received me awfully elegiacally. Her very welcome and request—"Dear Fräulein, will you not take a seat?" sounded like Thekla's sad: "What is life without the gem of love?" and was followed up by: "I am glad that you are pleased with Vienna . . ." which sounded like Desdemona's song of the willow.

When Frau von Weiszenthurn eventually asked me to drink a cup of coffee with her she almost melted in " sadness and delight."

To complete the portrait, friend Witthauer told me a little story about the sentimentality of Frau von Weiszenthurn, which was universally-known and even in the most ordinary matters most transcendent.

It was raining heavily, and Frau von Weiszenthurn, with a graceful stork-step, her clothes well tucked up, strides through the masses of water at the moat, pathetically balancing her umbrella. Unfortunately she has to pass a cab-stand.

"Cab, your honour?" the first cabby asks.

"Thank you, my friend, I have got an umbrella!" Frau von Weiszenthurn replies languidly, turning up her eyes and umbrella pathetically, as if she declaimed with Johanna: "The pain is short, but joy is everlasting."

The driver looks at her speechless. No. 2 repeats the ordinary cabby-question: "Cab, your honour?"

Without tiring, Frau von Weiszenthurn replies— "Thank you, my friend, I have got an umbrella!" only by a few tones more languidly still, and with an elegiac turning-up of her eyes and umbrella in the comparative, something like Gretchen's: "Ach neige—Du Schmerzenreiche—Dein Antlitz gnädig meiner Noth!"

But then burst forth the well-known wittiness of the frolicsome Viennese cab-drivers, and No. 2 breathed in a still more elegiac way in his Sunday high German—

"But, good gracious, your honour; why such a meek behaviour?"

"Who would ask such a silly question, Tonerl. Do you not hear: she has a 'schirm!'" (umbrella, screen, protection). That is the classical answer of cabby No. 1.

That is the signal, and it goes from *fiacre* to *fiacre*.

"Do you not hear, Tonerl; she has a 'schirm.' . . ."

"No, no! we will not drive; she has a 'schirm.' . . ."

Frau von Weiszenthurn says no more; she only sighs softly to herself, slips past as quickly as possible, and only from time to time casts a glance at the band of Korah, as if she swallowed the words: "Ich achte keinen Mann mehr!" (I esteem no man now!)

The Viennese received me kindly in my part of Suschen, but nevertheless as if they were a little disappointed. My "Madame Danville," which I had studied in Paris after the pattern of Mdlle. Mars, pleased less still. My Danville was considered too measured, not piquant and pointed enough. But the good Viennese thought it particularly unpardonable that Madame Danville ventured to appear before them in the same ball-costume, though a delightfully beautiful and certainly terribly expensive one, in which I had paraded at Baden in "Zwei Jahre verheirathet."

As the "well-brought-up young god-mother" and as "Margarethe" I scored gratifying successes, was applauded and called out, but I believe not by a pulse more warmly than a few days afterwards Karoline Müller's "angelic little hat" and "heavenly" new dress were received.

I sat in the pit to see "Die Folgen einer Missheirath," a piece I had not seen before. Pretty Peche gave the sentimental *rôle* with warm feeling, and a touching natural truthfulness, and looked exceedingly lovely in her simple dress of white muslin, as a poor sergeant's daughter. Not a hand moved, I only saw shrugging of shoulders and even heard: "How common! For such a thing one does not pay one's good money to be admitted into the Burg Theatre; such toilets one can see in hundreds in the 'Au' and the 'Prater' every Sunday."

Then Karoline Müller made her appearance in the second act, and was received with long-continued enthusiastic applause. "Well," thought I to myself, "she probably has a great and difficult part to perform."

Mais, point du tout! After some insignificant phrases she went away again rustling, and the dear audience were not satisfied till she presented herself ever anew. And I heard my neighbours who had so sharply criticized Peche a little while ago exclaim in ecstasy again and again: "Charming! Yes, Karoline Müller outshines all the rest; she is simply, overpowering. What an inventive talent!"

"What did she invent, pray?" I asked, still quite innocently. "Her part has as yet been very insignificant."

Then the stout Viennese lady looked at me with her big, round, fat eyes, in compassionate amazement, as if the terrible thought moved her heart. —Is the poor thing blind, or does she come from the backwoods of Poland?—Then from the hedge of her ingeniously made teeth there came forth an angry growl. " *Rôle* here, *rôle* there! what about that? Do you not see how charming is the effect of that clever combination of white and green in her dress? It reminds one of the Scottish tartan, but yet is much more original and piquant, and this new costume Karoline Müller invented. The day after to-morrow you will see it in the 'Prater' in the most diverse variations. And how enchantingly her toilet is matched by the delicate little hat with the moss-roses, a veritable model of fashion!"

" Ah, ay!" I said to myself with an angry sigh. " I forgot that we are in the fashion-period at the Burg Theatre at present."

Afterwards, when I came to Vienna for a second series of performances, I was thoughtless enough to accept battle with Karoline Müller also in the *toilette*. I appeared on eleven different occasions, and received for each performance 20 ducats, *then* a prodigious fee, *now-a-days* a mere trifle. The whole of this fee I sacrificed, with a heavy heart, to the Moloch of fashion, Behr, whose fabulous reputation had awfully increased with the credulous Ammonites of Vienna. Herr von Behr accepted my modest sacrifice with a gracious smile, and promised to adorn me "divinely." And all the Ammonites flocked in endless streams, night after night, to the temple of the Burg Theatre, and did homage to me *i.e.*, to the work of their great idol, Behr, with the full vigour of their hands and feet.

The greatest *furore* we—namely, Herr von Behr in the first, and Karoline Bauer in the second place—made as "Maria; oder Die drei Epochen." First of all the enraptured Viennese were introduced to a young lady in a charming poetic-ethereal costume, then to the same Maria as bride in a fairy-like ball toilet, and at last to the young widow Maria in a siren-like, infatuating pomp awaiting her second suitor.

A similar success "we" had in the "Ball zu Ellerbrunn," and in "Bürgerlich und romantisch" by Bauernfeld.

Such successes made me wanton, imprudent—and in spite of all well-meaning warnings I went into the snare . . . and I congratulate myself this day that I got off so cheaply.

Along with me there starred in the Burg Theatre, in 1837, my excellent Dresden brother-artiste, Pauli, who was greatly esteemed and liked in the Elbe-Florence. We had often played together in Albini's comedy, "Die gefährliche Tante," and achieved great successes. Indeed, I only know of one more "Freiherr von Emmerling," who put Pauli's excellent and masterly delineation of this character into the shade, and that was Theodor Döring.

Thus it happened that Pauli and I arranged between us, when in Dresden, that we would appear together on the stage of the Burg Theatre in the "Gefährliche Tante." I got the special permission from the manager-general in Dresden to take with me my beautiful, genuine aunt-costume of last century. A dress of heavy brown satin with yellow stripes, embroidered with flowers; along with it a huge white cap piled up to a tower.

Pauli made his *début* as Iago in "Othello," and was called after every act. "Master" Anschütz was an unsurpassable Othello, and Julie Rettich, who had accepted a life-engagement at the Burg Theatre a year before, charmed and moved wonderfully as Desdemona.

Everything promised well. Count Fürstenberg, the successor to Count Czernin in the office of intendant, gave a cosy little artiste-dinner in honour of the two guests from Dresden, and Pauli and I were highly delighted. The intendant, a friendly, courteous gentleman of about 40, made an agreeable host up to the dessert, when he suddenly dropped into a strange frankness, *à la* Princess Melanie Metternich.

A guest inquired about our approaching performance of the " Gefährliche Tante " . . .

" Oh, our Karoline Müller and Wilhelmi are unsurpassable, unrivalled as the 'dangerous aunt' and as 'Emmerling,' " the intendant thought aloud all of a sudden.

Pauli's eyes flashed like lightning, and about the corners of his mouth there played a bitter, sarcastic smile.

I endeavoured to start a new subject of conversation. In vain! His Excellency went on to "think" with more and more animation.

" What stage would compare with the Burg Theatre? Our artistes are the most brilliant, the only true stars on the theatrical horizon of the present. . . ."

" But, your Excellency, why then are the members of other stages so often invited to play at the Burg Theatre?" Pauli said, not without acrimony.

" In order to become acquainted with other talents too," his Excellency said, perplexed, and adroitly gave the signal for the clearing of the table.

During the rehearsal of the " Gefährliche Tante," Fräulein Reichel, who played the chambermaid, said to me —

"I hope you will appear in the costly cloak of red velvet, trimmed with real ermine, like Karoline Müller. It is a splendid match to the white satin dress!"

"No, I shall endeavour to appear like Adele Müller, who is engaged at a small provincial theatre, and is not likely to possess an ermine cloak!"

"Then you will not be received with applause on your appearing on the stage as Karoline Müller always is."

"But Adele Müller would have had to sacrifice more than a whole year's wages for such a costly cloak, you know, and yet she is but an actress, and has to keep her poor family."

Fräulein Reichel shrugged her shoulders, saying —

"Our public does not mind that!"

After the rehearsal, Weber, the good old hair-dresser of the theatre, stepped up to me officiously.

"Mein Fräulein," he said, "a word of the greatest significance. . . . How shall I arrange the little curls for the 'dangerous little aunt?'"

"Not at all, good Weber. I have brought with me my Dresden grey wig, well packed away. All is in first rate trim."

"Grey wig beneath the delicate lace cap?" he cried, horrified.

"No, no little lace cap, but an honest, old-fashioned, sturdy, great granny cap!"

"But will not that look dreadful along with the white satin dress with the long train?"

"Oh, keep your mind quite easy, good Weber; the cap is excellently suited to my hundred-year-old brown dress with yellow stripes."

"Brown, with yellow stripes?—a hundred years old—grey wig—great granny cap.—I am thunderstruck!" the little fidgety old man exclaimed. "And Fräulein Karoline Müller looks particularly well as 'aunt,' so beautiful and dainty, like a sugar-plum that you could just eat."

"But, my good Weber, the 'dangerous aunt,' you ought to know, must not look like a sugar-plum that you could just eat. She is, on the contrary, to inspire confidence in the obstinate Emmerling by a right venerable aunt-like appearance. . . ."

"True—only too true," the old man continued, plaintively. "But of what use is to us the 'venerable' if we make fiasco with it—a dreadful fiasco? . . . Watch what comes of it!"

All this ominous clamour had indeed caused my courage to sink greatly. During the hair-dressing operations for the first act Weber sighed quite piteously, and conjured me to send at once for the red velvet cloak trimmed with ermine. But I remained firm, even when the other ladies of the cast stared at my aunt-costume as Mrs. Lot did before she turned into a pillar of salt.

Pauli was the first to enter the stage—not a hand moved. I followed in a grey cloak. . . . Stillness of death! Thereupon a dismally increasing a-a-ah of disappointment, which, to my indeed somewhat spoiled artiste-ear, sounded like the tones from the last trumpet on doomsday. But I collected myself and bravely continued my part. The pretty scene with the chambermaid gave me an opportunity to introduce a nice little touch. I changed a few words.

When I presented myself to my admirers in a charming costly *négligée*, this bran-new prodigy of the magician Behr was greeted with due applause. The chief moment approached. With a beating heart, and accompanied by copious sighs on the part of Weber, I put my luckless cap on my grey wig, slipped into the ancient brown dress with yellow stripes of a hundred years ago . . . and the death-stillness that received me was, if possible, more profound than before, and the a-a-a-ah of disappointment rose to the sound of a trombone.

Pauli had lost his head completely—and did not find it again that evening. Only when we put little Marie carefully, tenderly to bed . . . softly—gently . . . not to waken the beloved child . . . then the heart of the Viennese grew warm, and their hands and mouths rewarded the efforts of the poor Dresden guests by applause and recall.

Weber stood as if relieved of a nightmare, and even squeezed my hand heartily, which, from respect for me, he had never ventured to do before, whispering: "You may congratulate yourself—I should never have believed that all would end so well—with such a dress and such a monster of a cap, and such miserable grey curls. . . . How you would have succeeded if you had decked yourself like . . ."

"Like a sugar-plum that you could just eat!" I interrupted him with a laugh. But at bottom I did not at all feel disposed for laughter, and at the conclusion, when Emmerling, seeing the aunt's costume lying on the floor, said: "Thank goodness, there lies the aunt!" then a perfect fury at the brown dress with yellow stripes once so beloved, came over me, and the head-dress also experienced it when I threw it into the band-box.

Afterwards, when I sat in the pit-stalls, my cheeks flushed, and my heart beat with expectation to see Karoline Müller as the "dangerous aunt," and the "sugar-plum," really ravishingly beautiful in her mantlet of purple velvet trimmed with ermine, and Spanish hat with plume—and again in a dress of white satin with train, richly ornamented with lace, and in a charming lace head-dress, *à la* Maintenon, and coquettish little curls — received by an almost mad outburst of applause of the house. . . .

* * * * * *

And once more I was to proceed to Hungary from Vienna on a starring expedition. My colleague Korn, who annually gave a performance for charitable purposes in Pressburg, and, in recognition of this, had been made an honorary burgess by the municipality of that ancient Hungarian coronation-town, requested me to appear together with him at Pressburg, in "Menschenhass and Reue," as Eulalie and Meinau! At the same time I was to be introduced to a genuine Hungarian autumnal festival in the vineyard of the burgomaster of Pressburg. Of course I agreed to accompany him thither.

On the way I asked Korn: "My dear colleague, tell me frankly, without the least reserve, why I, who am younger and more blooming than your seven actresses who play first parts, and, I may presume, not less able, why I, in spite of my best efforts, have not achieved greater successes at the Burg Theatre?"

Then he smiled archly: "You are not cunning and coquettish enough for us Viennese, and do not understand to place yourself always and everywhere in the most brilliant light. Moreover, you take too little trouble to win friends and patrons among our fashionable, influential cavaliers. On the contrary, our young counts and princes think you much too prudish and reserved. You must have hurt many a blue-blood heart. And that is not the way to play at the Burg with impunity."

I listened perfectly dumbfounded. Then I could not help thinking of those young, bare-faced cavaliers, who made me, so to say, run the gauntlet each time I passed through the corridors on leaving the theatre, twisting their moustaches, whirring impertinently: "Mein Fräulein, my carriage—a supper awaits you. I should like to become your friend." And on my hastening past them proudly, I heard them say, in their charming Viennese jargon: "She puts on confoundedly aristocratic airs! but a skin she has—the whitest, softest, most tempting skin in the world."

There was the clue! Korn continued: "Let us add to this, that the love of the Viennese for their resident artistes is of a touching constancy. They hardly notice that we gradually grow old with them. Were you not surprised that we old fellows, Ludwig Löwe and I—whose combined ages amount to almost a hundred years—still played with you the parts of youthful lovers? No stranger disciple of Thalia can rise beside us—and if Fichtner were not a native of Vienna . . . I declare you would have had to play 'the young god-mother' with me!"

I could not help laughing when I heard this. Besides, it just occurred to me that Vienna's " unsurpassable Korn" had but very moderately pleased the public during a series of performances he gave in Berlin in 1825, although Mad. Stich was greatly taken with him and fought for him. The Berliners thought their Rebenstein more feeling, and their P. A. Wolff more intellectual and ideal, and Korn's voice husky and his visage insignificant, and could not understand how this man of forty and upwards could still be the much-coveted Adonis of the youngest and most beautiful of the Vienna fair, and be overwhelmed with love-letters and rendezvous.

I found it impossible to understand *that* in Vienna either. But I must acknowledge that Korn was the most discreet Adonis! He never spoke of his romantic adventures, although this was *bon ton* in Vienna.

Such conversation about art and the stage shortened the monotonous way to Pressburg.. At four o'clock in the afternoon our coach stopped in front of the stately official residence of the mayor of the ancient Hungarian coronation-town. The exceedingly handsome son of the house did the honours of the house to us in a cavalier-like way—and soon made his court to me with the true fire of the Magyars. I see him still, in his handsome, becoming national dress, driving the team of four wild greys that drew us in a gallop out to the festival in the vineyard of his parents—I there see myself, high above the glittering Danube, dancing to the sounds of the stormy gipsy music, or turning in the intoxicating Czardas with the handsome, enamoured young Maurus amidst fizzing rockets and firewheels, a dance which I had just learned from him while laughing and jesting. . . . Was it the fiery Tokay which made my heart and head feel so oppressed? Was it the flaming kiss which Maurus imprinted upon my arm when he suddenly knelt before me in the Czardas? . . . I could not be angry with him.

During supper Korn declaimed Kastelli's "Nichts und Etwas," and I recited the significant "Na!"—which my Breslau friend, August Kahlert, had once composed for me as a pendant to Saphir's "Na!" and young Maurus never tired of cooing to me and repeating this "Na!" in all keys.

Next morning I saw a young Magyar buried by his friends, who had formed into a solemn procession. A thrilling sight: these handsome, blooming youths, in their dark national dress, bearing torches in their hands, sadness in their eyes. Maurus also was among them.

In the evening we played "Menschenhass und Reue" with great success; here we could emphasize more than was permitted at the Burg Theatre. During the parting-scene acted between Minau and Eulalie there was such universal weeping, that one might have cried: *Aux parapluies!*—as was done during the performance of the piece in Paris with Mdlle. Mars as Eulalie. At the conclusion Korn, for the first time, called me "Dearest sister in art!" Maurus, with his four greys, drove home in triumph, and afterwards accompanied us a long, long distance on horseback when we started on our nightly return-journey to Vienna. When he kissed my hand for the last time, the good moon could have seen a tear glittering in his eyes and mine. We never met again.

* * * * * *

After two short engagements in Linz and Brünn, and after a very fatiguing journey by Prague, we alighted in the Hôtel de Saxe in Dresden, about the middle of October, 1834. My joy was great when, on examining the theatre-bill, I found that Raupach's "Tasso's Tod" was to be given, with Emil Devrient and Julie Rettich in the cast.

My heart beat with impatience, and as early as half-past five I sat with my mother in a small private box of the small, ugly, old, theatrical temple.

It looked like an enormous pie turned upside down, and had a melancholy, dull green colour, and not a trace of luxury. Moreover, the house was but poorly lighted.

The audience took their seats noiselessly, and appeared in simple dress without show. There were wanting the brilliant uniforms of St. Petersburg, the elegant ladies of Vienna, the beautiful princes and princesses of Berlin in the royal boxes. But how I felt drawn towards this audience during the performance ; they sat there perfectly quiet, and listened with a devout attention. The applause was not excessive. Only now and then, when particularly thrilling passages occurred, it broke forth with great heartiness.

But what an ideally beautiful, lofty Tasso was Emil Devrient! and what a thrilling Leonore was the classical Julie Rettich, with her expressive Southern features! Porth was an imposing Duke Antonio, and hoary Werdi a venerable monk.

I went home with the burning desire to find a lasting engagement on this stage, and beside such a mime! And mother went on repeating : " Ach, Lina, if only I could see you play Donna Diana together with Emil Devrient ! "

The first visit I paid next morning was at the house of the celebrated art-historian, Hofrath Böttger, who had been a rector of a " gymnasium," and critic in Weimar in Goethe's time. He presented the picture of a happy old man, with good-natured features, a perpetual smile upon his lips, and small bright eyes, which looked intelligent, sometimes inquiring, but which during a conversation were, as a rule, half-closed ; then the stout old gentleman looked strikingly like a purring cat. Böttger was at that time already 70 years old.

"Have you been at Tieck's already?" was one of his first questions on hearing that I would accept an engagement in Dresden with much pleasure.

"No, I intended to ask Hofrath Winkler (Theodor Hell), whose acquaintance I made in Berlin, to introduce me to Tieck!"

Then the old gentleman put on a curious face, which I only understood afterwards. But he said harmlessly —

"Circumstances are very favourable to your wishes at present. Fräulein Rettich will not remain in Dresden; her husband cannot take Karl Devrient's place, the public treat him with an icy coldness, and his friendship with Tieck has ceased likewise. He does not praise her any more!"

"His once beloved pupil? How is that possible?"

"Hum! The pupil has grown independent, is no longer an intellectual slave, cannot afford to hear the 'master' read two or three times a week. . . . So the 'dramaturg' will do his utmost to secure you for our stage; firstly, because you are an excellent successor to Rettich—and then from revenge against Rettich. Whosoever offends Tieck's self-love is banished! So you had better be politic, dear miss! Tieck can be enchantingly amiable, and he reads aloud in an unsurpassed manner. You may learn a good deal from him. Moreover, you will meet in his house interesting personages. All distinguished strangers that come to Dresden pay him their respects, and his wife and daughter are truly lovable creatures. Seek to win the friendship of Dorothea, his eldest daughter; she is a girl of rare talents, and very good heart. But you must be especially polite to Countess Finkenstein.

"Who is that? Tell me," I asked, curiously.

"Tieck's—friend. This peculiar relationship has been in existence for many years. You will soon see through it yourself. I am exceedingly sorry not to be able to introduce you to Tieck, but I have fallen out with the Hofrath . . ."

"Rettich has fallen out with him—and you, too?"

Böttger smiled quite friendly, saying—

"Ja wohl, as many others! You will soon find that out. But I hope that we shall, nevertheless, remain friends. Tieck does not need to know it, of course."

Hofrath Böttger had gained in Dresden for himself the nickname of "The reconciling principle," because he honestly strove to say nothing but pleasant things to everybody! The following rare anecdote was related of him: When Sophie Schröder played the part of Phædra in Dresden, Böttger sat in the pit clapping his hands furiously—turning round at the same time and whispering to Mad. Hartwig, the Phædra of the Dresdeners, who sat behind him: " Still no Hartwig! No, no Hartwig."

Owing to this weakness of flattery Goethe called poor Böttger an ubique-nature, and Tieck has terribly lashed the Herr Hofrath in his " De gestiefelt Kater"—for which Böttger revenged himself bitterly in his "Denkwürdigkeiten." He died as early as November, 1835.

From Hofrath Böttger I went to Hofrath Winkler, editor of the Abendzeitung, who, as a skilful translator of the most popular French plays, was known by the pseudonym of " Theodor Hell." He lived at the Altmarkt, in a corner house, opposite Hofrath Tieck. Of course I was in the city of the much-mocked " Hofräthe."

The beautiful Frau Hofräthin received me in the politest way possible. She had heard already that I had been at the theatre and listened very attentively, that my mother looked so mild and aristocratic, nay, even that I had worn a charming little hat with white roses.

I was forced to smile at the dear " provincial" Dresden. Then the Hofrath entered and welcomed me in such a homely way, as if we had but yesterday dined together gaily with Clauren in Berlin, or in the Turkish tent in Charlottenburg. He went on with great volubility to speak in the Saxon dialect—

"Aye! my dear miss, it is truly lucky that you are come to visit our town just at this time. I will announce you to his Excellency the intendant this very day, for I hope you will become one of us, and appear with pleasure in my translations from the French. But you must soon call on Tieck. But who will conduct and introduce you to the Herr Hofrath? It is really unfortunate that I have just fallen out a little with him."

"You likewise?" I cried, really alarmed. "You are the third already who, as I hear this morning, has fallen out with Tieck—first Mad. Rettich—then Hofrath Böttger, and . . ."

"And many, many more," he said, laughing. "Emil Devrient, Pauli, Werdi do not attend Tieck's readings any more either—and that is always the surest sign that the old dramaturg is angry—and that his favourites are tired of his everlasting readings. But of that more by-and-bye."

Winkler, then almost sixty, had, since he left Berlin, turned almost uglier still. But this ugliness one forgot readily over his gay amiableness. He regarded everything in a rose-coloured light, and was a self-sacrificing friend and patron to young talent.

The manager-general of the theatre, Herr von

Lüttichau, was much superior to the intendant of Vienna and St. Petersburg He spoke with a kind of dignified pride of his institute, and I liked that. He showed an appreciation of true art, and a warm heart for his task and his artistes. When, however, we approached the terms of the starring engagement, and his Excellency spoke of 30 thalers per evening . . . then I stood somewhat amazed, for such a honorarium I had not been offered as yet, even by any of the provincial stages. I said somewhat pertly —

"Your Excellency seems to look upon your Dresden stage as such a lofty institute that stranger-artistes should deem it a very fortunate thing to be allowed to play upon it only for the honour of it!"

The fine courtier blushed, and answered with dignity —

"Mention to me a second Emil Devrient, a Wilhelmine Schröder, a Doris Devrient; Julie Rettich you have admired—Pauli, Porth, Werdi you will come to esteem. What town is there that has a dramaturg of Tieck's importance? You will have to confess that I may be proud of our stage!"

Now it was my turn to blush. I promised to make my appearance for a series of performances in Dresden in the coming spring.

Arrived at our lodgings, I met an old friend of

ours from Karlsruhe, Baron Sternberg, author of the novel "Bühne, Kunst, Liebe." His daughter was an early playmate of mine. Having been formerly intendant of the excellent theatre in Mannheim, he still took an interest in the stage. I used to read to him in Karlsruhe from time to time. He was quite angry with me once when I read Marianne in Goethe's "Geschwister" so coldly; especially: "Wilhelm, was war das für ein Kuss?" Nor was I ever very successful with these words afterwards.

Sternberg promised to introduce me to the dramaturg. Here, then, was at last one who had not fallen out with Tieck.

At the *table d'hôte* we met a dear friend from the time of my Berlin engagement—Baron Gotthilf August von Maltitz, who had been obliged to quit Berlin owing to his harmless philo-Polish play, "Der alter Student."

After a short stay in Hamburg he had settled in Dresden. He proved outwardly and inwardly unchanged. His wit was so cutting and sharp, and his fire consuming, but a pure flame. The expressive head, with the penetrating eyes, rested upon a mean crippled form, and in the heat of conversation he would throw his long, long arms through the air just as of yore. The world was less and less to his taste, he assured us seriously; but suddenly his features brightened up, and his gay laughter, which had so taken my fancy in Berlin, carried me away. His old honest good heart had also remained to him. He spoke with a loving enthusiasm of Tiedge, the poet of the " Urania."

" Is it not elevating," he cried, in his enthusiastic manner, " that an old man of eighty could express his sympathy for Poland in a poem with the full glow of his heart? You must make his acquaintance."

Next day Maltitz came for me to introduce me to Tiedge. On the way there he spoke with much affection of the strange friendly union which bound the composer of " Urania " for so many long years to the Baroness von der Recke, till she had died in Dresden in the spring of 1833. " But even beyond the grave, which at her request she found in the motherly bosom of the earth without a coffin, only wrapped in winding sheets, her anxious friendship for the revered poet reached. She not only bequeathed to him her whole large fortune, but also made such arrangements that Tiedge, in the cheerful old garden-house on the Elbe, and quite in his wonted way, as if Elisa was still with him, can bring the evening of his life to a peaceful close. Always an old friend, of either sex, is with him, who nurses him, and on birthdays, and other festive occasions, gets up small parties—just as in Elisa's lifetime."

Thus I found the old house, and in an old-fashioned, cheery room a company of very aged, world-forgotten ladies and gentlemen; and in a quaint dressing-gown of yellow stuff, with red tulips, seated in an armchair, I found the poet, then 82 years old, in his hand a long pipe, which he smoked constantly. He was about to rise, but I held him back in his chair with gentle pressure, and kissed his hand much moved, and looked up to his good, kind old face, and his mild, child-like, brown eyes.

I felt as if I was in a fairy-dream. It was solemnly still in the room; only the clock on the wall softly said its tick! tick! and the shadow from the foliage of the trees in front of the window played upon the flooring and on the walls, upon the portraits of his dead Elisa and the departed early friends: Göcking, Gleim, Clamer-Schmidt, Hölty, Voss, Bürger, and the two Stolbergs . . . and upon the dusty wax-figure faces of the old-fashioned gentlemen and the old, yellowed ladies in their narrow wedge-frocks, with broad girdles and large buckles, with tiny silvery locks under huge white head-dresses, and with faded smiles and colourless eyes.

It made an impression as if the angel of death had forgotten the whole of the company below here.

Not before, at Tiedge's request, I commenced relating something of my stage experience, of my engagements in Berlin and St. Petersburg, and my starring in Riga, Mitau, Vienna, and other towns which the poet had once visited as travelling companion of his Elisa, and when, little by little, I found again my old sparkling vivacity and treated them to all kinds of jolly adventures and theatrical anecdotes, came some life into this company of shades, although all started when my spoon would come a little into audible contact with the delicate little cup of Meissen porcelain. Even the whiteheaded old servant who handed round the coffee walked about as if on velvet soles. This habit dated from the lifetime of the departed Elisa, who was a great sufferer from nervous headache.

Tiedge was the liveliest of them, and showed a particular interest in my three years' stay at St. Petersburg, where his Elisa had once lived, highly honoured at the Court of Katherine, and in my engagement in Mitau and my acquaintanceship with Count Medem. A native of Courland, Countess Elisabeth von Medem, and step-sister of the celebrated Duchess Dorothea of Courland, she had, when 17 years old, married Freiherr von der Recke. This luckless union, which was untied again after a duration of seven years, and the death of her beloved daughter and of her brother, Friedrich von Medem, who had with a touching affection reared and educated her, led the religious enthusiast into the arms of mysticism, which was then alarmingly in vogue. Unfortunately, she made the acquaintance of the juggler, Cagliostro, in Mitau, who initiated her into the mysteries of freemasons, caused her beloved dead to appear before her, and, in the most impudent way, plundered her purse. She was the most enthusiastic pupil of his teaching, till she saw the revered Grand Cophta, to her greatest regret, unmasked as—a common thief and swindler. With tact and dignity she met the many ugly rumours about her relations with the adventurer in a pamphlet, and this book caused such a sensation that Empress Katherine had it translated into Russian, and invited the authoress to her Court, and indemnified her for the robberies of Cagliostro by presenting her with an estate in Courland, where Elisa devoted her talent and time quite quietly to the up-bringing of poor girls . . . till her nervous state led her to travel in Germany, to which her ideal friendship for Tiedge bound her till her death.

The couple lived for a long time in the Castle of Löbichau, the celebrated possession of Duchess Dorothea, where also Jean Paul, Theodor Körner, Eberhard, Schink, Böttger, and other literateurs visited.

When the Duchess Dorothea died, in 1821,

Elisa led her poet to Dresden, and lived there at first in great style; but she is said to have caused poor Tiedge a goodly amount of torment by her loving kindness. Thus, for example, the unhappy man was obliged daily to swallow the most diverse mixtures and sedative powders from her hand to keep him from falling sick.

Tiedge said of his Elisa, "Never did a more beautiful soul inhabit a more beautiful body!"

During the talking and chatting Tiedge turned more and more lively and kindly, and the pressure of his hand was agreeably warm, as if we had known one another for years. But when I spoke of my approaching visit to Tieck, a dark cloud passed over his genial face, and the shadowy forms looked at me in sheer horror. Afterwards I learned more of the long-continued enmity between the two families of the poets and their adherents. Especially had the late Elisa and Countess Finkenstein, Tieck's Egeria, hated each other cordially, which hatred was kept on the increase by all kinds of town-talk and story-carrying. Tieck always smiled very ironically when the talk turned upon Tiedge, Elisa, and their followers: "Yes, those are the pious—we the impious!"

When, on leaving, Tiedge asked me very heartily to be sure to call again very soon and very often, adding that this day had appeared to him like a laughing May-day of his own beautiful golden youth, the dusty, world-forgotten shadows chimed in with alacrity.

"What a happy, sunny evening of a life!" Maltitz said, as we went home. "Happy he who can await his approaching setting-sun with so clear and peaceable a countenance! Tiedge will soon have finished his earthly pilgrimage—but we? God knows what struggles and storms are yet in store for us! You, happy creature, who with so little trouble succeeded in conjuring-up, in his declining autumn, sunny spring with merry sounds and fragrant blossoms! Would that you, too—we also one day, when all around us has grown still and lonely—may not want youth—gay, laughing, radiant youth, that understands us, and desires to show us some kindness. Let us often go out to see Tiedge again. And when, at last, you alone remain, then let, in the dream of your evening of life, a genial picture of the poor, odd Maltitz, and of this minute upon the Elbe-bridge in Dresden, pass before your mental eyes."

And many a time did we go out across the Elbe-bridge to the house of Tiedge . . . "You come like the 'Mädchen aus der Fremde,'" the amiable old man said, jokingly. Three years later I walked the road alone; Maltitz had died, scarcely 43 years old, willingly! He was not happy, despite the very best, the richest, and most loving heart, and despite his successes as author. He felt lonely and unappreciated in the world. Tiedge survived his younger friend by four years. The majority of the shadowy figures that formed his surroundings had faded away entirely when I laid a fresh flower-wreath upon the coffin of the old man of nearly 90 years of age.

That I did not forget that moment on the Elbe-bridge, that I did not forget the golden words of the noble Maltitz . . . this sad spring-scented memorial will prove.

* * * * * *

On my way to Ludwig Tieck's house at the Altmarkt my heart beat somewhat anxiously. How will the much-lauded and much-censured poet, the great dramaturg receive you, I said to myself. I felt that my stay in Dresden would depend on this first meeting.

It did by no means serve to calm me that Baron Sternberg, my companion, said to me on the road, concerning the enmity between Tieck and Winkler and Böttger —

"There had been a party at Tieck's house one evening. The centre of conversation was a young and talented painter who had just lately returned from Italy, who had brought with him a large portfolio full of sketches, and quite a bag full of merry stories, and adventures. Tieck went about like a growling lion, for he could not very well stand hearing another, even for a time, play 'first fiddle.' He has accustomed himself, and the incense-offering world has accustomed him, to have the 'solis' allotted to the first 'romanticist,' reader and dramatist of his time—to Herr Hofrath Tieck!"

"But on that evening even his growlings were taken little notice of. Especially the young, curious world, who are fond of a chat and laughter, found too much enjoyment in the robber-stories and robber-sketches of the artiste, among them two small water-colour drawings representing the robber savage, with a wild black beard, bloodthirsty eyes, and the bandit-bride, luxurious with red cheeks, burning eyes, and black locks.

"'What have you got there, dear?' said Böttger, who had been conversing with a strange professor in a window-niche, stepping nearer with his sweetest smile.

"'Two portraits,' said Winkler, in his jocular way, giving us a hint, which meant—Now wait, just let me alone; we shall have capital fun! 'Do you not recognize the originals, Herr Hofrath?'

"'Of course, of course I do; why should I not?' said good Böttger, who was very short-sighted, holding both pictures up close to his eyes. . . . 'This one, to be sure, is our revered Tieck, and this—ah!

what a charming likeness—is our dear Countess Finkenstein.'

"The burst of laughter that followed cannot be described, the whole company joined in it, and Tieck's nonplussed face showed that he did not know whether he should join in the laughter or be offended. At last he condescended to a compassionate, world-disdaining smile, and for the rest of the evening he did not get out of it again. But within him there was dreadful uproar! To confound him with an Italian desperado, and the poor old elegiac Countess Finkenstein with a bare-faced, sturdy robber-bride . . . that was too much for his dear vanity. Moreover, he believes even to this day that the whole affair had been slyly preconcerted by the wicked Theodor Hell in order to make a fool of him. And Tieck never forgives—remember that, my dear young lady!—I say Tieck never forgives an insult, or an act of neglect. He took his revenge of Winkler and Böttger in every possible way. Ay, soon there were published the most cutting lampoons on both sides."

That was the prologue of my first performance at Ludwig Tieck's house. Not without a beating heart did I enter the famous grey corner-house at the Altmarkt, and walk up the dark stair. We entered a spacious, somewhat gloomy saloon. At the same time the door of the adjoining room opened, and before me stood the celebrated poet in his frank, enchanting amiability.

Tieck was 61 years of age then, but in his appearance, and especially in his manners, he had something exceedingly fresh, gracefully youthful. He wore a long gown-like frock of black velvet, with wide sleeves, "à la Raphael," and a little scull-cap of the same material. In his brown locks there was not a single white hair to be seen. Only his form was bent by gout, and, so to say, collapsed. The black velvet set off advantageously the marble whiteness of his beautiful, nobly-chiselled face, with the large, deep brown eyes, which looked so clearly and sharply, and the alabaster-whiteness of his small well-kept hands. And well he understood how to enliven the conversation by a few graceful movements of his hand. An enchanting smile played around his delicately-cut, almost youthful, blooming mouth when he bade me welcome to Dresden with the purest North-German accent. "I have heard much about your talent that is nice and creditable," he said, "and I am looking forward to your performances with pleasant expectations; "and," he added, with a graceful bow, "I hope that you will remain with us altogether. In the meantime, you are going to Berlin, I understand, in order to win new laurels upon the old boards."

"I should be grateful for a few flowers of remembrance and welcome—the laurels, Herr Hofrath," I said, significantly.

"Well, you will not want the flowers," he said, smiling, accepting the tribute as a matter of course. "You will meet with success wherever you show yourself—you are young and beautiful."

"Rahel Varnhagen's sister-in-law, the exquisitely beautiful wife of Ludwig Robert Torno, the celebrated Swabian Friederike, says I am pretty—only pretty . . . and her verdict in matters of beauty was regarded as beyond dispute in Berlin at that time."

"Ludwig Robert possessed a fine talent for the drama. Did you ever appear in his tragedy, 'Die Macht der Verhältnisse?'"

"Yes, in Berlin. It was a splendid cast: Ludwig Devrient in one of his master-characters, Beschort thrilling as father, besides Rebenstein, Lemm, the ideal Devrient-Komitsch, the beautiful Schröck with the sweet, enchanting voice. I had to play a small part only, that of the Gräfin."

"But a very difficult one, which does not merely require to be played, but to be studied and felt even to the minutest folds of the spiritual life."

"And to this small part I owe the first praise in a tragical character I won from Pius Alexander, which made me exceedingly happy; in comedy he was mostly pleased with me."

"A great artiste!" Tieck said, thoughtfully, as if lost in remembrance. "After the highly-talented Fleck and my great Bethmann, I used most to admire the couple Wolff in Berlin. They were genuine comedians of the good old school, devoting their soul and body to the much-revered boards. Wolff's death is an irreparable loss."

"And yet, Herr Hofrath, since I have seen your glorious Emil Devrient as Tasso . . ." But I stuck fast.

Tieck looked at me with his peculiar, large Cæsarean eyes, as if he would say: "You too, Brutus—and so soon?"

At the same time a friendly nudge from Sternberg reminded me that Emil Devrient had become a *persona ingrata* in these rooms.

"Did you ever see Sophie Müller, who had to part from us and from art so prematurely?" Tieck suddenly asked, bringing the painful pause to a termination. "Who would have thought when she played the blind Valerie in Dresden with so touching, so heartfelt, and thrilling a pathos . . . and yet so simply true, that those beautiful, intelligent, expressive eyes were so soon to close for ever."

"I saw her in Karlsruhe when I was a child, and afterwards in Berlin. But I know a spiritual sister of Sophie Müller."

"On which German stage?" Tieck interrupted, impatiently. "What is her name, do you know?"

"Not upon a German stage, Herr Hofrath. I mean Mdlle. Mars from the Théâtre Français. I have seen her play in Paris often—very often—and each time she reminded me of our Sophie Müller, by the depth of her feeling, sweet womanliness, lovely voice, and the moderation and reality of life in her whole delineation and play. Yes, Mdlle. Mars is the only French actress who plays in a genuine German style, and has from her own country-women adopted their inimitable gracefulness and their sprightliness."

Tieck listened to me with evident interest. He requested me to reproduce a few scenes of the "Blinde Valerie," as it were as a copy of Mdlle. Mars and Fräulein Müller dramatically, and praised the fine *nuances* of my imitation.

We had grown very lively. Afterwards I had to relate, to the great *divertissement* of Tieck and Sternberg, how Kotzebue's "Menschenhass und Reue" was represented on the stage of the Theâtre Français.

After the dramatist had inquired about my *repertoire* he said —

"I hope in time to see you in Dresden in the most tragical parts. You possess passion, a sympathetic tone, noble gestures."

"But no tragical face, Herr Hofrath!" I interrupted, in a tragi-comic manner.

Tieck smiled kindly, saying—

"The mind overcomes that too! I should like you, for once, to try the character of 'Marie Stuart.' I shall be glad to go through the part with you to show you how Friederike Bethmann played it. She, too, thought at first that she was created only for naïve or sentimental characters, and she became the greatest 'Marie Stuart' of her time. You shall now, through me, learn also from Bethmann how in the garden scene one can walk up to Elisabeth, saying, with queenly pride: 'For *I* am your *King!*' without appearing to have any intention of aiming a blow at her as many a modern 'Marie Stuart' likes to play this part," he concluded, jesting, but still a little contemptuously.

I thanked the "master" from my heart, promised everything, even to come with my mother to the reading that night, and went home enchanted. Tieck's entire and exceedingly amiable individuality, the magnetic power of his eyes, the enrapturing effect of his speech, the charm of his smile, had completely captivated me. Everything that I had heard about his vanity, love of power, injustice, sensitiveness, and petty love of revenge, as well as all that had made my own heart so heavy and distrusting, was as if completely wiped away from my mind.

Mother and I, in grand toilette, went that evening to Tieck's house.

"Lina, I wish he would read a comedy!" this maternal sigh mingled with the confused hum which surrounded us in the lobby.

"A large company?" I inquired of the friendly old female domestic.

"Oh, *only* thirty persons!" was her dignified reply. In this little word *only* lay the true and genuine domestic pride: "Yes, look here, we claim every respect, we are very much coveted and celebrated people!"

The saloon with three windows, three sofas, and many chairs was brilliantly lit up. Stately, friendly Tieck, in evening dress, stepped forward to meet us. He conducted us to a sofa and introduced us to a puny little dame, whose little, narrow face completely disappeared under tulle-ruffles and litttle kerchiefs of lace—Countess Finkenstein. Mother had to seat herself beside the Countess. The Hofrath conducted me to his daughters Dorothea and Agnes, who looked at me inquisitively with their intelligent eyes. Then the disagreeable gauntlet-running of introducing the guests began and lasted for a while. Among others, I was introduced to Baronin Friesen, Fräulein von Brunnow, Frau von Bülow, and Count and Countess Baudissin, etc., ... after which ceremony Dorothea took me to a quiet corner where her mother and Julie Rettich sat. Tieck's wife looked indisposed, and was leaning back in a high arm-chair, a sufferer in the gay company! But I felt at home immediately in the quiet nook, and I thought like Hebel's Haberkörnle: " Here I stay whatever may become of me!"

Tieck walked about among his court like a *grand seigneur*, now addressing to a guest a friendly word, and now favouring another with a smile. In spite of all his amiableness this manner of "doing the agreeable host" was not altogether without some little admixture of condescension.

At a royal signal of Tieck's the female domestic placed a small table with two wax tapers in the centre of the saloon opposite the three large historical reading-sofas of Tieck. First, a little moving of chairs, then a most absolute stillness . . . and behind the two tapers there sounded from the bolstered settle Tieck's voice: " 'Prinz von Homburg,' tragedy by Heinrich von Kleist."

It seemed as if a breath of relief went through the saloon. Frau Rettich whispered to me: " A happy choice; the piece is not so dreadfully long as those by Shakespeare and Calderon, and Tieck reads it splendidly." Tieck's wife had, in resignation, leaned back in her easy chair and shut her eyes; the tulle-ruffles of the Countess were gleaming; my poor little mother had also resignedly folded her hands over her handkerchief in her lap, and seemed to address a last petition to the nameless god of the nerves (the ancient heathens, of course, knew nothing about nerves), and I listened in breathless suspense.

The "Prinz von Homburg" had always had much attraction for me. The people in Berlin used continually to discuss the question if Homburg was a hero or the contrary! I always broke a lance for the "hero" in spite of the shudder of death which he shows when standing by his open grave. In the hot battle Prince Homburg would have had no fear of death.

And how Tieck did read Kleist's drama as I shall never hear it read again! At first he read over the names of the persons, then only at each new scene. But with Tieck's wonderful art of reading one fancied one saw the various persons acting on a stage before one. Above all, I was charmed with the lofty simplicity of his elocution. There was not a trace of hollow declamation or stilted pathos.

Tieck read quickly. In the thrilling scene when the Prince is tortured by anguish at the sight of his open grave, at the thought of the disgraceful execution, his words were chasing each other like thunderclouds! All the greater was the effect when the heavens cleared up, when the Prince composed himself and is resigned to give up his life too. That flowed from the lips of the reader like refreshing sunshine.

. . . When I expressed my enthusiastic thanks to the "Hofrath" for this enjoyable evening he pressed my hand with his enchanting smile, saying —

"Prove to me that you would like to hear old Tieck read oftener, and come back to Dresden with the first swallows for evermore!"

How gladly I promised that I should do so!

CHAPTER II.

IN BERLIN.

Return to Berlin after Five Years—A Short and Unsatisfactory Engagement—Farewell to Berlin for Forty Years—An Old Reminiscence—A Royal Tournament at Berlin.

At the end of October, in 1834, I saw Berlin again after an absence of five years.

How differently felt you, Gretchen, when, exactly ten years ago, I entered, for the first time, the gay, enticing, royal city, my young innocent heart full of hope for an artiste's and woman's happiness, my young laughing eyes full of sunshine! . . . How differently even then when, in May, 1829, I quitted Berlin so mysteriously and set out on that sad journey to the fortune I had hoped to find in England's mists!

How different was now everything in me and around me! Berlin had become a stranger to me, and so had I to the Berliners. Even towards the old faithful friends the former harmless, gay, sincere tone could not be restored again. Many I did not see again at all—thus, the family of the Deckers. That mystic flight to England had come between us. I even heard all kinds of delicate or rude allusions to it, or, at least, I could read them in the peculiar smile of the people's mouth and eyes.

Timm, the king's private chamberlain, gave a dinner in my honour, and the King made his appearance during the dessert to welcome me and hear from me about my experience in England, and about Prince Leopold, who had meanwhile become King of the Belgians . . . But I had the disagreeable feeling that only curiosity had invited me!

Also on the stage I felt a stranger and not at ease. Ludwig Devrient and Rebenstein had died in the interval, and artistes and public were divided into two parties that were fighting to the death, into Krelingianers and Hagnerianers, and I had to take sides with both. Also the two new rising stars on the theatrical horizon of the Königstadt Theatre, Bertha and Klara Stich, did not improve the chances for my short engagement—not to leave unmentioned the deadly hatred and the secret persecutions of Prince August.

Enough, I did not relish my Berlin starring at all although the critics and the impartial part of the public accorded me a friendly reception, and Berlin's first critic, Komödien-Schulz, styled me an "artiste of the first rank."

I appeared on eleven evenings with increasing favour. I was most appreciated in my part of "Donna Diana," which I had to repeat, and as "Blinde Gabriele." . . . But my old happy Berlin time was gone for ever—on the stage and in life.

With tears of sadness I said farewell to Berlin. I never appeared there on a stage again—I never saw Berlin again—for more than forty years.

Nor should I care to see Berlin again now. It is so sad to walk by the side of graves—of graves of beloved men—of dispersed gay hours of youth and golden dreams and destroyed ideals!

* * * * * *

A ROYAL TOURNAMENT IN BERLIN.

Under the flourish of trumpets, and preceded by heralds in a train varied with colours, there entered from the one side of the hall:

Francis I., King of France . . . Prince Wilhelm, son of His Majesty, of high, powerful and magnificent appearance, in the full bloom of fresh manhood, with his spouse Claudia, represented by Crown Princess Elisabeth, beaming in beauty and diamond bliss.

Henry d'Albert, King of Navarre, was represented by the Crown Prince, elegantly and characteristically. He wore a very becoming costume of white and blue satin. The very noble Prince led his aunt, Princess Wilhelm, as Renata of France, Duchess of Ferrara.

Duke of Alencon . . . the young, well-made Prince Albrecht.

Admiral Bonnivet . . . Duke Karl of Mecklenburg, the clever inventor and arranger of the festival, which had been performed once before with brilliant success in February in the Palace Monbijoy, where the Duke resided.

Duke of Lothringen (Lorraine) . . . Electoral Prince of Hesse . . . and a brilliant retinue of French nobles and Court-beauties, represented by the flower of the Prussian nobility. All Berlin had contributed its brilliants for the occasion.

After the French Court had taken their seats upon estradas the English Court, not less brilliant, entered the hall from the other side.

King Henry VIII. of England, Prince Karl, leading the Grand Duchess of Mecklenburg Strelitz as his wife Katharina of Aragon.

Queen-mother Elisabeth . . . Princess Blücher.

Duke and Duchess of Suffolk . . . Prince Wilhelm, brother of the King and the Princess Liegnitz. . . . Then I heard somebody beside me mutter : " *Ah ! Comme elle est fraîche !* " I looked ; there sat Mdme. Desarus-Lemière gnawing her underlip with jealousy. Yes, *she* was anything but fresh and blooming.

Our intendant, Count Brühl, represented the Lord Chief Chamberlain, the Earl of Salisbury, with much dignity. Some forty ladies and gentlemen concluded the brilliant train.

When the Court of France had saluted the English visitors in the midst of the hall, and both Courts had sat down on opposite seats, a quadrille of sixteen ladies and gentlemen of the higher aristocracy entered the hall in rich Polish costumes executing national dances. Then followed a Basque quadrille and a quadrille of the French Court, in which Duke Wilhelm, of Brunswick, and Prince Radziwill joined, as well as the beautiful lady-in-waiting of the Crown Princess, Fräulein von Brockhausen, of whom it was said that Prince Wilhelm would marry her morganatically if politics and etiquette for ever denied him the hand of his beloved Princess Elisa Radziwill.

During the ball that followed, Duke Karl of Mecklenburg, as "foreign knight" of the Crown Princess, presented to the Queen of Bavaria and the King poems of homage.

The four blooming sons of the King did the honours as hosts in the most charming way. The Crown Prince was in very high spirits. Now he was seen upon this side of the hall jesting, laughing, and carrying away everything with him in his sparkling merriment; then on the other side, in spite of his *embonpoint*, he would successfully risk bold *entrechats* ... Suddenly his eye caught our box ... and immediately there was raised behind us the red velvet *portière*, and His Royal Highness stood there with the most pleasant smile: " *Ah, Madame Catalani,*" he said, " *vous ici? Quel plaisir*!" and so he went on in a pleasant rattle. ... Even Madame Desargus received a friendly word, the first out of this mouth during her long stay of ten years, a compliment on the charming character-costumes that she had procured through her brother in Paris.

Ballet-master Hoguet forgot the rules of good-breeding by a reverential pantomime to invite the Crown Prince, who was still standing upon the threshold holding the *portière* uplifted, to step nearer ... and immediately all the enchanting amiability was gone from the round face of our visitor as if by magic. His Royal Highness the Crown Prince of Prussia stood proud and cold opposite his father's barely tolerated comedian-favourites, and in sharp irony there came over his curled lips: "*Très-bénin, Mons. Hoguet, très oblige*'!" He lightly bent his head and was gone.

Only with the clever Pius Alexander Wolff have I seen the Crown Prince sometimes exchange a familiar witty word.

When I saw, two years later, in the Odeon Theatre at Paris, the splendid representation of the "Duc de Guise," the costumes and characters represented reminded me vividly of this most enjoyable evening, and the Countess Montgomery's yearning for the forlorn happiness of the little actress Karoline Bauer almost broke her heart. . . .

> Wie anders, Gretchen, war dir's
> Als du noch voll Unschuld.*
> (How different feelings had you
> When you were yet full of innocence).

After Catalani had sung at the court before the King, and in the Thiergarten, † before the Queen-mother (Madame Beer), she appeared in the opera-house at double prices, and also in the garrison church as concert-singer. I was present during her first concert in the opera-house on 6th April. She was received with enthusiastic cheers. Her appearance was imposing. Heavy white silk-stuff enveloped her like a cloud, upon her shining black hair she wore a glittering diadem, brilliants on neck and arms, yea, on girdle, her notes in her hand, she stepped forward in proud attitude, like a sovereign accustomed to victory.

She sang—and the densely packed house was mad with rapture.

---

* Quotation from Goethe's "Faust."
† Park containing many villas in the West End of Berlin.

And yet the forty-eight-year-old cantatrice was as such already a ruin, though an interesting, grand ruin. Her tone was still powerful, but it was painful to see how her lower jaw-bone worked and shook from side to side, especially during the quavers, in order to force up the sound. She sang Latin, Italian, and English, even Handel's airs in English. Let us listen to two competent critics of those days about this singing. Ludwig Rellstab wrote thus in the " Vossische Zeitung : "

" What standard are we to employ, what compare her with ? She stands there so wondrously grand in her unique greatness that it is the easiest task for the will and the most difficult one for the deed to praise her. . . . She grew and went on growing ever more grandiose, more royal and worthy of admiration. She *must* carry away with her everything, and we are very happy indeed to be in a position to affirm frankly that since her last appearance in Berlin nothing has been able to stir up such an enthusiasm and such storms of applause as her wondrous appearance. Like a born queen the cantatrice stepped into the proscenium. The orchestra began the mighty melody (of " God Save the King "), and after having replayed it the songstress also began her stanza with a dignity, with a loftiness, nay, with a majesty for which we are unable to find epithets. The enthusiasm of the artiste communicated itself to every heart. The chorus joined in solemnly, and everybody felt carried away by the power of art as much as by patriotic* feeling. Ever higher and mightier arose the voice of the singer; every movement of her majestic form became one with the song, out of every one of her looks shone forth the fire which filled her own self, with which she penetrated every breast. At last she once more raised the organ-like tones of her singing over the whole chorus, and high as an eagle soars over the mountains, so hovered her voice over the streaming surging sea of sounds. Over such a performance criticism is silent, only the voice of transport may be raised. . . ."

On the other hand old honest "Musikmeister" Zelter writes to Goethe at the same time:

"It is a pity indeed! What a voice! A golden dish with common mushrooms. And we—one could curse one's self!—admire what is despicable. No man can believe it. A dumb brute would mourn. But it is impossible. An Italian turkey comes to Germany where there are academies, universities, old students, young professors, and sings German Händel's airs in English—ENGLISH. What a disgrace, if this is to be an honour, in the midst of Germany!"

* N.B.—The Prussian anthem is the same as the English as far as the tune goes.

It shocked me most how the Italian sang "God Save the King" in Berlin. She stepped forward like one in ecstasy, lifted up her arms towards the King's small private box and addressed her song directly to the King, so that the august Prince, terrified, disappeared behind the curtains nor did he again show himself.

The Crown Prince and the Princess had risen immediately at the beginning of the song, and the whole audience had followed their example, and now all sang and shouted and roared the "Heil Dir im Sieger Kranz" in a confused chaos together with Catalani, whose powerful tones now and then drowned the ecstasy-chaos.

But I was forced to think how many crowned heads the Italians had thus addressed already with the same "God Save the King!" and with the same ecstatic transport? Only lately the libertine King George IV. of England.

I was, moreover, forced to reflect that she sang this "God Save the King" at double prices, and that she netted that evening thousands, and was overwhelmed by the Court with rich presents, whilst Sophie Schröder shortly before in the same place had played her Sappho, Phædra, Medea, Isabella, and Iphigenie for fifty thalers per performance, and was scarcely taken notice of by the Court.

Oh, mankind! Oh, phantasmagoria of the world!

CHAPTER III.

THE DEMONS OF THE HEART.

This and the following chapter refer to Sophie Schröder—mentioned in the preceding one, " A Royal Tournament in Berlin "—and to her daughter Wilhelmine.

WHO of us could lay his hand upon his heart and say: Here in my breast there only lives the one, the pure, lofty soul?

None whose heart is yet bathed by the hot blood of youth. For in this hot blood there dwell the wild passions, the heart's evil demons. Happy are we if our heart is strong enough not to succumb to its demoniac passions for ever!

The combat of these two souls in our breast is human life!

And yet how does it happen that these words of Faust-Goethe, who knew the two souls from his own breast, always recall to me two gifted colleagues whose ways often crossed mine?

Their lives, which I was permitted to fathom

deeply, may furnish the answer. They are rich in long-forgotten love stories.

Their names are Sophie and Wilhelmine Schröder, mother and daughter.

Sophie Schröder, the greatest *tragedienne* of our century, when performing as guest at Karlsruhe, had even then filled my foreboding, longing child's heart with the highest delight and the profoundest awe, by her impersonation of Lady Macbeth. The sleep-walking scene, and all the torment and demoniacal passion she understood to put in those three famous sighs and into the one word, "blood," often caused me to start in my troubled sleep, and to this very day I hear that indescribable sound, "Oh—oh—oh—blood!" ring within me; and I behold her before me in my mind, a woman of about 40 years, not tall, well knit, wearing a waving long night-dress, her plain, almost masculine face enframed by her dark, dishevelled hair, the large sombre eye so fixed, a flickering light in her hand . . . the nervous rubbing of her ghastly hands to wipe away the murdered man's blood. . . .

And now in August, 1826, Sophie Schröder arrived in Berlin with her young husband, Wilhelm Kunst, to appear at the theatre. With what great expectation I looked forward to her playing! I might now not only admire without envy the great artiste, I was also to co-operate with her as an aspiring colleague, and learn from her.

Sophie Schröder had been engaged at the Burg Theatre in Vienna since 1815, and her fame as tragical heroine and hero-mother had long been European. She made her *début* in Berlin as Sappho in Grillparzer's tragedy. I was not in the cast, and in the pit of the crowded opera house I awaited in glowing excitement the appearance of my celebrated colleague. I shall never forget the overpowering impression produced by Sappho's appearance on the splendid scene in a white garment with purple mantle and laurel wreath, upon a triumphal chariot amidst the ever-renewed acclamations of the whole large house, imposing, majestic like a queen of ideal classical Hellenism, lofty, infatuating, adorable like a noble, pure woman and an inspired, enthusiastic poetess. . . . Sappho's wonderful large eyes sparkled like stars in the circle around her and there sounded like music from her lips:

> "Dank, Freunde! Landsgenossen, Dank!
> Um Euretwillen freut mich dieser Kranz,
> Der nur den *Bürger* ziert, den Dichter drückt,
> In Eurer Mitte nenn ich ihn erst mein! . . ."

Then her splendid sonorous voice, so remarkably capable of modulation, as I never heard another, increased like the sounds of an organ till in full, rare power and fulness of sound it vibrated at last through the whole large house. And how distressing, how overpowering then again sounded her groans of pain when Phaon repudiates and betrays her love! What a world of love and of pain she knew how to throw into this one word: "Phaon!" when she surprises her beloved with Melitta!—and what death-disdaining enthusiasm, yet shrouded in deep melancholy, rang through her parting words when she flung herself into the sea, giving herself up as a sacrifice for Phaon's and Melitta's love:

> "Die Flamme lodert und die Sonne steigt,
> Ich fühl's, ich bin erhört! Habt Dank! Ihr Götter! ...
> Den Menschen Liebe und den Göttern Ehrfurcht!
> Geniesset, was Euch blüht und denket mein!
> So zahle ich die letzte Schuld des Lebens,
> Ihr Götter, segnet sie und nehmt mich auf!"

He who did not feel his heart tremble in all its fibres on that occasion, could have none!

Yes, her chief strength lay in her delivery; she had made elocution an earnest and untiring study during all her stage life, and had attained an efficiency in it of which our contemporary stage has no idea. She came of the old classical, serious school of Friedrich Ludwig Schröder, in Hamburg, and had never given the lie to it. Each word, every movement, of hers was deliberate, tried, and fully justifiable. And yet that the whole streamed forth in the purest harmony, and the listener noticed naught of intentionality and long and hard study, that was just the never-surpassed art of Sophie Schröder. Hand in hand with this wonderful elocution went her most expressive mimicry and classical plastic art.

It is related how Friedrich Ludwig Schröder, the greatest representer of man of his age, succeeded in awakening and directing on its right course the wonderful yet slumbering talent of his young namesake and sister-artiste.

Soon after Schröder had abandoned in anger the management of the Hamburg Theatre in 1801, a cheerful little woman of twenty years, Madame Sophie Stolmers, divorced, whose maiden name was Bürger, the child of comedians, appeared on that stage first as Kathinka in the "Mädchen von Marienburg," then singing and dancing as Hulda in the "Donauweibchen," as naïve Margarethe in the "Hagestolzen," and as silent Julius in the "Abbé de l'Epée." She espoused in 1804 the good and handsome actor and singer Friedrich Schröder, who shone especially as Don Juan.

Friedrich Ludwig Schröder in the end could not put up with his rural still life at Rellingen, and he again turned his attention to the Hamburg stage, and to the talent of Sophie Schröder. Thus he writes on 1st December, 1808 : "'Aline, Queen of Golconda,' is the most splendid operetta I ever saw on this stage. . . . Mdme. Schröder might sing better, but I am glad the part was not allotted to a real songstress. . . ." Later : "The *Strudelköpfchen* gains very much through Mdme. Schröder." "*Eboli*, as performed by Mdme. Schröder is excellent; only I do not agree with her in one part of the soliloquy where she divines her rival. . . ."

It may have been this passage which impelled the maestro after the performance to go to the stage and put the question—

"Dear madam, good playing that, but what did you *think* when saying those words?"

The artiste looks at the questioner at first highly delighted, but then puzzled and speechless.

"Perhaps you thought nothing at all with them?"

"Nothing!" she says faintly and meekly.

"Little lady, that is a pity!" says the maestro with a friendly smile. "On the stage one must not merely feel, but think more still, and account to one's self for the impressions produced in clear words. Our great Lessing justly demands: 'The actor must everywhere think *with* the poet; he must in passages where the poet has blundered think *for him!*'"

These words fell like a divine spark into the breast of the young tragedienne. Within it, it grew clear and ever clearer. At first Sophie Schröder *felt*, then she *thought* her impersonations of men, and later on she was fond of relating about this Hamburg apprenticeship —

"I would read my part till I had wept my full over it, and then I began the real study, and seeking to reproduce the feelings I had experienced in proper proportion."

Thus grew out of her own self the great, unique tragedienne Sophie Schröder.

And yet mother Nature had granted to this favourite of the Muses and Graces so wretchedly few outward gifts and means for the journey over the world of boards. When, on the morning after the performance of Sappho, I saw Schröder, then already 45 years old, at the rehearsal of Medea for the first time in the very midst of everyday life, I got quite a start. Was this stout, large-boned little woman with the robust face, short massive nose, wearing a youthful-looking short dress of indienne and a coquettish head-dress, the ties of her shoes neatly crossed over her ankle—was she the queenly, idealistic, enchanting Sappho of the previous evening? Nothing reminded one of her representing beautiful Hellenism, risen again from the dead, but her expressive large beaming eyes.

Friend Krüger, who was to play Jason, saw my astonishment. He smiled: "Just be patient. Despite the crossed shoe-ties, you will soon find in Medea a worthy sister of Sappho."

And he was right! I was to play Kreusa; I undertook the rather thankless part not altogether without apprehension beside the famous guest. Schröder approached me friendly and kindly, telling me that she had heard already much that was creditable concerning me, my talent, and aspirations! And after the very first scene of the artiste, Kreusa had forgotten the crossed shoe-ties, the short print-dress, the coquettish head-dress, and the whole want of beauty in Medea. Yes, indeed, therein lay the magic of her art, that Sophie Schröder had so little need of the paraphernalia of the histrionic art.

What an extraordinary effect she produced on her hearers when she said —

"Sieh mich nicht so voll Verachtung an!"

It was said that a similar storm of applause to that which broke forth in the Berlin Opera-house on the evening of the performance after the words —

"Zurück, wer wagt's Medeen zu berühren!"

had never yet been heard before, and up to this day the terribly beautiful, demoniacal sorceress Medea stands life-like before my spiritual eyes.

Three times I had the good luck to play Kreusa beside this Medea, and with acceptance. A critic praises my Kreusa as being " graceful not merely in appearance, but also in delicacy of enunciation, and the expression of virginal feelings. A contrast so mild, so altogether womanly, compared with the unwomanly impetuosity of Medea, produced in the place and at the proper time a most agreeable, pleasing effect."

Sophie Schröder further played Isabella in the "Braut von Messina." I played Beatrice, and at this moment when my old heart, moved to sadness by remembrances, longingly dives once more into those times, I hear Isabella's cry that penetrated the very marrow and shook the heart in the last act at the corpse of Manuel —

"Es ist mein Sohn!"

And yet it was a cry of anguish that proceeded from the poor deadly wounded mother's heart rather than from the mouth.

Not less great was Sophie Schröder as Phædra, (I played Aricia), as Lady Macbeth, and as Margarethe in Houwald's long-forgotten little drama "Fluch und Segen." Besides, she recited Schiller's "Lay of the Bell," in a manner in which this wonderful lyric, I dare say, has never again been pronounced. The hearer saw the casting of the bell, with master and journeyman, and the whole rich inner-life almost literally taking shape before him and— spiritualized.

How matured and psychologically deepened was everything in these master-performances; how vigorous the expression, how lofty and great the tone, how picturesque all her attitudes—her mantle-play was classical—and still nothing of mannerism or artificiality! Everything came about so simply and naturally, as if no diligence, no calculation—nay, no art had been employed in it.

The master-artiste never produced splendid minutiæ, but always a full well-finished whole. Her powerful spirit, her wonderful fertile imagination, comprehended and penetrated the poet's work and appropriated it to herself.

Add to this her divine inspiration! What no subtilizing genius had found out she hit upon with amazing accuracy. If you inquire of her about the how? and why? she would shake her head smiling and say: "I cannot explain that in words—but here in my breast I find it, all written clearly and explicitly; thus and not other-wise!"

The ideal in art had become to her life-giving productive nature.

But the most wonderful thing in Sophie Schröder after all was her magnificent unique voice—the expressive mixture of vigour and mellowness—thundering fury and sweet-whispering love-cooing. How clearly she articulated every whisper!

And still this great artiste had a two-fold weakness—as woman! which she has had to atone for often and heavily.

In her youth she had given, without youthful beauty, naïve and sentimental lovers. She had a difficulty in severing herself from youth.

Once she appeared as Alvira in Müllner's "Schuld und Reue," before the people of Vienna. Unfortunately Count Hugo has to make reference to the girdle which he will lay "around Elvira's slender body" . . . and then the jovial Viennese laughed aloud at the little, stout, plain Elvira.

The wild, maidenly charms of which Jason speaks had to be scored out owing to the loud hilarity of the audience.

In Berlin, too, Sophie Schröder was destined to pay for this woman's female weakness.

She had insisted upon playing Mary Stuart and not Queen Elisabeth. The beautiful Auguste Stich used formerly to play the part of Mary Stuart in Berlin — and she was an enchanting Queen of Scots. Now there stepped forward an absolutely ugly Mary before the spoiled Berliners: moreover, she even looked, in the great Stuart head-dress, ten years older. Amalie Wolff, as Elizabeth, on the other hand, appeared young and beautiful. And so when Montime very unnecessarily said to Mary Stuart rather enthusiastically —

"Der bist das schönste Wieb auf dieser Erde!"

the Berlin audience laughed likewise, and even the enthusiastic adorers of the great artiste smiled.

I wonder whether the ingenious artiste had ever heard that, according to Goethe's injunction in Weimar, Mdme. Vohs played Mary, as being the most beautiful actress, and Frau von Heigondorf, as the cleverest, played Elisabeth?

But the part of Elisabeth had its difficulties for Sophie Schröder, and when in 1840 the Viennese, at the words of Leicester to Elisabeth —

> " Ja, wenn ich jetzt die Augen auf Dich werfe
> Nie warst Du, nie zu einem Sieg der *Schrönheit*
> Gerüsteter, als eben jetzt. . . ."

laughed at Sophie Schröder, the maiden-queen, who was then 59 years old—then she withdrew, deeply mortified and angry, from the stage, and went to München.

And even now—1826—Sophie Schröder, who, as much hurt in her dignity as woman as she was in mourning as artiste over the decay of tragedy in the Burg Theatre, left Vienna in a very angry mood.

This leads us also at once to her other weakness as woman, that of "derbe Liebeslust,"* of which Faust-Goethe speaks.

Her wild heart, which was still glowing with a blind passion, in spite of two unhappy matrimonial connections and plenty of sad experiences in love, had fallen in love with Wilhelm Kunst, blooming, handsome, 18 years younger than she. He acted the parts of heroes. The talented young man, coarse in mind and heartless, was well pleased

* Strong impulse of love.

with the attentions of the famous artiste, and believed himself, as the husband of Sophie Schröder, to be sure of the most brilliant engagements. Frau Schröder, with that view, had an audience of the Emperor Franz, and put as a condition of her continued stay, an engagement of her intended for first parts.

Then Kaiser Franzerl, who meant well by her, said in his way (and peculiar accent): "*Schröder, sein's gescheidt, bleiben's bei uns end lassen's die dummen heirathg'—schict'n auszi—bedenken's doch: so an alt's wieberl und so an jung's mannerl.*" . . . (Schröder, be wise, stay with us and leave those silly marriage affairs alone—consider, do: such an old wifie and such a young laddie.)

"I an old wifie?—not quite five-and-forty yet, your Majesty," was her angry reply, in the tones of a Medea.

"*Nu—nu—i mein ja nur im verhaltniss zu dem jung 'n mannerl—konnt' ja halt fast zweimal ihr sohn sein*" (Well, well, I only mean in proportion to the young laddie, you see—he might be almost twice your son forsooth) said the Emperor, pacifying her.

That was too much for the loving heart of Sophie Schröder. She married the handsome Kunst and went with him touring as stars, intending not to return to the ungrateful Vienna. Thus, after a mutual engagement in Hamburg, the couple had come to Berlin, but there was already much talk about the bad matrimonial quarrels, although not six months had elapsed yet since their wedding.

I saw Kunst for the first time appear as Jaromir in Grillparzer's "Ahnfrau," which was a surprise to everybody in the opera-house, since this antiquated tragedy that was quite out of date or fashion, was not able to fill the much smaller "Playhouse" on other occasions.

At present curiosity had attracted the Berliners to see the notorious young husband of the celebrated old Schröder. But Jaromir was judged before he appeared on the stage. It was known that he had married the great artiste only on speculation and from vanity, and people knew that he treated his unfortunate spouse rudely and heartlessly, and only indulged his evil passions. So Wilhelm Kunst was received with an icy silence. Quietly and coldly his play was allowed to pass over. And yet Kunst, who was but 27 years old then, was a bewitchingly handsome, fiery Jaromir, with a highly sympathetic, sonorous voice, which was put in the shade only by the precious metal of his wife.

Wilhelm Kunst was the most brilliant realistic player of his period, but he lacked the true culture of the mind and heart, the discipline of self-education and self-criticism and every ideal flight. He was in his life and in art a *mauvais sujet*.

What a motley, debauched life lay behind him, though only 27, before he came to Berlin!

How often he had broken his contract! It was said that he had never yet left a theatre otherwise than by bolting. And he remained faithful to this character also in Berlin—and during the whole of his after-life.

Born in Hamburg in 1799, and the son of a poor cobbler, Wilhelm grew up in indigence, and almost without schooling. He was servant to several actors, and in this manner came first in contact with the theatre, where he was employed in petty supernumerary parts. His thirst for adventures led him first among the Hanseatic, afterwards among the French troops, with whom he lived a rather profligate life in Mecklenburg; thereafter he went to Münster, where he deserted. Apprenticed to a Hamburg merchant, he was sent away again. Being a handsome, smart fellow, he tried his hand at the mimic art, in a wooden booth in the horse-mart, and successfully, in a modest amateur theatre "un grunen Teich." In quick succession he got engagements in the suburb of St. Georg, in Mölln, with 1 thaler 12 groschen* weekly wage, in Preuszisch-Minden, in Lübeck, where he already played successfully "Aballino" and "Wetter von Strahl," in Stettin, Danzig, Bremen, Cologne, Düsseldorf, Würz-

* 4s. 2½d.

burg, München. . . . Of course, this quick change of engagements was rendered possible only by frequent bolting.

In 1825 Wilhelm Kunst came to Vienna with "director" Karl—and here in the city of brilliant appearances and easy fast life, the handsome, wild, fiery comedian was in his element. He delighted and enraptured the Viennese in the then popular dramas of knights, robbers, and horrors—thus, as "Otto von Wittelsback," in a golden suit of armour—as madman in the "Irrenhaus von Dijon" —and as Karl Moor, in Schiller's "Räuber." But he was not afraid to use the commonest tricks to cause sensation. Thus he played the robber Moor in the most motley, impossible costume, and at the words: "And may this flame burn in your bosom till eternity grows grey! Away, monster, never show face again among my band!" without ceremony pulled a pistol from his belt and shot the highwayman Schufterle dead on the open stage, amid the philosophic cheers of the audience.

And for this "Kolossale Leistung" (prodigious performance) Schiller's son had presented to Karl Moor, with a flattering dedication, a copy of "Die Räuber" which the poet himself had used.

More realistic and naturalistic still, was his get-up for "Otto von Wittelsbach." In the scene where Otto kills the Emperor, Kunst rushes into the side-scenes ... but staggers back to the stage, having his huge sword painted blood-red to the hilt! No wonder that Czar Nicolas of Russia—this "born comedian"—this Apall in a slave's body—presented, by way of admiration, to this bloody-drastic Otto von Wittelsbach, on the occasion of his casual appearance in the German theatre in Petersburg, a silver suit of armour and a gigantic sword with silver hilt!

Such was the brilliant hero-actor, Wilhelm Kunst, whose Jaromir Berlin allowed to pass by so coldly—because it wished to wreak vengeance on the insolent, brutal fellow on account of his deceived spouse.

With very natural curiosity I looked forward to the rehearsal of "Phœdra," in which Sophie Schröder was to play the title-*rôle*—her husband, Theseus—and I, Aricia. I watched the two, who were by that time living apart. Sophie Schröder did not deign to speak or to look at Kunst—and was only Phœdra! Theseus feigned smiling ease, arrogance, and scorn ... but at bottom he was perplexed, and cut a melancholy figure, since the rest of the cast also turned their backs upon him. It was a rehearsal full of the most trying situations for all of us.

When Sophie Schröder, at the conclusion of the rehearsal, gave me her hand, I felt how she trembled. A ghastly colour had come over her face, and her eyes were bathed in tears. I heard her say to Lemm excitedly: "If you please, dear colleague, give me your arm home—my self-command and strength are at an end!"

On the evening of the performance Phœdra was overwhelmed with demonstrative applause, while the really brilliant Theseus was, if possible, received more coldly still. Nay, some hisses were hurled at him.

Next morning Wilhelm Kunst had secretly left Berlin, his starring engagement, and his poor, deluded, befooled spouse, for ever!

Sophie Schröder appeared yet several times with increased success. But it could be seen that this latest experience gnawed at her heart. Yet its demons—the consuming passions of carnal love—were to continue to rage through the mysterious heart of the great artiste for many years to come.

This she hints at when, in after years, she was urged by her friends, and particularly by her children, to write her memoirs. At last she yields, and begins: "But I can only agree to write about my professional life, in that my private life has too many dark sides which would compromise others more than me. Moreover, the grave has covered much; often I should be compelled, besides, to cut into my own flesh, and altogether am I of opinion that the interest of the public is intended for the artiste rather than the woman—whose up-bringing and situation in life could mislead her into many great errors, and never caused her to act badly and heartlessly. What pleasure could the reader experience in encountering horrible wickedness, of which our time unfortunately has abundance! Therefore, I will pass by my private life, and allow it henceforth, as I did for so many years, to fall into total oblivion, so much the more, since, on my part, everything has long been forgiven and forgotten. I shall only touch upon it if it immediately and unavoidably mingles with my professional life. . . ."

But these memoirs either never got beyond mere preliminaries, or were later, in 1854, burnt together with all her other writings, in an evil hour. Certainly a great loss for the history of the German stage.

* * * * * *

Years had to elapse before I was to see Sophie Schröder again, when she appeared in Dresden during a visit from Vienna. It was my good fortune to be allowed to admire her in two new characters: as Sibylle, in Raupach's "Kaiser Heinrich VI.," and more still as Goethe's "Iphigenie." It was said that the veteran artiste had faced with trembling and reverence this most idealistic part to which she devoted an affectionate study during her long professional career. I own that I, too, did not without trembling look forward to her appearing in this character, when I thought of this nobly-beautiful priestess and Grecian, and of the robust little old woman who was to embody it for the beauty-spoiled people of Dresden.

And on the evening itself when Iphigenie came up to the foot-lights in white flowing robes, her thick massive head wrapped in white cloths, making it appear broader still, then I was almost startled at this uncomely old priestess of Diana.

But scarcely had she opened her magic mouth and begun:

> Heraus in eure schatten, rege wipfel
> Des alten heil' gen dichtbelaubten Haines,
> Wie in der Göttin stilles Heiligtum
> Tret' ich noch jetzt mit schauderndem gefühl. . . .

when my fears, and the whole corporeality of this Iphigenie, were completely forgotten. I listened with rapture to her wondrous tones, which irresistibly captivated ear and senses. The power of her enunciation and delivery, mimic and plastic, appeared to me in the aging woman more conquering than ever. Here was no demoniacal passion, no wild raging of a Medea captivated by storm; here all was lucid Greek repose and pleasing grace, animated by a true, warm, human heart. Her longing after her lost home and her lamentations for the fate of her beloved brother poured forth from her wounded bosom like the song of the wailing nightingale on a balmy spring night.

Even Ludwig Tieck, who in his peevish, fault-finding manner rarely acknowledged a dramatic talent which had not issued from his school, and who, years before, had caused this harsh sentence to be printed: "Sophie Schröder has, by her glaring manner, contributed much to make the German stage worse!"—I say that even this old egotistically-whimsical dramatist, in face of this Iphigenie, confessed: "Yes, there one may see how much genius, diligence, artistic education and warmth of feeling may prevail over the poor bodily frame! Old Schröder looks like a sutler, but she plays and speaks like a goddess!"—he, too, who himself was so famous as a reader, owing to his beautiful metallic voice, was most taken by Schröder's noble, clear, full tones, now rising into the mighty roar of thunder, now melting into the sweetest whispering of love.

At the same time Tieck related one of his favourite anecdotes: When Friedrich Schröder, who, like no other mimic, knew how to imitate comedians and common mortals, was asked to mimic for once the great Eckhof, he said, shaking his head: "First give me his voice!"

That could be said of Sophie Schröder likewise.

But what never wearying diligence, up to great old age, did the artiste employ in the perfecting of her organs of speech that were so richly gifted by nature already!

When she appeared in Hamburg in 1834, her son-in-law, Dr. P. Schmidt, heard her repeating aloud her often-played part as early as five o'clock in the morning, and now and then going over the same verse twenty or thirty times in a loud angry voice. This she herself afterwards explained at breakfast in these words —

"I recited aloud, as I always do, my part for the evening, and there I encountered a word which would not go over my tongue in its wonted manner and then" (raising her voice) "then I have no peace, the tongue must pay for its obstinacy till it obeys—no, in that I am unrelenting."

The same diligence she employed in the spiritual perfecting of her parts. She studied whole libraries on the life of the ancient Greeks for her Medea, Phædra, Sappho, Iphigenie. And before she undertook the part of Sibylla, in Raupach's "Heinrich VI.," she applied herself to a profound study of Raumer's "Hohenstaufen."

During the twelve years that had elapsed since I saw Sophie Schröder last in Berlin, new storms had raged in her eventful life, and among them some had struck her heart. Her blind weakness for Wilhelm Kunst, and the disagreeable divorce-suit, had not only destroyed her and her children's happy family life, but also disordered her pecuniary affairs. With Vienna she was out of favour more particularly through Kunst, who was still scoring great successes there upon the suburban stages in his knight-robber and horror plays with his splendid physical means. Moreover there were misunderstandings between her and the management of the Burg Theatre . . . and so Sophie Schröder resigned, but she availed herself of a professional tour in 1829—before her contract had expired—not to return to Vienna any more. This rash, passionate deed caused her many troubles and disappointments.

Now began a restless, often enough starving, roaming comedienne life for her. In the depth of winter she went with her younger children through Russia as far as Moscow and St. Petersburg. At the instigation of the Austrian Embassy she had to break off a starring engagement splendidly begun. Disappointed in her hopes, sick and weary, she returned to Germany. Count Redern, the intendant of the Berlin stage, at first refused her a temporary engagement, probably having regard to her breaking the Vienna contract. But the artiste almost impetuously accosted him, saying—

"I *must* play, your Excellency—for I *must* have bread for me and my children."

"How? A Schröder—and come so far?"

And she did play in Berlin with her old Vulcanic passion, after the Vienna contract had been successfully cancelled, but she did not find the desired engagement. Also attempts to re-establish relations with the Vienna Burg Theatre failed. Then King Ludwig of Bavaria, who had always thought very highly of "Germany's greatest tragedian," as he called her in every letter, offered her a permanent place at his Court Theatre, with considerable sacrifices from his private purse. In München Sophie Schröder, now already 50 years old, in enthusiastic co-operation with Esslair, called into existence her "Iphigenie," "Civa" in Schenk's "Krone von Cypern," and "Sibylle."

To this period belongs King Ludwig's piquant saying:

"Schröder, your whole gracefulness lies in your Grecian upper arm!"

Nor did the King resent it in his greatest tragedienne that she, after a stay of but five years, gave up her engagement in München and returned with a pension of 1,200 Bavarian gulden to the reconciled Burg Theatre.

But her time was over. She only added three small parts to her old master performances, that of Claudia in "Emilia Galotti," Armgard in "Tell," and Anna Lambertazzi in Halm's tragedy. But what did she make out of these small parts? When Armgard threw herself with her children in front of Gessler's horse the deepest emotion ran through the house.

Three years later Sophie Schröder requested her dismissal in Vienna likewise, and retired, with an additional pension of 800 gulden, at first to Augsburg into private life, full of gratitude towards King Ludwig and Emperor Ferdinand, who had made the evening of her life one free from cares. She used to say: "Hapsburg* and Wittelsbach have been the guardian angels of my life, and nothing can equal my veneration and gratitude for these august houses!"

This gratitude even inspired her to these lines:

> "Hapsburg und Wittelsbach!
> Zwei Namen die mir tief in's Herg geschrieben
> Denn beide lenkten gnädig mein Geschick,
> Hoch werd 'ich sie verehren, treu sie lieben,
> Ihr ew' ges Heil erflehn, wie hier ihr irdisch Glück!"

In Augsburg, Sophie Schröder lived with her beloved son Alexander, who was in garrison there. But now and then the old comedienne felt impelled to reappear in the world of boards—to approach once more to the footlights. Thus in 1842 she also came to Dresden, where her talented daughter, Wilhelmine Schröder-Devrient, shone as prima donna.

At the desire of the Court the old dame of 61 once more appeared on the stage on two occasions. I played with her in "Emilia Galotti"—she Mother Klaudia. Through her wonderfully touching tragic art she raised the third act to the most important

---

* The reigning houses of Austria and Bavaria.

of the whole tragedy. Besides she gave the "Königin von Cypern."

With her daughter Wilhelmine she drove over to Leipzig, and gave a concert in which she recited Bürger's "Leonore," and Klopstock's "Frühlingsfeier," as only she could do it.

Felix Mendelssohn writes about it, on 28th Nov., 1842, to his mother in Berlin—

"Three days ago the concert of old Mdme. Schröder took place, in which I had to play and conduct the overture to Ruy-Blas. The old declamatrix has thoroughly delighted all of us with the vigour and liveliness of her voice and her whole nature.

"Her daughter Wilhelmine, looking younger and wilder and more madcap-like than ever, sang likewise, and will sing again to-night in Döhler's concert, and a week which she spends in a place is not the quietest either for her acquaintances. Besides Tichatschek, Wagner, Döhler, Mühtenfels, the whole of last week was a constant commotion and bustle. . . ."

During that somewhat protracted stay of old Mdme. Schröder in Dresden, the great artiste and the interesting, genial woman also came into nearer personal contact with me. We met in various social circles: at Tieck's, at von Lüttichau, the intendant's, at the house of Count Bandissin, at the

Baroness Brunnow's, and more and more I learned to esteem Sophie Schröder's great amiability, goodness of heart, freshness of mind, and solid accomplishments.

Once when I said to her that with my 35 years I should also have soon to think of discarding the first "lover" and to embrace the older parts, she shook her head.

"I should not advise you to do so. It is not good to play too long. One outlives one's self and one's fame, and becomes for the public like a familiar object of every day. I, too, have played too long, but only from need—for my daily bread. I had to play on till I had acquired the right to a pension, before I might, without cares, retire into private life. You do not require to do so. You are still young enough to marry. That is better than to play comedy."

On another occasion she said to me—

"I intend to note down the reminiscences and experiences of my professional life. You should do that by-and-bye too. Both of us have lived through enough, and also possess the mettle for putting it on paper."

I shook my head at that time sceptically, for I could not then foresee that later the complete isolation of my life and heart, the most despairing desolation in and around me—nay, despair of life—

would make me take up the pen, to forget the gloomy present in writing about the sunny past!

What of her more eventful stage-life Sophie Schröder wrote down, no man's eye has ever seen. In 1854, when the cholera was raging in Augsburg, she also burned her "Reminiscences," together with other papers.

But let us return to Dresden—1842. In the select spiritual circle at the house of the wild, madcap-like Wilhelmine Schröder, who liked to hear the popping of the champagne cork, her mother also frequently grew extravagant and wild, excessively merry and witty, as if the many thorny experiences her heart had gone through in her varied life had not touched her perceptibly.

Once the talk was about sweet, cruel love, and Wilhelmine Schröder had much to say about it. Then her mother, the dame of 61, suddenly rose and said excitedly, and with the gesture and in the deepest tones of Medea —

"This vile passion I have renounced—for ever—for ever. . . ."

At first we looked at one another speechless. Then a wanton spirit came over me too, and I asked harmlessly —

"Since when have you renounced this—vile passion—for ever?"

Most serious, and in her deep sonorous tones of old, the tragedienne answered —

"Since—two years!"

Did not we laugh!—of course Wilhelmine leading as the wildest and most extravagant.

This little trait excellently characterises the *woman* Sophie Schröder.

She herself once wrote about her passionate heart and its amours —

"We are wanted to represent to you on the stage the passions in their whole truth. Why do you chide us if we feel them also?

"He who will cure a sick heart through severity and harshness has either no heart himself, or is a bad searcher of deep, feeling hearts.

"If in some way or other, through fate or circumstances, we must lose or renounce what we esteem, honour and adore, this will cause, no doubt, an ever burning pain, and the heart is drenched in tears, and inundated till it breaks; but it is crushed under feet, torn to pieces, and all the furies of hell take up their abode in it when the monster, conviction, steps before us and shows to us that love, veneration, esteem, adoration, were thrown away on an object that was not worthy of it. Would that the Almighty rather broke that heart, closed those eyes for ever, than that we should arrive at this conclusion!"

From these words it becomes clear how deeply and sorely Sophie Schröder had suffered through that "vile passion" of her heart.

With all that, Sophie Schröder was truly religious, very generous, and of great goodness of heart.

In her residence there were found these words by her hand:

> "An Gott will Keiner mehr glauben,
> Doch lasse ich ihn mir nicht rauben,
> Ich fühle ihn thronen in meiner Brust,
> Fühl' nahe ihn mir in Schmerz und Lust."

Her last words on earth were:

"To-day the dear God will put an end to my career."

Here may follow two more traits of her touching goodness of heart.

During the last nights of any temporary engagement one might always see in Sophie Schröder's dressing-room a little basket upon the toilette-table with many weighty little parcels in white paper and sealed. The different parcels were inscribed: "For the female attendant," "the theatre servant," "the prompter," "the property-man," "the lamp lighter," "the stove-heater," "the carpenter," "the janitor," &c., &c.

Nobody was forgotten. These little parcels contained the parting-gratuities for these subordinate theatrical servants, generally the artiste's share of the drawings of one evening. Had she drawn much she gave away much. To cause joy to others was as necessary to her as food and drink. And her feeling of justice told her that these badly-paid *employés* of the theatre, who year after year have to labour hard for the welfare of the whole fabric, should have a share, too, in what she so readily won by her talent. Sophie Schröder used to say:

"I like to see happy faces around me—and no grudging, envious ones. I know that these good people always hail my coming, and I do not take it ill that they also rejoice at my going away, owing to the light golden shower connected with it. During my engagement they do everything they can to please me. And I could not calmly and with happy mind leave a town without having satisfied my heart by these little money-parcels!"

I was so much pleased with this, that henceforth also at the conclusion of my tours, the little basket with the paper-parcels was not wanting upon the dressing-table.

Neither old Schröder nor I have carried riches with us from the theatre into private life.

Another trait proves the rare lofty generosity of Sophie Schröder, such as will hardly be found matched upon these boards of cabal and intrigues.

The tragedienne was starring in Stettin. The first "lover" there, a beautiful and talented girl, had to play second parts beside her, such as Kreusa, Aricia, and Beatrice, and her vanity was hurt by it. Moreover, she was envious of the triumphs of the celebrated artiste. She carried on intrigues in order to interrupt the inconvenient appearances of the stranger, or at least to put them off. Now she was ill, now she took an unreasonable time for the study of these hateful secondary parts. Sophie Schröder, in her peculiar frank manner, did not conceal her displeasure. That was throwing oil upon the fire.

Well, during this time of frictions happened the benefit-night of the resident "lover." In her wantonness she chose one of the most brilliant parts of the celebrated "star," Civa in Schenks; "Krone von Cypern." Sophie Schröder shrugged her shoulders and waited.

The day of the benefit arrived, but the beneficiant, owing to nervous excitement, having become quite hoarse, had to report herself sick.

What now? According to the bye-laws of the Stettin Theatre a benefit could not be put off. And the sick actress, who had to maintain her mother and younger brothers and sisters, required the proceeds urgently.

Then Sophie Schröder took her revenge on the jealous sister-artiste—in the noblest way. Spontaneously and unexpectedly she appeared at the rehearsal, where all was confusion, and revised the chief part; and in the evening, she, instead of the beneficiant, played the same before a crowded house, and renounced every share in the splendid takings. The jealous sister-artiste was put to shame, and cured of envy and cabal.

Ziegler, an actor, at that time stage-manager in Stettin, and afterwards my respected colleague, told me the particulars of this unique deed of a comedienne.

I have not seen Sophie Schröder again since those happy November-days in 1842, but have often heartily thought of her, especially when her name would run through the papers once more, and thus reached my gloomy solitude.

The tragedienne appeared on the stage for the last time in a whole part in 1847, in Hamburg, where once the cradle of her fame had stood, half a century before. She played Isabella in Schiller's "Braut von Messina" with unaltered vigour, and was overwhelmed with applause and honour. How many things must have moved the heart of the aged artiste on that night!

In the spring of 1854 Vienna, too, saw for the last time her greatest tragedienne once more upon the stage of the Burg Theatre, to take her farewell for life. Deeply moved and deeply moving she recited Schiller's "Lay of the Bell."

Then, on 24th May, Grillparzer wrote into the album of his loftiest "Sappho" and his sublimest "Medea," in "old friendship and admiration":

> "Zwei *Schröder*, Frau und Mann
> Umgrenzen unsers Dramas höhern Lauf
> Der *Eine* stand in Kraft, als es begann,
> Die *Andre* schied—da hört's wohl, fürcht'ich, auf!"

Friedrich Hebbel added:

> "Unvergänglicher Lorbeer in schnell verbleichender Locke
> Welch ein gewaltiges Bild menschlicher Grösze und Kraft!"

And Ludwig Löwe, as the conclusion of a very successful sonnet:

> "Dir rief die Kunst ihr gold-durchglühtes Werde!
> Dir ward Posaunenklang, wo Andre lallten,
> Und einzig stand'st Du da auf deutscher Erde!"

In October, 1857, Sophie Schröder took her leave of Berlin, too, with the "Lay of the Bell." The last appearance in public of the artiste took place in München, in November, 1859. It was on the occasion of Schiller's centenary that Sophie Schröder, at the special desire of her old friend and patron, King Louis I., appeared again before the people of München at the great age of 78. An eye-witness reports thus:

"... The appearance of Frau Sophie Schröder was anxiously awaited. Every eye was turned towards the door through which the celebrated hoary artiste was to step. She appears on the hand of Stage-manager Richter. She is received with enthusiastic cheers. Her very first words: "The Lay of the Bell," by Schiller, betokened that her voice defied old age, and was yet possessed of great vigour. But not only much vigour, she has also kept all her feeling, and passion flashed out of her highly-artistic delivery at the proper moment. The whole house was carried away with admiration, so that the artiste was certainly more than six times interrupted by a perfect storm of applause. At the conclusion of her recitation the cheering only stopped when Sophie Schröder had three times in succession appeared on the stage thanking the public with silent gesture under great emotion. King Ludwig leaned forward in his box and conveyed his applause to the artiste, formerly also admired by him, in the lively manner peculiar to him by applauding, nodding, and gesture."

How gladly would I, the envied Polish countess, have changed places with the old comedian who had always remained faithful to herself and her art, that evening, and for ever!

In the same month of November, 1859, the old heart of Sophie Schröder was to be shaken by an announcement of death in connection with a name that was once very dear to her heart: Wilhelm Kunst had died in Vienna. . . . It was followed, a year later, by the death of her most gifted and favourite daughter, Wilhelmine.

But on 1st March, 1861, all Germany celebrated the 80th birthday of its greatest tragedienne. From all parts, especially also on the part of the former colleagues during her golden days of glory, arrived congratulations, addresses, poems, medals, presents, and all kinds of acts of homage.

On 25th February, 1868, Sophie Schröder died, gently and peacefully, in the arms of her beloved son, Alexander, at München, in the 87th year of her life. Her last words I referred to already.

"In death she was beautiful. Long-suffering and majesty were impressed upon her face!"

Her funeral was solemn and dignified. The muse wept at her grave. A white marble bust crowns the mound to-day.

An enviable, peaceful death.

I alone was forced to remain silent and forgotten by the beloved companion of better days. My lord and master did not like to be reminded that once, in the heat of passion, he had chosen a comedienne to be his companion for life. . . . "Karoline Bauer— la comédienne est morte à jamais!" How often have I had to hear those icy words! Karoline Bauer was dead—and Countess Plater did not live! What a wretched existence!

Seven years more Sophie Schröder lived after that rare feast of her 80th birthday. Her loneliness and dulness of hearing she relieved by reading and a diligent study of art. Thus she once said—

"Every winter I peruse Shakespeare's works from beginning to end, and every time with greater appreciation and increased admiration. Do you know what part I should like to play? Richard III.! For the sake of this part I have often regretted not to have been a man!"

Only sometimes she was heard to utter angry words about the downfall of the art she always had cherished so highly—falling on account of the indifference of the public and the want of artistic acting on the part of the actors. Her words were these —

"I was often ungrateful towards the public. I was ashamed of their tokens of favour; for when I compared my intended acting with the actual performance, I would often say to myself: 'Good God, they know nothing about it! . . .' Art has perished, handicraft conquers. The greater the glitter, the rattling, the rustle, the greater the cheers! Great names—small artistes. And the so-called artistes? Dress, dress—that is all they can do! But enthusiasm—passion, without which there cannot be any dramatic art—good gracious!—yea, a passion that makes you beat your head against the wall—a passion even if accompanied by bread and water and a linen dress—but, for goodness' sake, let us have a passion!"

But such a passion does not exist without the demons of the heart!

CHAPTER IV.

Wilhelmine Schröder-Devrient.

Wilhelmine Schröder had inherited from her great mother the grand dramatic talent, but also the hot, most passionate heart with its evil demons.

I met Wilhelmine Schröder-Devrient for the first time in Berlin. From Dresden, where she had been engaged as first dramatic singer since Easter, 1823, she came, in December, 1828, on a professional tour to Berlin, the "capital of music" as the French violin-virtuoso, Boucher, used to call it. She appeared after the triumphs of a Catalani, Henriette Sontag, Nannette Schechner, Sabine Heinefetter, Constance Tibaldi, and yet she had taken the Berliners by storm on her first appearance in Weber's "Euryanthe." She conquered through her grand, most realistic acting, through her captivating, highly expressive singing, and through the combined charms of her individuality, so that she was called before the curtain vociferously, immediately after its lowering, at the conclusion of the second act, an honour no Euryanthe had yet attained in Berlin, although she was far surpassed by the Schechner in the rich metallic ring of her wonderful voice, and by the perfect technique of Sontag's singing. Both these highly famous songstresses sang, it is undoubted, with their brilliant throats—Wilhelmine Schröder-Devrient sang with her burning soul.

In her second character, that of Rezia in Weber's "Oberon," the talented artiste occasioned no less enthusiasm among the Berliners, especially by the powerful air "Ocean du Ungeheurer!" Through her singing was heard the wild rolling and grumbling of the raging sea.

Rellstab wrote at that time: "Madame Devrient has conceived Rezia with such a depth of feeling, and in such highly productive fancy, that she has given us, both in a musical and dramatic sense, entirely new views about this character."

And how she succeeded in captivating in the part of the charming Swiss girl Emmeline!

On the Königstadt stage she sang the title-part in Paer's comic opera, "Largines, oder der Zögling* der Liebe," and Anna in Boildieu's "La dame blanche"—one of the chief parts of Sontag—with great success, which, however, did not prevent the merry, witty Berliners, who had already heard

* Student of love.

many a piquant little anecdote of Wilhelmine's hot, passionate heart, remarking, in their agreeable accent: "What? she claims to be a student of love? She might very well succeed as professor of love!"

Even at that time it was my good fortune to come into nearer contact with this great artiste and much admired beautiful woman. Her most enthusiastic admirers gave, in her honour, a splendid artiste-fête, with music, poems, flowers, laurel-wreaths, and other signs of homage. I had been requested with several ladies to do the honours. What I most admired in our beaming queen of the fête were the mobility of her very marked features, her sparkling, laughing blue eyes, her wonderfully rich fair hair, and the rare combination of high spiritual giftedness with sweet naïve cheerfulness.

Pressed by everybody to sing something, she immediately sung the simple, sweet little Swiss air—

"Auf der Alm bin ich so gerne,
Denke Dein, Du süszes Lieb. . . ."

playing her own accompaniment on a guitar she had sent for.

What a charm lay in this plain song! A warm, loving human heart! That called forth from our eye a cheering tear. Everybody listened, deeply moved, to the sweet, heartfelt sounds. A rapturous *encore* Wilhelmine accepted with a grateful smile.

But merry Spitzeder understood splendidly how to bring us back from the soft mood into most jubilant, festive spirits. He asked for the guitar, and in his most comical way he began to sing a classical Viennese street-song full of the most grotesque nonsense. I can only recall a few lines —

> " Mein Madel
> Das kocht Knadel,
> Der sind grosz als wie sin Kopf.
>   (*Softly*)
> —Hat kein Wasser in dem Topf!

Then —

> Dort auf der Birkenspitz
> Sitzt ein alter Stiegelitz,
> Der pfeift in guter Ruh. . . .
>   (*Softly*)
> —Und hat den Schnabel zu!"

To understand our roars of laughter—nay, laughter that brought tears and nearly knocked us off our feet—one would require to see the arch-comical face of Spitzeder's. But the green sward of the churchyard in München has covered it for nearly fifty years.

What a really happy day that was in December, 1828! And Wilhelmine Schröder the merriest and most frolicsome of us all. . . . To-day, I dare say, I am the only one left to give an account of it.

Wilhelmine was at that time exactly 24 years old, and in her merriness and liveliness, with her burning cheeks, her flashing sea-deep blue eyes, and the wreath of fresh flowers in her waving, luxuriant locks, beautiful and enchantiug—like a Bacchante.

She was but three years older than I; but what a motley, agitated, wild life lay behind her!—a life lashed and torn by the demons of the heart. She was a divorced wife, and mother of four children— and yet childless! The law-court had given the custody of the children to the father, having found Wilhelmine Schröder guilty of adultery.

Her very childhood was restless and homeless, as is the case with most children of comedians. She herself relates as follows:—

"As soon as I was four years old I began to work. I had to begin early to gain my bread. . . ."

Her mother, Sophie Schröder, rather susceptible and carried away by an idea, caused her little girl to be instructed in the art of dancing by a Mulatto dancing-master living in Hamburg. As early as in her ninth year Wilhelmine appeared on the stage of Hamburg in a *pas de châle* and a *hornpipe*, and was applauded—a little felt hat, with blue ribbons, on her head, and her feet in clogs. "I only remember of this my performance that the spectators lustily cheered the clever little monkey, that my teacher was very much gratified, and that my father carried me home upon his arms. My mother had presented to me, before the beginning of the performance, the prospect of a pretty doll, or—a whipping, depending on my success or failure on the stage; and I am sure it was anguish that made my little limbs light and supple, for my mother's whippings were sore. . . . As to my education, I can say nothing. It was undoubtedly very much neglected, as indeed, up to my twelfth year, I was not put earnestly to any other study than that of dancing. But my fancy was even then wide awake.

"The war-tumult (1813) was to exercise a decisive influence also on my parents' fate. During the occupation of Hamburg by the Russian General Tettenborn, my mother had, in the occasional play, 'The Russians in Germany,' worn a Russian cockade on her breast. Afterwards, when Davoust occupied Hamburg, he demanded that the French cockade should be used in the play. My mother was long in carrying out this order, but when she could no longer evade it, to the merriment of the whole audience, she appeared with a tricolour cockade as big as a soup-plate. She was cited before a court, and was to be carried off to France a prisoner. Thus we had to flee; and I remember that my greatest fear was that the French could take away my doll from me, wherefore I hid it carefully under my sash."

The Schröder family—father, mother and four children—now begin a restless peregrinating comedian-life, doubly vagabond owing to the troublous time of war. Wilhelmine, then ten years of age, and her younger sister, had to assist in the performances, young as they were, in their dancing shoes, to help to earn the daily bread.

The roar of the cannon, caused by the battle of Hanau, drives the poor comedians again northward from Frankfort-on-the-Main. At last, they find an engagement with director Liebich in Prague. Wilhelmine and her little sister have to take an active part in the children's ballet. About this she says afterwards: " The remembrance of this makes my heart bleed even now. We were exposed to the most brutal treatment, surrounded by the worst examples, and learned nothing but dancing and tricks."

When Sophie Schröder and her husband, in 1815, found an engagement at the Burg Theatre, in Vienna, their three little daughters entered the then famous children's ballet of Horschelt . . . the most dangerous schooling for the inquisitive eyes of a child, and the tender, guileless heart of a child! Nor did poor Wilhelmine dance under these palms with impunity! The children's ballet of Horschelt was by-and-bye put a stop to by the police on account of grave breaches of the moral law. A certain Count Kaunitz, a son of the sybaritical minister of the Empress Maria Theresa, would, at that time, have got penal servitude if indeed he had not been—the aristocratic Count Kaunitz. What demons sprang up at that time in the young heart of the charming little ballet-dancer, Wilhelmine Schröder!

The greatest misfortune for the young wild Wilhelmine was the early death of her good, loving father. She acknowledges this herself much later in these words —

"I can never without emotion recall with what circumspection, care and kindness my father looked after our bodily and mental training. How often did I awake in the dead of night by his coming to our beds to convince himself of our sound sleep; and with what gentle firmness he sought to restrain our wildness, and to accustom us to order and regularity! Oh, if death had not snatched away from me that father at a time when I needed him so much—how very different my life might have shaped itself! But I was not to have a loving hand to smooth my path of life for me, I was to hurry along over cliffs and abysses; though heart and soul of mine were to break like the surging sea, what did it matter?"

What an accusation one may read here between the lines—against her mother! Perhaps not altogether without reason.

Sophie Schröder, at that time, was the much

admired Sappho of the Burg Theatre. The Phaon
of her heart was Daffinger, the popular Viennese
miniature-painter, who painted his Sappho in the
32nd year of his life, that is to say during Friedrich Schröder's lifetime.

Wilhelmine, soon after her father's death, was
trained for the stage, under her mother's directions.
She was not quite fifteen years old when Phaon-
Daffinger made the discovery that she would be the
most charming Melitta beside this lofty Sappho.
And one day, Sappho found her Phaon and the
fair-haired, blue-eyed Melitta in very affectionate
intercourse. A passionate scene followed. Sappho
entirely forgot her part, She did not bless Phaon's
and Melitta's love, and plunged not in noble impulse
of self-sacrifice into the sea. She treated the lovers
to boxes on the ear.

So, young Wilhelmine early learned to know the
"vile passion of the heart"—through the lover of
her mother.

Indeed, her early training in the house of her
mother had much sinned against her heart, and had
much to answer for her whole life, the scene of many
violent passions. There she saw and heard much
that was not fit for the eye or ear of a chaste
maiden. Mildew had attacked the tender bud before
it could develop into a full bloom.

On 13th October, 1819, Wilhelmine Schröder,

who had made some attempts previously on the amateur-theatre of Stegmeyer, appeared, when not yet fifteen years old, for the first time as Aricia, with her mother as Phædra, on the boards of the Burg Theatre. Her first critic writes thus about it—

"Her appearance is pleasing; her acting, considering her age, is remarkably deliberate; her pure and sensible elocution showed what school she comes from. When the public called her at the conclusion of the play, her esteemed mother led her forward by the hand and recommended her not only to the *indulgence*, but also to the *strictness* of the audience."

At that period Wilhelmine also played with acceptance Luise Millerin in Schiller's "Cabale und Liebe," Ophelia in "Hamlet," and Beatrice in Schiller's "Braut von Messina."

But a greater surprise yet was in store for the Viennese, on the part of their fair-haired favourite. Thus writes old, quaint genius, Kanne, a musical-critic who afterwards ruined himself by drink—

"On 20th January, 1821, there appeared for the first time on the stage of the Court opera-theatre, at the Kärntnethor Gate, as Pamina, Wilhelmine Schröder. Her prudent mother had not allowed the young lady to sing previously in any private circle; nobody knew that the girl was possessed of musical accomplishments, and thus a singer had, so to say, dropped down straight from the clouds. The wonder was all the greater, therefore, to find her possessed of a pretty, well-trained voice, a perfectly pure intonation, and an execution simple, indeed, but very agreeable, and free from all ornamentation. These advantages, coupled with a dramatic talent such as few great songstresses have yet exhibited, engendered a peculiar charm, and thus delighted the unexpecting audience, so that the house echoed with applause."

Still greater enthusiasm she awakened soon afterwards as Emmeline in Weigl's "Schweizerfamilie." "Her acting was masterly—you may call it lofty— full of feeling, simplicity and truth. She sang plainly and feelingly as the part requires it. . . . The public love her already. . . ."

She was dressed in that simple, genuine, substantial Swiss costume which showed no trace of the theatrical gaudery then in use—"beautiful as the dawn"—and soon all the women in Vienna wore "Emmeline-frocks," à la Wilhelmine Schröder.

As Maria in "Bluebeard" she filled the audience with compassion and awe "by her heart-penetrating tones and gestures that really sprang from within. She played the whole part with equal, nay, towards the conclusion of the opera, with ever-increasing vigour, and so highly creditably did she act, especially during the two last acts, from the moment of her rushing out of the room of terror to the end, that it might be difficult to give this character more realistically and more stirringly anywhere."

And this Maria was but sixteen years and six months old! But she was no longer a harmless child. As such she would not have been able to represent "Bluebeard's" wife in so stirring a manner. She herself had eaten already of the tree of knowledge—she had lived and loved.*

Soon after she sang Agathe in the "Freischütz," when she was perfectly charming and bewitching.

"A charming 'blondine' of sixteen years combines, with a splendid sonorous voice, the deepest feeling in her delivery, and a rare degree of the mimic art, which seems partly inherited from her mother, and partly acquired by study!" And Weber, who, the year after, conducted his opera personally in Vienna, is reported to have said, even then: "She is the first 'Agathe' in the world, and has surpassed anything I thought to have put into the part."

And then—in November, 1822—Wilhelmine Schröder impersonated for the world—for immortality—poor old deaf Beethoven's part of "Fidelio," which had till then been misunderstood, nay, con-

---

* "Ich habe gelebt und geliebet," "Des Mädchens Klage," by Schiller.

sidered impossible! Her dramatic art and the fire of her life-sparkling heart knew how to embody the music of the master as neither before nor after her any singer has done. Nor has our artiste ever in any other part met with such triumphs as in this her master-impersonation.

Beethoven sat in the orchestra, during the performance of his opera, so completely wrapped in his cloak that only his burning eyes shone out of it. And he *saw* his Fidelio before him as he had pictured to himself in his melody-filled dreams, this lofty woman in the garment of a man, with the great heart ready for sacrifice. And after the performance he went behind the scenes to his Fidelio, and his eyes, usually so gloomy and misanthropic, smiled and thanked the young songstress for giving life to his favourite musical form, and he stroked her cheeks and promised to write a new opera for her . . . and she kissed his hand much affected. . . .

A solemn, never-to-be-forgotten moment in the life of our artiste! And what she vowed to herself and to the great master at that time she has kept splendidly : in an exultant triumph she has carried his Fidelio through the world, and conquered for it even in reserved England and negative France a brilliant throne of victory even to this day!

With Fidelio, Wilhelmine Schröder made, in the spring of 1823, her brilliant entry into her new engagement at Dresden. To this stage she belonged fully twenty-four years as its greatest ornament, and there we became afterwards more intimate colleagues.

It was likewise in Dresden that the wild demons of consuming passions got more and more the better of this young, hot, unbridled heart, till this poor heart and an entire human life, so richly gifted and wonderfully dispositioned, perished under its withering breath, as Semele did under the flaming kiss of Jupiter.

Wilhelmine Schröder was eighteen years old and full mistress of her own person, having an income of 2,000 thalers, when in Dresden the youthful hero and lover-player Karl Devrient paid his addresses to her. He was handsome and full-blooming, like Antinous—scarcely five years older than the charming, fair songstress, who was idolized by all the world—and he read in her eyes the blazing fire of love. . . . They soon loved each other like turtle-doves.

In July, the lovers came to Berlin for a short run, which proved very successful. There in the Jerusalem church they were privately married. Then both played in Hamburg, and here, for the first time, the soon world-renowned name, "Wilhelmine Schröder-Devrient," stood on the play-bill.

They were a wonderfully beautiful, happy pair

who returned to Dresden, and, for some years following, traversed the world together in their own elegant carriage on starring-tours. They put old Königsberg especially into a perfect frenzy of delight, in the spring of 1825—both on the stage and in society. The good people of Königsberg had still much to say about this when I, three years later, appeared there, also in spring. Those days in Königsberg were probably the happiest in Wilhelmine's life.

She did not only delight, move, and deeply affect her audience as Agathe, Emmeline, Donna Anna, and Leonore-Fidelio—but in order to enjoy the happiness of playing together with her beloved husband, she also appeared in a dramatic character at that time strange in theatres. Thus she gave Preziosa and Louise Millerin—he the most ideal Don Alonso and the fieriest Ferdinand von Walter. The jealous love was still so great with Karl Devrient at that time that he mixed one evening as a hunter among the supernumeraries to be able to catch his swooning Euryanthe in his own arms. . . . And after three short years, what had become of his happiness and his love? The jealous husband appeared at the court and claimed divorce from his culpable, faithless wife!

A pretty story is told of the enthusiasm which the happy Wilhelmine Schröder-Devrient stirred up upon the stage and in Königsberg society.

The artiste did not disdain to play and to sing the part of Luise von Schlingen in Holtei's farce "Die Wiener in Berlin," which was much admired at that time; she charmed old and young hearts in it. She had scarely finished, under tremendous applause, the inserted couplet:

> " Einmal noch die schöne Gegend
> Meiner Heimath möcht' ich sehen . . ."

when in the pit there rose an art-enthusiast, and, stretching up his hands imploringly to the stage, said —

"Ah, my divine Madame Devrient, if only I could have a copy of this charming song!"

And "Frau von Schlingen" smiled down into the pit-stalls with irresistible waggishness, saying—

"Exceedingly sorry, my dear sir, but M. Bäuerle in Vienna has only allowed me the song for singing. I must not *give* a copy of it. But should you demand to hear the song again of me, and have paper and pencil with you, then—"

A thousand voices cried: *da capo! da capo!* shaking the house. "Luise von Schlingen" repeated the song, and a hundred hands wrote it down. Next day the whole of Königsberg—at that time certainly not "the town of pure reason"— upon all the streets and in all salons sang: "Einmal noch die schöne Gegend. . . ."

Fanny Lewald, who belongs to Königsberg, and

who was at that time fourteen years old, gives us, in her reminiscences, a charming picture of the irresistible charm of the artiste and the woman:—

"... Her youth, her beauty and loveliness corresponded perfectly to the idyllic part of Emmeline; but even at that time she was in possession of great tragic power, for the gentle wailing of Emmeline, her home-sickness, her innocent longing for love, became so affecting in Mdme. Devrient's representation that the audience could not repress their tears, and men and women to whom such an early love was foreign were as if rejuvenated by this performance. The air, 'I am so merry, so cheerful!' grew, in her mouth, into a most touching lamentation of love, and the painful sighs and the sound of repressed tears, which always were heard through the assurances of her cheerfulness, were deeply affecting.—Next day I saw her at a party in the country seat of a family with whose daughter she was acquainted. Both sexes surrounded her, blinded by her beauty; we young girls gazed at her from a distance. It was in the height of summer; she wore a dress of white taffeta, with rose-coloured stripes; arms, neck, and bosom bare, the abundance of her fair hair wound in tresses and puffs around her magnificent head. One of the gentlemen present chaffed her about the deep dimples in her chin, 'Yes,' she said,

'God himself has stamped that upon me. When I was created He gave me a little push with His finger, and said, "Now go! Now you are finished!" This was the origin of the dimples!' She said that quite charmingly, and when, later in the evening, she stuck some of the roses that had been plucked for her in her breast and her fair hair, she looked so beautiful that I was vividly reminded of her words twenty years afterwards when for the first time I saw Titian's Venus in the Tribune at Florence. Not that the picture had resembled her, but it was the same luxuriant magnificence of youthful womanly beauty."

Also my old early companion Friederich Tietz, who was studying at Königsberg at that time, and afterwards honoured me in Berlin with Königsberg marchpane, spoke of the charm which Wilhelmine exercised not only upon the ear, but almost more still upon the enraptured eye. He saw her with her husband in the travelling-coach—"a couple whom God seemed to have created in His best humour. He, a handsome man with finely-cut, very spiritual features—she, a blondine of 19 summers, with a lovely complexion and angelic countenance. . . . She appeared as Emmeline, in which part the truly German singing of the young wife caused a strangely emotional effect, but her personal appearance heightened the impression in a really magic manner. When, in the third act, the window of the hut opened and the singer appeared, her girlish face enframed in waving tresses, her hands folded, her moist, beaming eye lifted up to heaven, on her knees for the morning prayer—struck by this sweet Madonna-tableau in the frame of the green encircled window, the audience broke forth into most rapturous expressions of delight, which seemed never to end, and which retarded the beginning of the song for a long time."

And—scarcely three years later!—a new demoniacal passion had seized the luckless wild heart of Wilhelmine, and Karl Devrient obtained a divorce, for adultery, from his wife and the mother of his four children; the court gave him the custody of their children, having found the wife guilty as charged....

That proved a terrible blow to the poor mother's heart. From those days these words of Wilhelmine are quoted —

"If I were a Roman Catholic I should take refuge in a cloister!"

But as she was not a Roman Catholic she took refuge in the arms of love to stupefy herself and to forget, at least for moments, her inward wretchedness and the dismal desolation of her heart . . . and when one love was used up she snatched, with a greedy hand, another. . . . the rule of the demons in her heart became ever more unbridled;

but ever more demoniacal was also her influence, and her victories as a great artiste. Her whole life became a feverish chase from transport to transport, from triumph to triumph. . . . Despite this, she continued to act, for six years longer with her former husband on the Dresden stage! What bitter meetings! What situations! What new agitations daily! Karl Devrient was generous and—left.

On her first starring tour in Paris the artiste was allowed, in Weimar, to sing to Goethe, then 80 years old, his "Erlkönig," in Schubert's setting. The poet was so much moved by her highly dramatic lifelike singing that he took the singer's beautiful head into his two hands, kissed her upon the brow, and said —

"A thousand thanks to you for this magnificent artistic execution! I have heard this composition once before, but without liking it; but represented, as by you, the whole takes the shape of a visible picture."

In Paris Wilhelmine Schröder-Devrient, after her very first appearance, became the lioness of the day, and the queen of all hearts. Indeed she was the very first artiste who was buried in flowers upon a Paris stage; to obtain her favour was the cause of quarrels among the most famous heroes of the *entr'acte*, and of fights with sabres and pistols in the *Bois de Boulogne*. Soon the frequenters of the Boulevards had so many piquant stories to tell of the love adventures of the beautiful German cantatrice that a literary manufacturer found material enough to write and publish the "Secret Memoirs of Mdme. Schröder-Devrient."

But she also won the distinction of having gained over France for Beethoven's only opera. Her wonderful impersonation inspired the Paris critics to these words —

"Behold this woman whom Heaven seems specially to have made to be Beethoven's Fidelio. She does not sing as other artistes do; she does not speak as we are accustomed to hear it; her acting is by no means in conformity with the rules of art—it is as if she did not know at all that she stands upon a stage. She sings with her soul more even than with her voice; her sounds spring from the heart rather than from the throat; she forgets the audience, she forgets herself, in order to immerse herself entirely in the being whom she represents. . . . The heart-moving play, the charm of her voice, the fire-soul of Madame Devrient have displayed their whole magic. . . . The precious qualities of this songstress are a gift of nature. Fidelio does not call forth our sympathy in his sorrows and joys because he has recourse to professional tricks. The dramatic action of Madame Devrient harmonises so well with her enunciation and emphasis, she plays with such an accord of gesture and voice that one is unable to resist these two powers, which are, moreover, strengthened by the charms of her personal appearance. This talent is sublime, and the effect it produces immeasurable; the silence of the deeply-affected audience, the tears which were in everyone's eyes, are more reliable securities of her new success than the bouquets, crowns, and bravos which accompanied this triumph."

And a year later, in May, Beethoven, Fidelio and Madame Devrient, in the very zenith of her fame and beauty, made again their triumphant entry into the hearts of the Parisians. The fair German cantatrice was, if possible, received more enthusiastically still than on the first occasion. An attempt was even made to attach her permanently to the great opera. But she was prudent enough to refuse this honour. On the other hand the two following winters she appeared, with credit, in the Italian Opera at Paris, beside a Malibran, Pasta, Karadori, and Tadolini— and beside a Rubini, Nicolini, Bordogni, Lablache, Santini, and Graziani.

In "Othello" Malibran sang on her benefit night the black title part; Wilhelmine sang Desdemona. On the last dropping of the curtain a tragi-comic scene ensued. Othello has strangled his Desdemona and then stabbed himself, not noticing that both corpses have come down too near the footlights. Now, when the heavy curtain slowly rustles down, the dead Desdemona, to her terror, notices through her winking-eyelashes that it must inevitably smash her head the next second. . . . Then, quickly resolved, she jumps up, makes to the audience a tragi-comical gesture of excuse and pulls the dead Othello by the sleeve as if she asked, " Brother Jacob, are you sleeping ? " till he, too, rose from the dead, and the curtain fell amid great and universal hilarity.

In May, 1832, Wilhelmine Schröder-Devrient appeared for the first time in London as Fidelio, in a German opera company—with what splendid success may best be gathered from an English criticism, which says —

"The sensation produced by Fidelio, in 1832, will never be forgotten. The Italians, whose troupe was not strong, were honestly beaten off the field by the Germans. Everybody felt that the intense musical power of Beethoven's opera, interpreted in the chief part by a songstress who has never before appeared in England, was a surprising novelty."

An early friend of mine, who lived in London at that time, Moscheles, calls this Fidelio " unsurpassable, and the audience so enthusiastic during the whole evening that it *encored* the *overture, canon, chorus* of the prisoners, and at last (after the artistes had been called and retired again behind the curtain) the whole of the *finale*."

A scarcely less enthusiasm Wilhelmine stirred up in the cold English by her Lady Macbeth in Chelard's opera. She was placed on a par with the Lady Macbeth as *played* by Mrs. Kemble-Siddons.

Thus a critic says —

"One could not look at her without at the same time being reminded of the ideal which Mrs. Siddons is said to have created of this 'great satanic character.' With seductive and dignified gracefulness of deportment she combined a portentous look, a piercing expression of the eye, the effect of which was all the more awful because it contrasted so strangely with those colours and forms which we are accustomed to interpret as the symbols of innocence and tender sentiment. That which makes the skin shudder at the expression, 'the white devil', spoke out of every feature of Mdme. Schröder-Devrient, out of her honey-sweet and humble smiles when she welcomed the king that was destined to be murdered, out of that mixture of cruelty and flattering caresses which she knew how to express in the scene of the murder, out of the awful soliloquy of the soul which wakes whilst the body sleeps. . . . She was one of those visions which may cause young men to go mad and the old to lose their heads. . . ."

However much our artiste might be satisfied with her successes upon the English stage (her Fidelio had won for her the name of Queen of Tears!), she was highly indignant at her position in the exclusive English society, she to whom in Germany princes did homage. She was, indeed, invited into the most fashionable society, but as paid professional singer, and also treated as such. It is only to be wondered that a Schröder-Devrient suffered that— that she at all responded to their invitations. She allowed no occasion to pass without venting her anger about the fashionable English society. Thus, for instance, in Moscheles' house, where Felix Mendelssohn, Meyerbeer, and Hauser were playing at that time, she sang to her heart's desire, and she would say —

"Ah, my dears, for you I sing with pleasure; but imagine a stiff English *soirée* where I require to stand as still as a stick, and the ladies watch how I behave myself; that takes away my breath. Nor do the conductors always accompany as I want. Enough, I do not feel free as I do among you."

At the house of Moscheles she was all the more lively. Thus, one day at dinner, when relating how Romeo draws his sword, she seized the table-knife, aiming it with such violent gesture at her neighbour, the tenor Haizinger, that the English waiter, to the amusement of all present, could not hide his dismay.

After a separation of eight years, I met Wilhelmine Schröder again. My "bright still-life" as Countess Montgomery in England and Paris, an engagement in St. Petersburg, lasting three years, and a somewhat protracted professional tour through Germany and Austria-Hungary, lay between. When, in the spring of 1836, I entered upon my last and longest engagement in Dresden, whose greatest and most celebrated artiste Schröder-Devrient continued to be, the latter had, shortly before, entered upon a leave of absence of 15 months, for a starring tour.

In the winter of 1836, Hermann Michaelson, on the part of director August Haake, came from Dresden to Breslau in order to contract with me for a rather long cycle of performances for the spring following. The terms were unusually decent, the parts proposed for the performances very acceptable. I was not obliged to demand classical plays in addition to the comedies customary in provincial theatres. Mary Stuart, Emilia Galotti, Romeo and Juliet were offered me, and a worthy cast guaranteed. I had made Haake's acquaintance when he appeared on the Berlin stage, and found in him a thinking actor of the old school. As stage manager and director, he had made a name for himself long ago in the theatrical world. Gladly I signed the contract, which was favourable also in a pecuniary respect.

On a sunny spring day, on 23rd April, 1836, my

mother and I drove into the snug old town on the Oder.* The wonderful alleys of the celebrated promenades around Breslau were then shining in their first, fresh verdure. Good gracious! what enormously high houses, and what strange signs on so many of them: lions and lambs, bears and hens, horses and hounds. That in Breslau everybody lives on the fourth or fifth flat I had heard in Dresden; but soon my feet were to experience it when making calls. And always the question forced itself upon me, "Who in the world lives in the first, second, and third storeys?"

The "Golden Goose," a handsome hotel, received us kindly under her wings. The elegant and amiable stage manager, Baron Perglass, was in attendance, and welcomed us in the name of the director and his colleagues, and conducted us into the rooms reserved for us. Whilst we ascended the stair, a wonderfully warm, impressive voice above us sang, with captivating passion:

> "Die Sonne dünkt mich hier so kalt,
> Die Blüthe welk, das Leben alt,
> Und was sie reden leerer Schall,
> Ich bin ein Fremdling überall.
> Wo bist du mein gelobtes Land?
> Gesucht—geahnt—und nie gekannt?
> Das Land, das Land so hoffnungsgrün,
> Das Land, wo meine Rosen blühn,

---

* Breslau, situated on the River Oder, capital of Silesia, a province of the Kingdom of Prussia.

> Wo meine Träume wandeln gehn.
> Wo meine Todten auferstehn,
> Das Land, das meine Sprache spricht,
> O Land, wo bist Du?
> Ich wandle still, bin wenig froh,
> Und immer fragt der Seufzer : wo?
> Im Geisterhauch tönt mir zurück :
> Dort wo Du nicht bist—dort ist das Glück!"

It was a voice full of soul and fire of delivery, which touched my heart and brought the tears to my eyes. Whilst my mother and Perglass walked on, I stopped listening on each step. I never had heard such singing . . . and yet the voice seemed familiar to me. . . . Suddenly, when Schubert's "Wanderer" was finished, another song, a simple Swiss couplet, vibrated through my soul as coming from a great distance :

> "Auf der Alm bin ich so gerne,
> Denke Dein, Du süszes Lieb . . ."

Of joyful memory! And this song the same voice had sung eight years ago in Berlin. But the voice then sounded differently — more child-like. Ah, what storms had blown over this singing heart meanwhile. The singer was Wilhelmine Schröder-Devrient.

Baron Perglass told us that the great artiste had arrived in Breslau as early as the beginning of the month, but that she had stayed for a fortnight with a friendly family, after her professional tour and her bewildering triumphs, in order to take a rest. Four times she had appeared since as Norma, Romeo, and Fidelio, amidst ever increasing enthusiasm, at double prices, and before crowded houses. . . . I own that my heart sank within me a little when I heard this good news, although I had grown very fond of Wilhelmine in Berlin; and jealousy, much less artiste or professional envy, was not one of my dark sides at any time. But, if the people of Breslau expend their enthusiasm and their money on Schröder-Devrient, what would remain of both for Karoline Bauer? And I, too, had dreamt of earning some green and golden laurels in Breslau; for without such a dream one does better to remain quite quietly and snugly at home with the Penates of one's own safe stage, especially if one is bound to, and connected with it by contract for some years. Going from Dresden to Breslau at that time still meant a slow, fatiguing, and expensive journey by coach. And now it had perhaps been undertaken for nothing; for what theatrical enthusiast could burn to-day for Fidelio and to-morrow for Mary Stuart, and who could pay the ruinous prices?

Baron Perglass, a perfect gentleman and man of the world, may have guessed such mournful reflections under my deranged travelling toilette, for he said, *en passant:* "Celebrities of the opera and drama are no dangerous rivals in the favour of the public. You will see that to-morrow on your first appearance as Donna Diana. All the boxes and reserved seats for the performance are sold already, and the other places will not suffice for our Sunday audience."

This restored to me my self-possession. Had not my Donna Diana been everywhere a success!

Scarcely had Baron Perglass left us, when the good old theatrical manager, Voigt, from Posen, rushed into our room, greatly excited, his face as red as scarlet. I had played on his stage at Posen on two occasions, and brought golden luck to his coffers that were usually somewhat consumptive. The good fellow had in return enclosed me in his honest and harmless heart, and obtained from me, as the highest favour, that he might be allowed to call me by my christian name. I had consented laughingly, as the honest old man was truly devoted to me. Voigt was somewhat asthmatic, spoke in short sentences, besides emphasizing every first word after each new breathing-pause. Now, add to this the high stairs of Breslau and his excitement, which made him almost literally pant for breath: "*Dear* Karoline—*come* with me to Posen—*rather* do not unpack at all—*your* guardian angel has brought me to Breslau—*here* the hottest boards are awaiting you—*fourfold* trouble is ready for you—*firstly*, the Schröder has snatched away all applause—*secondly*, exhausted every purse—*thirdly*, your manner of acting is new here—*you* play too simply, truthfully—*Breslau* wants to be struck, dazzled—*fourthly,* cabals await you here—*friends* of Mdme. Dessoir have resolved not to let you have a chance on any account—*dear* Karoline—*if* you were hissed off the stage—*hissed off* the stage—*imagine*, Madame Bauer*—*I* tremble at the very thought of it—*do not* expose yourself to that danger—*dear* Karoline—*come* with me to Posen—*there* people know how to value you—*ugh*! *I* can say no more!" And, almost breathless, the zealous old man sank down upon a chair, mopping his red face with a huge blue pocket-handkerchief.

Although good Voigt in his excitement looked rather too comical, yet I felt anything but ready to laugh as was my custom. I said, nervously: "How, dear sir, you advise me cowardly to flee the battle-ground before I have even set foot upon it? My adversaries are to triumph even before I have tried to break a lance with them? And you counsel me so and pretend to be my friend? *La garde meurt et ne se rend pas*! I will, I must, and I shall play in Breslau, at least a cycle of six parts. And, if after that I have not gained for myself an honourable place on Breslau's boards also, then—"

"*Then*, dear Caroline—*come* you to Posen—*to* your old, faithful friends?"

Now I was obliged to laugh: "Ah, that is your

† My mother.

meaning ? Is the draught on your coffers in Posen again so great that only Caroline can help ? And this draught has had no small share in making the Breslau boards so burning hot for me ? . . . But why must you give my mother such a fright ? . . ."

"Karoline," the honest fellow cried, horrified, and bounced off his chair as if mad—" *dear, Karoline—how* do you misunderstand my heart—*only* of you I thought — *innermost* conviction prompted me to speak—*would* that all may go well—*nobody* shall be more delighted—*than* your most faithful friend—*courage* then, dear Karoline—*to-morrow* after the performance—*I shall* inquire again —*now* I will work for you, canvass—*dear* Karoline . . ." And still more excited than on his arrival, Voigt rushed away.

Scarcely had my mother and I somewhat recovered from this new annoyance, than when busy unpacking and arranging our things, an elegant billet was brought me with the remark: the footman was waiting an answer. I broke the seal in expectation—gummed envelopes were not known then—who might be writing to me? Why, I had no acquaintances in Breslau. I read with great gratification the following, in large, clear, steady characters:—

"How nice that I am enabled to meet her in Breslau, my dear sister artiste, whom I hold in affectionate remembrance from Berlin, having been unable to pay her a visit in Dresden. How many years have passed since merry Spitzeder sang us his funny Vienna 'Schnadahupfel,' and how much have both of us gone through! Can we not meet this very day? You are expected impatiently by your

"WILHELMINE SCHRÖDER-DEVRIENT.

"Can a sister-artiste meet you in a more amiable manner?"

I sent word that I should follow the servant in two minutes. When I ascended the stair, there stood an admirably beautiful woman, her full, soft form enhanced by a tight-fitting dress of pale blue silk, her sternly classical head enframed by gold shimmering locks. She nodded gracefully, smiled slyly, and sang softly, in charming drollery copying poor, merry Spitzeder, who had long since grown "a silent man" in the churchyard of München —

> Dort auf der Birkenspitz',
> Sitzt ein alter Stiegelitz,
> Der pfeift in guter Ruh . . .
> *(Pause then softly),*
> Und hat den Schnabel zu.

The amiable sister-artiste embraced me heartily, and drew me into her room.

Wilhelmine appeared to me in Dresden almost more beautiful still, her animated features more telling, more expressive than in Berlin. At that period she was after all suffering more from the divorce suit and its result, including the loss of her four children, than she owned. Now her eyes, that possessed a magic power of attraction, beamed in cloudless merriment. She told me very cheerfully of her great tour, and her latest triumphs in Leipzig, Braunschweig (Brunswick), Hanover, Nürnberg, Brünn, Vienna, Pesth, München, Augsburg. . . . She was at present triumphing in Breslau. And she spoke in childlike rapture of these triumphs, and the enthusiasm of the people of Breslau for her Romeo, Fidelio—her Lady Bluebeard, and Emmeline in "die Schweizerfamilie."

This recalled to me all the spectres of my faithful knight and director from Posen, and my own bad visions of empty houses, and indifferent hearts, and dumb mouths and hands, and I sighed a very deep sigh, saying: "How shall poor I fare under such circumstances beside your playing?"

"I fear, not well!" she said quickly, with a frank smile. "This time, my dear colleague, I have snatched the Breslauers from you; they have had to bleed already pretty freely. When I sang here last summer, the prices were quadrupled during the wool mart. First come, first served. Another time you take your revenge, and I will stand by very patiently and cry *bravo*! . . . But," she continued with good natured laughter, when she perceived my alarmed face, "I have only to sing on seven other nights, then you are rid of me, and the field is yours!"

Her frankness rather struck me at first, but afterwards prepossessed me all the more in favour of the rare woman. Later on, in Dresden, when I spent agreeable years on the same stage together with the artiste, and came into ever closer relation to her, I found out (a very unusual thing) that Wilhelmine never was untrue, never dissembled or flattered. Even when she was perfectly conscious of how much stating the truth would harm her, she could not make up her mind to speak against her conviction. And this rare virtue won many friends for the artiste and woman who remained faithful to her till her death, even though they could not always approve of her licentiousness.

When I saw that supper was being prepared in the next room, I rose. At that moment an officer entered the room rather brusquely—a good-looking, dark-complexioned man. Without embarrassment, Wilhelmine introduced her friend, saying: "Herr von R. will sup with me. . . . In spite of all, then, dear colleague, let us be good friends, both now here and by-and-bye in Dresden!"

This supping admirer was yet to cause much vexation in the engagement of the great artiste that had begun so brilliantly. The youth of Breslau, especially the academical youth, the natural rivals of sabre-rattling, flirting lieutenants, felt offended at the beautiful woman whom they idolized, because she never appeared without this shadow in cloth of two colours, and had neither eyes nor smiles for the homage of these most enthusiastic youths.

The rehearsal of "Donna Diana" heightened my courage for the evening. This most subtle and graceful of comedies was excellently got up, everybody knowing his part splendidly. Ludwig Dessoir as Don Cesar was not particularly handsome, but full of character, and readily and successfully reciprocated every shade in my acting and intonation of Donna Diana. Baron Perglass acted the part of Perin with humour and gracefulness, and an elegant volubility of tongue, so that we were enabled to take the scenes à *trois*, at a great rate, by which the play gained very much. He was a genuine "fish without fins." We, as it were, almost threw at each other playfully the sparkling *bon mots* of Don Augustin Moreto. That must necessarily also take with the audience in the evening. Director Haake conducted the rehearsal with a critical eye, with earnestness and energy, so that I was able to tell him, from my fullest conviction, that this conscientious co-operation reminded me in a lively way of the rehearsals of the Berlin Court-stage, at the time of Count Brühl, Ludwig Devrient, Pius Alexander, and Amalie Wolff.

In the evening my heart was in no small agitation when I stepped from the dressing-room on to the stage. I knew well that my first appearance would be decisive for my whole professional visit in Breslau. For a superfluity my faithful bird of ill-omen also panted up to me from the side scenes —

"*Dear* Karoline—*I* must tell you that yet—*that* you may be prepared—*do* not lose your self-possession—*if* no hand is moved for your reception—*criticism* of the sharpest kind awaits you—*all* leading men are there—*August* Kahlert, Epstein, Braniss, Mosevius, Hilscher—*already* they are engaged in a lively debate on your merits—*I* shall take up my place near the most cutting 'pens'—*courage*, dear Karoline, otherwise everything is lost—*ah*, would that we were safely in Posen—*after* the play I shall call again—*if* you will depart with me to-morrow—*how* my heart beats—*dear* Karoline. . . ."

He meant well indeed, honest old Voigt. But was this encouragement of his likely to give me courage? Rather the contrary. My position was rendered worse by the thought of my poor mother, who sat full of anxiety, and lonely, in the parlour of the theatre, not having the heart to be present at my first appearance and the Breslau reception—or rather non-reception—with her own seeing eyes and hearing ears. I really stood behind the scenes with very uncomfortable feelings whilst the first scenes were being played before me between Don Cesar, Don Louis, Don Gaston, Don Diego, and Perin, and making no impression on either the audience or myself.

But was not this the proper frame of mind for a proud, men-disdaining Donna Diana?

The moment arrived in which I had to appear for the first time on the stage before a Breslau audience. . . . Stillness of death! Coldness of ice pervaded the whole of the crowded house. That was new to me. And I felt, with unerring stage instinct, created by a long practice on the boards, that I had enemies in the house! People had been prepossessed against me!

Strange! My heart did not fail me; it rather reared proudly, saying within me: "Do you want to fight? Donna Diana is prepared for you." And coldly and proudly, as if I did not at all notice this icy temperature of the house, I said: "Read on, Laura!" I fancied how the mercury below (in the audience) was sinking a few degrees below freezing-point yet. . . . Just after my long speech to the wooers:

> "Verbergen will ich Euch nicht meinen Sinn,
> Und was, tief in Gemuth, ich fest bewahre."

I felt a breath, like a soft breeze in May, wave gently through the old house, which in those minutes did not vainly bear the name of "Zur Kalten Asche."

The rigid eyes and hearts began to melt visibly, and their frosty tongues and hands thawed gradually.

In quite a peculiar mood for battle, I adorned myself for the ball and garden scene. Since it was not Don Cesar alone who was to be overcome—but my enemies also—not only *one* heart of flint was to be conquered, but a thousand:

> "Der stolze Thor, er soll mir nicht entrinnen,
> Mit tausend Fäden will ich ihn umspinnen."*

But now I spare them no longer, not alone because I was eager for the fray—but also because I was hopeful of victory. That was an important forward move, and after every fall of the curtain the little bulletins I carried to my mother into the parlour of the theatre sounded more hopeful—more confident of ultimate victory.

When at last Diana's proud heart is conquered, and I could employ the soft language of the heart:

> "Weh mir! nicht zweifeln darf ich. Ja ich liebe!
> Was mich ergreift im tief bewegten Herzen,
> Es sind der Liebe nie gefühlte Schmerzen."

—then I had gained the victory! a splendid victory!

I was called three times with enthusiasm. Three times!—a small success to-day where "claque" and "clique" lead the applause; then, however, a glorious victory, obtained honestly with my own

---

* "Thou shalt, proud fool, not escape from me,
   A thousand threads I will forsooth spin round thee."

means. I expressed my thanks to the Breslauers in heartfelt words, as the moment and my overflowing heart inspired them; they thanked me in their turn with hands and mouth ... and the treaty of peace and friendship was concluded between us for ever, as long as, indeed, I crossed the world of boards.

The director and his colleagues heartily congratulated me on my success. Quite in flames, Voigt rushed joyfully upon the stage, crying: "*Victory*, despite all, *victory—dear* Karoline, how glad I am—*though* I have lost you for Posen at present—*but* next spring you will come to Posen, won't you? Now is your chance! *delight* them as poetical Käthchen—*move* them as Suschen—*enchant* them as Preciosa—*divert* them as poetical Frau von Lucy (in "Junge Pathe")—*and strike* them with wonder in Mary Stuart ... *dear* Karoline, all Breslau is yours."

I embraced my good mother with tears of joy. Thus concluded my first evening in the little old playhouse "Zur Kalten Asche!" What warming and kindling sparks had flamed forth for me from the cold ashes—after so much anxiety! If only the dear public could also cast a few glances into the poor human hearts of their artistes who are called upon to divert them, they would regard the stage with milder and friendlier eyes.

My second and third character—Käthchen von

Heilbronn and potato-peeling Suschen, in the "Bräutigam aus Mexico"—also won for me the more feeling hearts of Breslau—and Mary Stuart, which I played on Sunday, 1st May, 1836, for the first time, was really to conquer by storm the minority of the public who were still cautiously suspending their verdict, as Voigt had prophesied. All seats were engaged during the day. The orchestra was changed into reserved seats. The crowded house was in a perfect fever of excitement; breathless silence alternated with thundering applause. I played the magnificent part with enthusiasm and love; it was the only tragic part for which the compass of my voice sufficed, and which I played to my own satisfaction. The great master, Ludwig Tieck, in Dresden, had directed my studies of Mary Stuart, influenced by his animated and animating recollections of Friederike Bethmann. And even this day I hear his wonderfully sonorous, charming voice : " Well done, my child, almost the same as Friederike Bethmann ! "

On the "Busstag,"* according to use and wont, an "Academic" took place for the benefit of music director Seidelmann. I was glad to be allowed to appear beside Wilhelmine Schröder. Of course the songstress had the lion's-share of the evening in the performances. She gave two scenes from "Faust,".

---

* A day of general humiliation, commanded by the State, when no theatrical performances are allowed.

according to Prince Radziwill's composition. I
heard her for the first time speak on the stage:

> "Es ist so schwül, so dumpfig hie!
> Und ist doch eben so warm nicht drauss',
> Es wird mir so, ich weiss nicht wie. . . ."

—till she passed on to the singing of the "König
in Thule"—and afterwards the scene in Frau
Martha's garden—as a worthy daughter and pupil
of her great mother. Had not Wilhelmine Schröder
preferred to be an illustrious, world-renowned songstress, she might have occupied a place among the
best tragic actresses. The "König von Thule," and
Schubert's "Erlkönig," she sang in her warm,
sonorous voice most affectingly and touchingly. Her
tones flowed like the warm blood of the heart
through the soul of the listener. No other singer
has been able to efface the impression which those
ballads then made upon me. Spohr's "Emma-
Lied," on the other hand, sounded like the rustling of the wood and the warbling of birds. Beethoven's "Adelaide," like the soft yearning of
love!

I recited August Kahlert's beautiful poem, "Pa-
pagei und Brille."

It came to pass that I "got rid" of my dangerous
competitor on the Breslau stage a few days sooner
than she had laughingly announced to me on our
first meeting. Although this benefited my per-

formances—and, to confess the truth, also my pocket—yet the reason why the amiable sister-artiste had suddenly to break off her engagement filled me with sincere regret.

Wilhelmine Schröder intended to sing in the great hall of the University on 3rd May, in a concert given for the benefit of the Beethoven Monument. Her envied shadow, in cloth of two colours, accompanied her to the rehearsal. Making use of an old privilege, the students filled the body of the hall, their faces threatening mischief. I know not on which side the contest began. Two different accounts were current in Breslau at that time. Enough, the cantatrice entirely ignored her academical audience. "Provoking!" growled the students.

The parts of Madame Schröder came in their turn: "Adelaide," and Beethoven's fiery air, "Ah perfido!"

She did not sing, she only marked. Subdued groans upon the students' benches. The singer shrugs her shoulders, and laughing, turns talking to the officer and the musical conductor, her back turned to the auditory. Then the storm burst; loud groans, hissing, scraping of feet . . . a great row, in fact. And when the songstress, on the arm of Herr von R., left the great hall, walking proud and disdainfully through the ranks of the surging students, then insults are showered upon her which were

not aimed at the artiste—but at the woman. . . .
Nevertheless Wilhelmine sang, with great self-command and fortitude, in the large hall of the University on 3rd May, and as Romeo in the theatre two evenings afterwards. Then the students in the pit resumed the fight, by laughing and whistling, although the noise was somewhat drowned by the applause of the impartial audience. Having been called at the conclusion, after much opposition, the artiste appeared, and thanking her friends, she addressed a few dignified words to her opponents: " I am not conscious of having provoked such disgraceful treatment, still less of having merited it."

Immediately the storm broke out afresh, and a few voices were heard from the students' pit: " You are not wanted to appear again! Do not return! Pereat!"* mixed up with coarse invectives aimed at the " woman " (meaning her character as a woman).

Wilhelmine abandoned her two remaining performances, and left Breslau in anger. When in September, during the coronation of the Emperor Ferdinand, I played in Prague, together with her and Emil Devrient, her brother-in-law, her voice still trembled when she spoke of that insult: " Never! never will Breslau see me again."

But as years roll on, the joy and the sorrow, love and wrath, pass away. Her friends in Breslau

* The reverse to vivat! say, *down with her!*

called her. The generation of students had changed. Three years afterwards Wilhelmine Schröder again performed in Breslau; she was received with great enthusiasm; and in June, 1842, she took leave of it for ever, under laurel-wreaths, flowers, and tears of joy and sadness, after having played as "Mary Stuart" and in "Bluebeard." That bitter hour of parting in May, 1836, was entirely effaced.

I shall revert to our mutual appearance in Prague when I relate Wilhelmine's and my experiences with with Prince Felix Lichnowsky.

From Prague we returned together to Dresden. After an absence of 18 months Wilhelmine appeared once more on her native stage, in September, 1836, being received by the people of Dresden with enthusiasm. For almost eight years we were now to live together in the same city, belong to the same stage, and come into nearer social contact.

Wilhelmine was a good comrade, kind, obliging, helpful, although in her jokes she was often very drastic and rough; and because I was not fond of entering upon this peculiar mood she liked to call me, mockingly, "the Court lady," but with so charming a mockery that I could not be seriously angry with her.

She could, however, be very furious with those poor "wooden puppets," "callous creatures," "dummies," "drones," with whom she had to co-operate on the stage, when they did not at all support her in her passionate acting. Many a yearning "lover," who did not know what to do with his hands except to lay them now upon his dear loving heart, then to stretch them up to the cruel heavens, had not merely to feel her scourging derision, but sometimes also her weighty hand. First as Donna Anna she sang her Don Octavio, as Euryanthe her Lysiart, as Desdemona her Othello completely down; then she threw the poor lover "like a bundle of rags" across the stage, hither and thither.

In the tragic dungeon scene of Fidelio, on the London stage, Schröder-Leonore hands to her Florestan-Haizinger the piece of bread which she has been hiding for three days in her bosom. But as he showed no signs to accept it she whispers to him in great temper: "Perhaps you would prefer it buttered?"

When she, the most fiery Romeo, had at last sung her moonshine-pale, tiresome Julia into the coffin, she could not resist tickling the unfortunate corpse very sorely—on the soles of her feet covered with silk stockings.

For a similar serious offence in the sight of the audience, offered to my youthful townswoman, Pauline Marx, of Karlsruhe, who was likewise engaged in Dresden between the years 1840-45,

Wilhelmine Schröder was, according to the by-laws of the stage, condemned to the smart fine of a month's salary.

She could grow exceedingly wroth when she saw actors play their characters in a thoughtless, mechanical way, doing only exactly what was scantily prescribed for them in their parts; in a word, when they did not entirely identify themselves in thought and character with the person they represented, and did things on the stage they would not have done in life had they been those persons in reality whose character they had assumed on the stage. For instance, if they would carelessly throw an object—a handkerchief, a sword, a bouquet—they no longer needed into the side scenes, before the very eyes of the public. "Automatons! Puppets! They do not respect their lofty art!" she might be heard to say, angrily.

With the same care and fidelity she would likewise always arrange her own costume. Everything, down to the minutest thing, had to be in keeping with the character of the part and the time represented. Her thoroughly true nature hated all theatrical gaudery.

Thus as Emmeline she wore a green dreadnought, a scarlet bodice, white shirt-sleeves of coarse linen, a coarse round straw hat, her hair in long plaits, long two-coloured stockings with horizontal stripes, which after the manner of the Swiss "Sennerin" (herd-girl) left the feet bare. . . . And yet she was far more beautiful than all the other Emmelines, in their motley, silk, fancy costumes!

The drapery of her Norma, Vestalin, Iphigenia, was strictly arranged according to the antique pattern, and left uncovered as much as possible of her nobly beautiful form, and the whole length of the arms and the feet above the sandals. Then, when some prudish soul would beseech her at least to wear flesh-coloured tights, for the sake of our modern sense of decorum, she would answer with an ironical smile: "With pleasure, dear madam, as soon as you have proved to me that the Greek and Roman priestesses also put on flesh-coloured tights, or when once I have grown old and ugly!"

She risked much upon the stage, more perhaps than any other great dramatic artiste has ventured. But only *she* durst venture it: with her classical plastic beauty of body in every movement and pose, with her affecting mimicry and profound characterization of the parts, and with her altogether fiery, lifelike acting.

Just as an old saying about Raphael is fondly repeated, that he would have been a great painter even though he had been born without hands, so one could say of Schröder-Devrient, that had she been born dumb, she would nevertheless have been the great dramatic artiste!

Her by-play as Fidelio, Donna Anna, Valentine, Romeo, Maria in "Bluebeard," produced a no less stirring effect than her expressive, highly dramatic singing. Most affecting she was as Fidelio, when anxiously wandering up and down through the files of the prisoners, trying to recognise Florestan in every face. . . . Then as Bluebeard's spouse, when in blank dismay she rushes out of the forbidden room from the corpses of the murdered wives and tries to hide her trembling form in a corner, and when Bluebeard drags her furiously by her flowing fair hair across the stage.

Thus her grandeur and profoundness of characteriztion in by-play and in plastic representation also justified our artiste during her occasional performances in appearing sometimes as "Stumme von Portici" (The Silent Maid of Portici), and, after the pattern of her mother and Mdme. Händel-Schütz, in representing in several *tableaux vivants* Niobe and her grief about her slain children.

When I met Wilhelmine Schröder again upon the stage of Dresden certain fine-eared critics of music asserted even then that her voice had lost its beauty and was fast declining—nay, that in reality our songstress had never had a great voice, and had not even been properly trained to sing like Sontag and Malibran. But for me and other unprejudiced hearers and spectators she was still the great, unique, dramatic songstress who carried away her audience irresistibly by the fire of her feeling, her expressive intonation, her heart-warming *mezza voce*, her rich creative fancy, and by the genuine demoniacal passionateness of her singing, and her acting which was ever in harmony with it.

One evening I shall never forget; it was in the spring of 1838. Meyerbeer's "Huguenots," then quite new, was being performed. Wilhelmine understood how to make Valentine one of her most brilliant and lifelike impersonations, in which there raged quite a volcano of passions, just as in herself. On the occasion of its first performance she had in an impulse of gratitude handed the laurel to the composer, and Raoul Tichatscheck placed the wreath she had scarcely less merited upon her locks. As Valentine she was always and everywhere sure of the most beautiful victory, and yet I found her that evening in the most ill-humoured excitement, with long steps walking up and down behind the scenes. Angrily she called out to me: "Court lady, I am beyond myself! Fancy, I have only just now learned why the Huguenots was fixed for to-day. Her Excellency Countess Rossi, wife of the Royal Sardinian Ambassador, has arrived here on her way to St. Petersburg, and has been pleased to express the wish to see Schröder-Devrient as Valentine. She pipes, and I must sing! Just watch how graciously she will eye me through her glasses from her private box, as if Henriette Sontag had never belonged to us common theatrical folk."

"You wrong the Sontag there, Wilhelmine," said I. "On the contrary, she would rather prove herself never to have belonged to the real theatrical folk if she did not feel the most ardent longing to sing Valentine in your stead, and to sing the part as successfully as Schröder-Devrient."

"Wise Court lady, you are right!" Wilhelmine cried, as if electrified. "I will sing Valentine, sing and play it as I have never done before, and the Countess shall die of yearnings because she no longer belongs to us theatrical people, can no longer devote her life to free art, and by her song turn the heads of a thousand hearers with rapture."

And she sang and played as she had never done before, especially in the great, most affecting duo with Raoul Tichatscheck, who worthily supported her both with his beautiful tenor voice and his vivid dramatic acting—the first hero-tenor and the first singing tragedienne of their time!

Wilhelmine, whose eagle eye did not rarely glance at the box of the Sontag, had the satisfaction of seeing with what emotion the ambassadress followed her acting and singing, and how she, stealthily, dried tear after tear.

Tears of yearning after the forlorn splendour and glory of the intoxicating boards?

Wilhelmine Schröder and I were still to live to see Countess Rossi return to the theatrical folk, in order to earn a fortune for her children by her voice.

Twice only did I appear on the stage together with Schröder-Devrient. It was on the 12th April, 1841, on the occasion of the inauguration of the new theatre in Dresden—Semper's splendid structure, long since a prey to the flames, which afterwards rose again from the ashes a renewed Phœnix. In an allegorical prologue by Theodor Hell I represented "Love," and Wilhelmine Schröder "Romance."

I, in these words:

> "Nehmt mich auf, ihr Bühnenräume,
> Nehmt mich auf in euren Schoots!
> Alle süssen Jugendtraüme
> Pflege ich am Herzen gross;
> Alle Blüten der Empfindung
> Wecke ich mit mildem Wehn,
> Und in seliger Verbindung.
> Fei're ich ihr Auferstehn . . .

And the conclusion:

> "Und so lasst die Liebe walten
> Ewig neu, doch ewig gleich."

"Romance" introduces the poet, Emil Devrient . . .

> " Ob Du mich Romanze nennest,
> Die den freien Aufschwung öffnet
> Und die Schranken überflieget,
> Die zü strenger Norm gezogen,
> Oder Phantasie mich heissest,
> Die dem Kalten Glut und Wärme,
> Dem Gefesselten die Freiheit,
> Und dem Todten Leben leihet—
> Mir gilt's gleich ; ich bin dieselbe,
> Und der Zukunft fernste Tage
> Werden mich noch so wie heute
> Bei dem echten Dichter schauen ! "

And how the spirited artiste contrived to give life and loftiness to these weak verses !

Soon after, Frau Ungher-Sabatier, a lady and artiste universally admired and liked in Dresden, who appeared here with the tenor-singer, Moriani, in the summer of 1841, took leave of the stage for ever. For her last character but one she had unfortunately chosen Norma, Schröder-Devrient's most brilliant part.

The latter sat among the spectators, and the friends of the parting colleague took it very ill of her that under the storms of applause of the audience she alone remained apparently indifferent, and moved neither hand nor lip to express her thanks.

But Wilhelmine Schröder was too conscientious an artiste, and too honest and sincere in her character. She would have had to sham applause on this evening, and that was repugnant to her. Norma's aging voice sounded harshly, and on several occasions did not suffice for the higher notes. It broke down.

But that nothing was further from Wilhelmine Schröder than petty envy or jealousy the good people of Dresden were to learn on the last appearance of Frau Ungher-Sabatier in "Belisario." The greatest ovations had been prepared, and the whole evening the artiste was overwhelmed with applause, flowers, and poems, in her really grand dramatic impersonation; pretty carrier-pigeons fluttered on the stage; but Wilhelmine and I had prepared a greater act of homage still as a surprise for the parting artiste. At the conclusion of the last act I stepped forward upon the stage, dressed as a muse, in a white-rosy garment, flowers in my hair, addressing to her with much feeling some farewell verses, at the same time offering her flowers. Tears came into the singer's eyes; then a melodious voice called to her from the opposite side. It was Wilhelmine, likewise dressed as a muse; she offered to her sister-artiste a full laurel-wreath, with heartfelt words. Deeply affected, the parting songstress sank into the arms of her still more famous rival, and I heard her whisper, with sobs: " And that you—just you, should so nobly embellish my parting. . . . How happy that makes me!"

"May I thus say farewell to the stage, too, one day!" was Wilhelmine's answer.

The house, taken by surprise, took the warmest and most demonstrative interest in this parting-scene; all were moved and enraptured. Exultant cheers were now lavished both on the parting Sabatier and the generous Schröder-Devrient. I am at a loss to compare the dramatic-singer Wilhelmine Schröder—with her absolutely demoniacal passion and power that carried along everything with it—to any other artiste except her own mother, the most brilliant tragedienne Sophie Schröder. As the latter wished to be a man, to be able to play the part of the satanic Richard III., so her daughter wished to be a man, in order to sing and play the wild Don Juan. "Oh, and what would I make of this part? Do I not feel in me the boiling of the real, wild, love-mad blood of a Don Juan? And how would I turn the heads of the poor, pretty little maids and wives, and make them fall in love with me, one dozen after another? Believe me, children, such an ingenious playing of a Don Juan, with all its thousand arts of hell, is a far higher enjoyment than love's sure possession."

With this she shook in bacchanalian wildness her rich, fair tresses, and her eyes glistened with inner fire, and her white teeth laughed—like Heine's Frau Venus. . . .

As her mother, Wilhelmine, too, might say—

"Enthusiasm—passion, without which there can be no dramatic art! Yea, a passion that makes you beat your head on the wall—a passion, even if accompanied by bread and water and a linen dress; but, for goodness sake, let us have a passion."

This passion was her greatness—and her misfortune. The demons of wild passion exercised a stronger sway in her heart than in that of Sophie Schröder. Therefore the daughter through her sweet, sweet love was to be far more wretched yet than her mother. During her whole life as a woman she always followed only the impulse of her unruly heart, and the whims of the moment.

Wilhelmine Schröder, like her mother, never was without some great or small passion of the heart— or of her hot blood. Beside the love that satisfies the heart, she allowed to the toying *amour en passant* likewise only too much free play. Upon her professional tours amorous simpletons fell by dozens at her feet, and she had her choice in the picking up.

Schröder-Devrient loved much in her life— perhaps more than any other theatrical beauty, But nevertheless, she stands morally, too, a great deal higher than most of the loving stage-heroines. Blinded by wild passion, she sometimes threw herself away, perhaps; but she never sold herself and her love!

The devotions of love were as indispensable to her existence as were those of art. Her hot, thirsty heart would otherwise have pined away. When serious friends entreated her not to rush wilfully to her ruin, not to risk her character as woman so madly, endanger her health, her voice, and throw away her fortune, she would answer, with a sad smile—

"Leave me just as I happen to be. 'Were I sober-minded I should not be called Tell!'* Nobody escapes from his fate, and nobody from his own heart. My heart is, perhaps, my curse; but it is also my happiness. And I cannot make it other than what it just is. The dear heavens themselves have stamped upon me a psychological contrast, and given me upon my life's journey the struggle of the demons in my heart. In the hour of my birth (6th Dec.) a violent thunderstorm was raging. Under thundering and lightning, a furious snowstorm swept through the streets of Hamburg. Is it my fault, then, that for ever lightning, storm, and thunder reign triumphantly in my heart? And forbid the silkworm to spin! says Goethe-Tasso, and *he* has once deemed me worthy of his hallowing kiss."

But dismal wailings found vent in her wildly-agitated heart, and in her writings—sad laments over mistaken love—a mistaken life. Thus she writes:—

* Quotation from Schiller's Wilhelm Tell.

"I was but 23 years old when my first matrimonial union was severed; but even then I had already lost all the sweetness of youth, all illusionary fancies that embellish life. Even then I could say with perfect truth: I am a stranger everywhere!

"Oh, it is awful to have to roam about in this insipid, empty, commonplace world, one's breast filled with warm, true, infinite feelings. . . . There is a burning, hot spot just in the middle of my heart; from it goes out an unspeakable woe to impart itself to my whole existence. . . .

"Canst thou not dissolve, mighty pain? Not even tears! Then it surges and wallows in the deepest part of my heart—it burdens my breast like masses of rock, and no deliverance! Oh, my God! *no* life—that were best for me! I feel as if I should be relieved and better if I could bore a deep, deep wound into this poor heart! Then this feeling of oppression, this anxiety, would cease—air! consolation! tears! . . .

"What demon often dwells in man that can neither be conquered nor banished! Weak, wretched nature—and yet no weak, miserable soul, a soul capable of all good and noble impulses.

"A true, genuine artiste requires a heart, but a blessing it is not. If you knew what a curse it was. to me! You stand with your hot heart so entirely alone. For who understands warming himself by its fire and is not afraid of the danger of burning himself at it?"

This poor, hot, wild heart consumed itself on its own fire!

When I came to Dresden, Whilhelmine Schröder's heart, her whole thought and being, were filled by a hot passion for a very handsome young officer in the Saxon army. A single look had been decisive for both hearts. While staying in an hotel of a small garrison town in Saxony during a journey, the young artiste was on the point of leaving her apartment one evening, when, perchance, in the same moment the door opposite opened, and Wilhelmine stood face to face with a blooming man, much younger than she; it was a Lieutenant M., the son of the first Minister of State in Saxony. . . . They stand speechless! But how she looks at him! As the serpent does at the little bird—with an entwining, engulfing, electrifying look! From her eyes flashes hot passion, already in high blazing flame. . . . So they face each other—dumb, eye to eye. . . . Then she slowly retraces her steps, without taking her eyes off him . . . and he follows her—spell-bound, step for step, as the bird does the magnetic look of the serpent.

This Lieutenant M. may claim the longest spell-of Wilhelmine's fidelity, namely, six years. He followed her to Dresden, and I have often met him in the house of his mother, the widowed State Minister's wife. His younger brother was *my* warmest admirer. Wilhelmine Schröder was not received in this house.

A marriage between the lovers was often spoken of. But the Minister's widow peremptorily refused to consent to it, and for very good reasons. Moreover, the lovers wanted the means that would enable them to resign their respective positions, and to live as circumstances then demanded.

And then a new passion—the wildest and most reckless of her life—flashed through her luckless, love-thirsty heart. . . . She made the acquaintance of Lieutenant von Döring, and parted with her true and faithful friend M. Döring was generally known as a coarse, profligate *roué;* but in her love-paroxysm, which was an altogether incomprehensible one, she had neither head nor heart for anything except her lover. Everybody warned her against the wicked fellow, who spent her money in profligacy, and in the company of his brother-officers paraded the love-mania of the aging woman—she listened to nobody except her own wild heart.

At that time (1842) there lived in Dresden the Countess Ida Hahn-Hahn, together with her lover,

Herr von Bistram. Her "Faustine" had just been published, and everybody spoke in rapturous terms of this wondrous novel. In certain æsthetic circles a perfect "Faustine-worship" was carried on, as if this was not at the same time a worship of free love. . . . Did not Faustine, with surprising facility, break troth to, and the heart of, two men whom she at first loved with idolizing affection, just as you would break a stick of barley-sugar?

Then, one day, Wilhelmine asked me right offhand: "Court-lady, do you, too, find that I bear such a great resemblance to Countess Hahn-Hahn's Faustine? People here assert that I have sat as a model for the character of this heroine."

Really, I was a little puzzled at this bold question, and the still greater boldness of the good people who reminded Wilhelmine to her face of her wrecked matrimonial union with Karl Devrient, and her hot, wild heart and its many mad romances.

"Well, why are you thus staring at me, as if I were Don Juan's 'guest of stone?' I myself find that I bear some resemblance to Faustine."

"Yes, certainly. You are like her—beautiful, enchanting, have golden locks, are witty, a prodigious singer."

"Court-lady—paragon of a Court-lady!" she interrupted me impatiently—"you do not want to understand me. No, no; the resemblance lies in the character, in the nature of Faustine—and, as far as it goes, pretty much in the fate too. May it not be proved that a Countess Hahn-Hahn has so brilliantly depicted me!"

"You, too, Brutus, in the spell of this literary siren?" said I now, laughing heartily. "How, in the world, did Countess Hahn-Hahn ever succeed thus in infatuating and confusing the commonsense and the honest heart of a Wilhelmine Schröder? Would you not eventually even enter a convent in order to finish your portrait of Pauline? Nonsense, Wilhelmine! You a Faustine? You have a genuine warm human heart in your breast, capable of the sincerest and most self-denying love, and Countess Hahn-Hahn and her Faustine in their turn only carry in their cashmere-bosom love caprices and whims. Countess Ida and her heroines boast of a 'prodigious soul,' but which must be terribly empty, for how could otherwise so much insipidity, artificiality, and idiocy strut about in it? Wilhelmine Schröder has proved by her art-creations, by her Fidelio, her Norma, and Vestal, that she is a great strong soul. Faustine breaks troth to her unfortunate husband, with the handsome Andlau, and when her husband fires at them with a pistol, she flies with the wounded lover to Italy. After a conjugal happiness of seven years, when Andlau is away on a journey of some months' duration, the charming Faustine hastened to let Count Mengen fill up the immense emptiness of her immense heart, although she asserts that she loves her Andlau still, nay, idolizes him. . . . But nevertheless, she discharges him in a letter, renouncing her love for him. Fortunately, Andlau returns, in order to bring Countess Faustine Mengen—in spite of all still loved by him—his affectionate greeting and pardon, and then to die happily in her arms. . . . That is the cue for Faustine—to abandon her adored husband, her son whom she loves intensely, to enter a cloister repentant, and after praying, singing, and organ-playing during eighteen months to ascend as a saint direct into the seventh heaven. Has Wilhelmine Schröder the miserable heart and the immense soul, is she possessed of the immense emptiness necessary to make three beloved men unhappy, with perfect consciousness, from pure caprice and vulgar selfishness, in order to be able afterwards to play for a time the part of the repentant in the cloister with the most refined stage trickery? Yes, then you are the original of Faustine."

"Court-lady, you are quite fire and flame!" and Wilhelmine held out her two hands to me in her hearty way. "Yes, you are right. My wild heart has often carried away my better self into wildernesses and abysses; but for a dear man whom I loved thoroughly with all my heart, I would leave my life before I would betray and ruin him."

And yet when I read years afterwards, after Wilhelmine's death, in my loneliness, the fragments of the diary of my old sister-artiste, published by Klaire von Glümer, I was quite startled by a Faustine-trait in these pages. "Everywhere we are met by the complaint about the emptiness of the heart and its loneliness, the horror of being alone, the longing after another loving heart that might fill this emptiness, quench this everlasting thirst for love."

The following may be found on one of those pages:

"When overwhelmed by applause, I returned home all burning with delight in my art, I was *alone!* And I had not a soul who understood me and rejoiced with me! I feel a sort of fear and misgiving! Would that I had a living creature about me, a faithful dog, any creature which was devoted to me! How I yearn for a sincere exchange of thoughts—but so alone! And to write what agitates my heart I cannot. Here the warm living word from mouth to mouth is lacking, and where the word suffices no longer, the look into an eye which penetrates into the depth of our soul. It is a hard privation to have to wander through life so uncomprehended. . . . To-day I acted as sponsor to a child of the labourer Lorenz, and have seen human misery in its most lamentable form. God, how is it possible that man can live thus ? . . . And yet who knows if the poor woman upon the straw is not happier than I upon my silken pillows? She has her husband, who nurses, supports, and watches her; she has her children. What is left to me ?

" Why can I not accustom myself to be alone in this life, as it is my lot to be? Cruel fate! Thou hast given me a heart full of gentle feelings, a soul which only feels that one want: to be understood and loved—and just that I have to want. I have nobody in this wide world, and I feel my loneliness more and more painfully—feel how my heart bleeds, how in its anxious yearnings for the unattainable it wastes away, and how my whole inner harmony is disturbed by it. I am absent-minded, thoughtless, impatient, peevish. I would fain rush out into wind and storm as far as my strength would carry me—if possible, to die, for it is a sad, bitter destiny to be alone in the world ! "

And in this anxious horror of being alone—in the ever more burning thirst to be loved, the more the time of love, her spring of life, faded—the unhappy one fell into the hands of that terrible Döring. . . . With the anguish of despair and the horror of desolate abandonment she clung to his frivolous declarations of love. ... She did not *wish* to see clear. She did not *want* to awaken out of this delirious love-dream! She *would* not believe those of her friends who daily brought for her new proofs of Döring's unworthiness! ... With the whole ardour of her wildest imagination, and with her ever busy "art of invention," which grew up with her, she ever belied herself anew, and convulsively worked herself into the most torturing love-delirium.

He who heard her sing at that time —

> " Glück ohne Ruhe
> Liebe bist du ! "*

might have an idea how this poor luckless heart of a woman—tormented by reckless passions—suffered—" staggering from desire to lust—and in lust dying with desire." †

Her outward appearance also participated in this restless haste. She rushed from one starring tour into another—almost without joy in the art she had once so highly valued—to obtain new intoxicating triumphs ... and new glittering lusty gold. ... For Döring required much, very much gold to indulge his noble passions—and he never hesitated to accept it from his mistress and—to demand it.

What blind love-paroxysm the poor woman, who

* Happy without rest—that is love blest.
† Quotation from Goethe's Faust.

was now almost forty, indulged in, her letters testify, which were partly published after her death. I shall only quote a few characteristic passages about her relations with Döring.

"Dantzig, May, 1843. . . . I felt clearly that I stood at a turning point of my life, but what shape my fate is to take in the nearest future I do not yet see quite clearly. Only do not talk to me of peace, there is none for me in this world. I must away— away without stopping, and whatever comes in my way I carry away with me. Whether the stream of my life lead to a precipice, or may ultimately lose itself quietly in the sandy plain of triteness— who can tell? Now I hasten on with my sore bosom from effort to effort, from excitement to excitement, from triumph to triumph, and every step leads, God be thanked, nearer to the grave. I have everything, and the world envies me, and yet have I never more ardently longed for death than just now."

"Königsberg, June, 1843. . . . I fear that your prayer to God to grant at last peace to my heart will not be fulfilled until this heart shall entirely cease to beat; for, alas, I see more and more that I am hunting after phantoms, never shall reach what I am striving after, and so shall always remain unsatisfied. Therefore, dear friend, the sooner this restless heart ceases to beat, the sooner my hottest wish will be realized. . . . Life lies heavy, yea, heavy upon me, and my soul strives violently to free itself from the disagreeable prison."

"Zürich, September, 1843. . . . I should think that it was not an altogether mistaken aim of life to help to lighten the existence of the best, most lovable, and amiable man who is not particularly favoured by fortune, instead of withdrawing from him the hand he has seized full of assurance and confidence. Anxious care for my own future will now make me all the less renounce him, because he is unhappy and has no friend but me in this world. I shall only act according to his will, and only his will can sever me from him. Hitherto I have in all my actions followed the advice of others, and not seldom I have had cause to rue that I did not follow my own way. But this time I am firmly resolved to act as independently as possible, and merely to submit to the will of that one in whose hand, after full deliberation, I have placed my lot."

"Nürnberg, June, 1846. . . . Nothing will shake my resolution to devote my whole life, with all its noblest faculties, only to him. Do not call me eccentric, dear friend; thus it will, and cannot be changed. I am given back to life and art, and now go to meet, with new vigour, with revived courage, all the plagues which may yet be in store for me till autumn."

On the 29th August, 1847, Wilhelmine Schröder-Devrient was privately married to Döring at Kleinzschocher, near Leipzig—in spite of the warnings and prayers of her friends.

Shortly before the wedding the deluded one received another such warning letter. The Duke of Coburg wrote :—.

". . . The news that your relations with Herr von Döring do not merely continue, but are even to be consummated in wedlock, has filled me with the profoundest terror. You must know that this Döring has been depicted to me long ago, and on all sides, as the most despicable man, as a man whose sole object is to prey upon you, and who besides boasts of the luxury he carries on with the money taken from you. The latter fact is said to have even induced his comrades several times to deliberate whether it was compatible with their honour to continue to serve with him. I repeat how exceedingly grieved I am to have to tell you so painful a thing; but also repeat that, as your true friend, I durst not conceal what I have said."

With what feelings must the unhappy woman have stepped to the altar?

In such a desperate, scornful, care-nothing mood she had, shortly before the marriage, signed, without reading it, the marriage contract drawn up by Döring.

Their marriage trip consisted of a new professional tour to hunt up gold, more gold, ever more gold, for her lord and master could never get enough of this metal to spend in extravagance. And now, having the marriage contract in his possession, he assumed a more and more regardless—nay, brutal conduct towards the woman who had sacrificed *all* to him!

On the 29th December, 1847 — exactly four months after her wedding-day—upon her tour to St. Petersburg, Wilhelmine sang in Riga the part of Romeo for the last time. If any one had told her that evening, when she was overwhelmed with laurels and applause: "You are taking your leave with this from the stage once and for all—you will never again tread the boards of your glory and your highest earthly happiness!"

On they went to Dorpat. . . . What there happened between the husband and wife we do not know, but it must have been something dreadful. . . . Even Wilhelmine only ventures to hint at it: " Suddenly Döring threw away his mask, and before me stood—a devil incarnate. . . . I was crushed, undone, a beggar, sick to death in body and soul, and without hope ever to be able again to rise from my wretchedness. . . .' With an insulting scorn this "devil incarnate" pointed to the contract of marriage, in which the spouse had made over to him everything: that which she actually possessed and ever might possess, nay, even the half of her Dresden annuity.

With this contract of marriage in his possession, Döring hastened back to Saxony and took possession of the belongings of his wife. She took legal steps to procure a divorce from him at Berlin. How much she suffered appears in a letter dated—Berlin, July. It runs thus—

" . . . I am dead for this world. . . . I must confirm what you fear : I have grown dumb—and for ever—and what you hope will not be fulfilled, for I shall neither appear as blood-thirsty Lady Macbeth, nor as avenging Medea ; and even if the magic power of the latter were actually at my command, I should make no use of it, for my Jason is not worthy of pursuit ! I was and am unhappy beyond expression, and the awful events which discharged themselves over my head, like a heavy thunderstorm, during the past six months, have caused such a complete ruin, both within and without, that even on that ground there never can be any question again of my appearing in full vigour once more. My soul is wounded to the death, and the slightest touch causes it pain. I have not sung any more these six months, and I can scarcely bear to hear singing. . . .

" . . . I am wretched and sick—*but free!* The *coup de grâce* I received through the death of my daughter, who died in my arms in Hanover, on the 22nd May.

" For the last three months I have been living here in noisy Berlin, all alone, secluded and totally forsaken. I wanted to await here the end of the lawsuit against Herr von Döring, but this proves so protracted that I probably shall not live to see its termination. . . . My pecuniary situation enforces upon me the strictest economy, as Herr von Döring has claimed all I called my own. God only knows whither fate may yet cast me; but what about me?"

Döring gave his consent to a divorce only after receiving payment of a considerable sum which Wilhelmine's friends raised for her. At the end of 1848 she was free—but broken down for life.

The awful desolation of her soul—the unnatural fermenting state of mind and heart, the confused impulse to stupefy herself through deeds, and her old tormenting horror of being alone—led the forsaken wife and the wrecked artiste, who could never hope again to win laurels upon the stage, in a wild frenzy into the arms of the Revolution. . . . And she never in any place, or at any time, concealed her revolutionary sympathies.

Late in the autumn of the wild year 1848, she had returned to Dresden—as annuitant of the Court Theatre. What a sad return to the places from which her brilliant fame as artiste had spread into all lands, a quarter of a century before! Where she had tasted the spring-time of life even to the last blossom! And now everything faded and gone!

A few days after it had become known that Robert Blum had been executed in the Brigittenau by Vienna, on 9th November, Wilhelmine Schröder walked over the Brühl terrace with Ernst Benedikt Kietz, a painter, and intimate friend of hers. This is the same artist who painted the magnificent crayon which represents the great singer in profile, a fur dolman over her bare shoulders. The picture was lost years ago, during the burning of the beautiful Dresden Theatre for whose artist's gallery it was painted—along with the glorious marble bust of the artiste which Rietschel had executed for the playhouse in 1839; also the costume-drawings which were to mark my artistic career were lost on the same occasion.

My friend Kietz has related to me afterwards at the lake of Zürich the following scene:—

"Wilhelmine Schröder had already compromised herself by many a bold revolutionary word, and openly acknowledged herself a democrat. She was very intimate with Robert Blum. His death had filled her with deep affliction, but also with bitter resentment. She had just vented her wrath to Kietz. At that moment the Russian Ambassador, Baron Budberg, accosted her, and said with a sarcastic smile —

"'Beautiful dame! You wear on your neck a black velvet ribbon. Is that to express your affliction at the death of the barricade-hero Blum?'

"'No! My grief for the murdered friend I bear in the depth of my heart—but, Baron,' Wilhelmine said, kindling up, 'should you ever be hung up by the people on the first lamp-post they come to, as you have honestly deserved, I shall exhibit my sympathy by a burning red ribbon on the neck!' Thus saying, she left the dumbfounded Ambassador.

"These words Herr von Budberg never forgave her—and Frau Wilhelmine von Bock has had to suffer for it heavily."

Also in the May revolt of the following year that took place in Dresden, Wilhelmine Schröder, who had returned but the day before from Paris, is said to have taken a part, along with Richard Wagner and Gottfried Semper, in haranguing the people, and urging them on to erect barricades.

But, deeply affected by the contrast between the blooming, laughing spring all around on the banks of the Elbe, and the ringing of the tocsin and all the terrors of devastation and bloody death in the town, once so flourishing and joyous, now dedicated to destruction, she hastened on to Berlin.

Fanny Lewald, a friend with whom she was connected by revolutionary sympathies, and who encouraged her to devote herself to dramatic recitations, received the following reply, accompanied by a sad shake of the head:—

"I can do nothing without music! Music is the

element which liquifies my powers and sets them in motion. And if I were to try it, if I wanted to play the parts of my mother, I would appear to myself a wretched copier, for the parts which my mother played cannot be given in any other way than hers, and I must act! work! myself produce! Moreover, you forget that there are situations in which it is absolutely forbidden to fail. Where should I try what I can do? And if it failed? I, Schröder Devrient, may suffer shipwreck in my life, that only concerns myself—on the stage I dare not shipwreck."

Then it almost seemed as if that poor, much-agitated heart, with its many demons, was yet destined to enjoy rest. Herr von Bock, a landed proprietor in Livonia, and afterwards "Landmarshal," a highly-accomplished virtuoso, and a man of noble character, whose acquaintance Wilhelmine had made in Paris, had the courage to offer to this woman with the evil reputation, and the motley past life, and the wild heart, his hand, his wealth, and his pure name. The marriage took place in Gotha, in the spring of 1850.

Frau von Bock was animated by the best intentions to be a faithful companion and an anxious housewife to her husband—"a noble, gifted man, full of tender love and care for me." She followed him to his estate in Livonia—but her restless heart did not endure this solitude for a year. As the flower thirsteth for the sun, so she thirsted for the air of her German fatherland, and German homage.

The following summer she was back to Germany. . . . Then she was arrested in Dresden owing to her participation in the May revolt, but set free on finding caution. The inquiry, however, was quashed by the King's mercy a few months after. Now the Russian Ambassador likewise remembered the scene between himself and Robert Blum's friend, on the Brühl terrace—and the consequence was that Frau von Bock was expelled from Russia on account of her revolutionary sentiments.

After many fruitless efforts and great pecuniary sacrifices, Herr von Bock succeeded at last in having this decree of banishment revoked. In the spring of 1854 Wilhelmine was allowed to prepare for her return journey to Livonia. In a parting letter she says—

" . . . I shall now shortly return to a country to which I, according to my whole nature, shall ever remain a stranger, into which nothing calls me back but a sacred duty and veneration for the best and noblest of men. I descend into an open grave, and as the Russian toll-bar sinks down behind me, so also for me sinks and vanishes everything that otherwise may embellish a life. Art and poetry, intercourse with men from whose rich knowledge one may draw refreshment, industry, and great historical events —all those remain on the other side of the toll-bar.

But I shall find there a home, order, and rest, at least outward rest, and live by the side of a man who is to me a faithful and loving friend. I shall not be alone in the wilderness which awaits me, I have the faithful friend, the beloved husband, and—myself."

But she deceived herself. She, who in the most animated, artistic, and erotic life, in the surging sociality of Dresden, and upon her exultant triumphant wanderings from stage to stage, was tormented by the horror of being alone—how could she have found repose in the solitude of Russia?

And thus she laments anew, after having hardly settled in Russia, in her letters to Germany —

" . . . I cannot live where my 'grand' does not keep in tune; you know that I am half dead if I cannot produce a sound from my throat. Add to this a winter of eight months' duration! . . .

" . . . During the first time of my sojourn in my new home, I was much occupied in bringing light, order, and cleanliness into the chaos that surrounded me, as far as this indeed is possible here, and at least to give to the apartment I inhabit a touch of poesy, without which I find it altogether impossible to live, but which was attended by endless difficulties; for here all is prose, naked, bare prose, in its most unlovely form. . . . An irrepressible feeling of discomfort has taken possession of me here . . . an uneasiness which lies upon my mind like a dark cloud. . . ."

This was rendered worse by the restless, distressing gnawing of vain thoughts at the heart spoilt by triumphs. In the distant Germany you are already forgotten as artiste! Here, in the wilderness, you are buried alive!

Who could better realize Wilhelmine's feelings than I, who suffered the same gnawing torment for fully a quarter of a century among the lonely Swiss mountains, till my name revived in my "Stage Reminiscences," and Karoline Bauer once more became a celebrated artiste in Germany!

This fear of being forgotten is heard plaintively in one of Wilhelmine's letters to a distant friend, dated 1855 —

" . . . Who in Germany troubles about the Schröder-Devrient at present? . . . Last winter I often sat with a bleeding heart in the theatre (in Berlin). . . . Was it not shown then? How then can it be that not a trace has been transmitted of what I could defend before the assembled Olympus. The audience who saw and heard me too, cheered and clamoured more than they ever did to me. Then a quiet tear would roll down my cheeks, and sighing, I exclaimed: 'Nonsense, thou prevailest, and I must succumb!'* There is, perhaps, no more painful feeling extant than that of having lived in vain! But is not the whole world a great Bedlam at the present time? Wherever one

* Quotation from Schiller's "Jungfrau von Orleans."

looks a caricature has stepped into the place of divine reason. Truth and naturalness have disappeared, especially from the representing art, and the only aim hunted after is—a full purse, indifferent as to the means by which it is filled. For the greater number of the artistes of the present are hypocrites on the stage as well as off it—and where there is no truth in life there is none in art either."

In this old horror of solitude, and in this new fear of oblivion, Wilhelmine, who was fifty-two by this time, had no peace on the rich Livonian baronial estate, till in April, 1856, she had sung in the Berlin "Sing-Akademie," from Schubert's 'Erlkönig', "Rastlose Liebe," and "Ich grotte nicht"—with a voice that was almost extinct, but with the old fire of feeling and the vigour of her dramatic delivery—and till she had won new triumphs as interpreter of songs. During the following two years she sang repeatedly in concerts in Berlin, Dresden, and Leipzig. Nay, she was preparing to appear on the stage again in Weimar, and then, like Sontag-Rossi, to win in a triumphal tour laurels and gold in America. She also wanted to write the story of her life: "It is just the old story, over which one's very heart will break. The world has only seen the roses upon my path of life, but knew not how their thorns have torn my flesh. However, I am anxious that my German fatherland should know from what pains the artiste developed, whom by its joyous acclamations it often made to forget the thorns."

Then, in the midst of this nervous struggle for new life and new triumphs, death, death in its most awful form, knocked at this poor restless, passionate human heart.

As late as the 6th March, 1859, Wilhelmine Schröder sang publicly at a concert in Leipzig— with broken vigour—her swan's song. Then she sank down upon a long couch of pain . . . never to rise again.

She suffered terribly; but yet she would not die. All the demons of the heart awoke once more upon this death-bed, and clung with desperation to life, and to—alas! its so hotly cherished wreaths of joy and crowns of fame. . . . Besides, her fear of being forgotten rekindles again and again! Its trembling accents may even to-day be felt in a letter, one of her last—

. . . "How sad is the fate of the mime! We are able to influence chiefly the mass, but are unable to imprint deeper traces than light sand would receive —a gentle breeze blows over it, and all is effaced —forgotten. The blood of my heart I have sung away to them—and now? . . ."

Frau Ungher-Sabatier, to whom Wilhelmine and I once handed the last parting wreaths on the Dresden stage, visited the dying sister-actress, and afterwards related most affectingly how distressfully she had struggled and murmured against death—a picture of horror, like dying Queen Elizabeth in Steuben's picture.

And yet the couch of agony of the dying artiste was not without a friendly angel—the consciousness not only of having gladdened many human hearts through her god-inspired art, but also of having dried many anxious, bitter tears in the eyes of poverty and wretchedness.

Wilhelmine Schröder was beneficent in the grandest sense. Her humane heart never, in spite of many a bitter experience, grew tired of mitigating human distress. In this respect, too, she was the worthy image of her mother.

Here on her death-bed, before her grave closes, I would relate some traits of her deep love for her fellow-creatures. Posterity will then judge more leniently this poor, weak human heart which so often erred and stumbled.

With the poor in Dresden the "dear, good" Mdme. Schröder-Devrient was a great favourite—and perhaps the most popular lady in the town. Nobody in all Dresden was so often asked to be sponsor; and always she came herself, even into the most wretched hut to hold the child at the font, to provide a cheerful christening feast, and to establish order and cleanliness as far as she could.

At Christmas there was always great joy in her dwelling near the Theaterplatz; then she gave presents to the poor, and in the heartiest, most pleasant manner. She knitted all the year over, during hair-dressing operations, to provide for this Christmas.

When her eldest son Wilhelm—to-day a farmer in Livonia—was being brought up in an Institute in Dresden, he durst not come to his mother's Christmas-tree without bringing some poor children with him whom he himself had picked up, and giving them of his own gifts—" for the boy is early to accustom himself to remember the poor!" said his mother.

And how often has Wilhelmine Schröder-Devrient sung in the concerts and benefit-performances of poor artists, not even fearing a costly and fatiguing journey to effect her purpose—to secure for her needy colleagues a good house by means of her name.

The whole of her Romeo-fee in Berlin, 25 Frd. d'or, she sent to the sufferers by fire in a village near Weimar.

She had purchased a new " grand," and advertised her other instrument for sale. Thereupon a shabbily dressed young man came into her house, and was about to go away at once when he had learned from the chamber-maid the price, and whose it was. But at least he would play a single tune upon the instrument that had so often accompanied Schröder-Devrient in her singing!—he could not resist that temptation. The maid had told him that there was nobody in the room. And so he grew absorbed in his playing upon the beautiful instrument, and poured out his young, warm heart in musical sounds, till Wilhelmine, in her most bewitching amiability, stood smiling behind him, calling out *Bravo!* She had soon overcome his shyness, and his life and heart lay open before her. She knew he was poor, and that he could not think of spending so much money for a piano; but that its possession would make him the happiest of mortals.

She dismissed him affably; and next day sent him the instrument, desiring him to accept it as a souvenir of Schröder-Devrient who knew no higher joy than to cause joy to others.

When a matter-of-fact friend of hers reproached her for this new extravagance in thus failing to provide for her old age, she said, with a mild, almost melancholy smile —

"These few dollars are, in this case, not at all worth considering—that is an affair of the heart. But you have no idea of how one feels who is to part for ever from such a silent companion! Before this instrument I have for years poured out all my joy and all my pain; and long since I felt pain at the thought of having to give up my old confidant into the hands of the first indifferent comer for vile money. Now I am heartily glad to have found for it a home with a good fellow who loves and knows how to treat it!"

For a dancer who had broken a leg she bought a circulating library to support himself with.

At Elgersburg, in Thuringia, where she took the waters, she used to converse with an old woman who herded the geese; her she furnished with a warm cloak, writing at the same time: "It is true the woman is said to be without morals or manners; but *à qui la faute* that these people are thus? For all that, you cannot allow them to starve or die of exposure; we must do for them what we can."

To *this* Wilhelmine Schröder-Devrient old Tiedge, the author of "Urania," who spent the evening of his life in Dresden, dedicated the following atoning words —

> " Hoch vom Ruhm empor getragen
> Strahlt Dein Nam' im Glanze *dieser* Welt;
> Was Du thust in stillern Tagen,
> Das wird in ein Rechnungsbuch getragen,
> Das ein Engel dort in *jener* hält ! "

This angel has kissed the last breath from her dying lips. After long and dreadful sufferings she died *gently* at Koburg on 26th January, 1860.

At her grave there was sung, at her request: "Es ist bestimmt in Gottes Rath!" und "Ein' feste Burg ist unser Gott!"

But even in the earth this restless heart was not at once to find rest, because in her written papers, left behind, the wish was expressed that she would like to repose in Dresden earth! Herr von Bock caused the coffin to be exhumed, and to be interred in the Trinitatis-cemetery in Dresden, where the grave was adorned with a granite-column, upon which is inscribed —

WILHELMINE VON BOCK
SCHRÖDER-DEVRIENT.

* * * * * *

At these two graves at München and at Dresden the wild demons that raged so furiously through the living heart of mother and daughter grew dumb.

But the question forces itself upon us whether Sophie and Wilhelmine Schröder would have become such great, unique, heart-moving artistes of the stage *without* these demons of hottest passions in their hearts?

Hardly! A word about this by Sophie Schröder I have referred to before. I here repeat it —

"We are to represent to you upon the stage passions in their grand reality. Why do you chide us if we ourselves feel them?"

A similar word by Wilhelmine Schröder an eye and ear-witness has preserved for us. The artiste was fulfilling an engagement in Pesth, under the frenzied enthusiasm of the hot-blooded Magyars. She always appeared with a brilliant suite of admirers, among whom Count Koloman Majláth was regarded as the favourite; he was the son of the unfortunate Count Johann Majláth (the friend and biographer of my famous colleague, Sophie Müller), who in

January, 1855, tired of the struggle for existence, with his daughter in his arms, sought and found deliverance in the Starnberg lake.

My authority, the Hungarian Kertbeng, writes thus concerning Wilhelmine's appearance in Pesth—

"... I remember the end of an act in which the Devrient as Fidelio uttered that famous heart-rending cry, and then, still trembling all over her body, rushed into the wings, that a circle of enthusiasts who awaited her there were applauding even more madly than the audience in the pit. The great artiste was panting, and threw herself upon a chair in the dressing-room, whilst all those admirers were standing around her singing her praises. Suddenly she jumped up, seized one of the most loquacious by the collar and cried violently: 'Has my representation really pleased you as much as you are at pains to assure me? Very well; but I have been told that beside this art-criticism, you, Doctor, are very much concerned also about criticizing my private life! Ah, my most respected sir, do place one of your so very moral citizen-wives, for whom I have the greatest respect, out there upon the stage, and let one of these calm, sedate dames sing and play Fidelio as I did. When I am to represent a passion I must have one too, for only that can carry you away which you feel yourself....'"

No, without the unfettered demons of the heart,

Sophie and Wilhelmine-Schröder would never have become such great, unique, heart-moving artistes as they were, standing out unrivalled in the annals of the German stage; but certainly they are happier women who would make others happy!

CHAPTER V.

FRIEDRICH VON UECHTRITZ.*

FRIEDRICH VON UECHTRITZ was among the most gifted and striving young dramatists of the day at Berlin —one of my warmest admirers, till I had offended his *amour-propre* as a poet by my excessive fondness for laughing.

Uechtritz was a supernumerary "Referendar" at the Berlin tribunal, a disciple of the romantic school of Tieck, which expected great things from him. When only two-and-twenty years old Uechtritz had written three very promising dramas: "Chrysostomos," "Rom und Spartacus," and "Rom und Otto III." He then belonged to the highly-intellectual, exuberant circle of Berlin authors that gathered in the 'old club' around Heine, bizarre drastic Grabbe, talented Köchy, and the satirical Ludwig Robert over a glass of punch; or in the evening in Lutter and Wegners "Weinstube" (tavern) around the wine-loving Ludwig

---

* The story of this young dramatist is introduced here as connected to a certain extent with Karoline Bauer's last appearance on the Berlin stage.

Devrient, who would at times, when animated by a few bottles of Burgundy or champagne, treat the excited guests to a performance of the diabolical Richard III. and Goethe's Mephisto, which the broken-down artiste was no longer allowed to play on the stage.

My dear god-father, Court-actor Wilhelm Krüger, had introduced young Baron Uechtritz at our house. He was just then busy writing his new comedy "Alexander und Darius," which he and his followers expected would meet with tremendous success.

One day Krüger invited me to take part in a private reading of the new tragedy by Uechtritz. This reading was to test the play before Uechtritz presented it to the Intendance. But it was added that Teichmann, the secretary of the theatre, Count Brühl's right hand, had read the tragedy already with much gratification, and would also assist at the proposed rehearsal. The poet, who was, as was well known, dreadfully smitten by me, would, as a matter of course, assign a fine part to me in the performance of the piece. . . . I, together with my mother, put in an appearance at gossip Krüger's house that evening in high spirits, and without any suspicion. I there found the author, terribly excited, the secretary of the theatre, Johann Valentin Teichmann—Schulz, *alias* Komödien or Spuck-Schulz (comedy or spitting-

Schulz)—a certain Dr. Wilke, an art-æsthetic—and the much-dreaded critic Saphir, who wrote favourably for the Royal stage at that moment because he was paid for it.

Saphir had arrived in Berlin soon after me, in the fall of 1824, after having been expelled from Austria by Sedlnitzky, the chief of the Vienna police and censorship, by Metternich's command. The following pun was among his literary sins; he wrote: "Yesterday a slater fell off the roof of the Hofburg. Never yet anything has come so quickly off the *offices* of the Hofburg!"

He was almost unknown when he came to Berlin. For shortly before, the Stuttgart Morgenblatt, in criticising the "Poetische Erstlinge," by M. G. Saphir, wrote: "Saphir? Well, whether the name be fictitious or true, it suits the man. Although still neither cut nor set, and though no bright-sparkling diamond or dark-flaming ruby, it is a precious stone nevertheless."

The name Saphir is said to have the following peculiar origin. His grandfather, a Hungarian Jew, was called by the name of Israel-Israel. When the Emperor Joseph commanded that the Jews who dwelt in Austria should adopt a fixed surname, old Israel, too, was cited to appear before the Sheriff for that purpose. But he could not make up his mind as to a strange name. Then the Sheriff said to him, in a dictatorial way: "Thou wearest on thy finger a ring with a sapphire stone, thou shalt be called Saphir!"

The grandson of this first Saphir, Moritz Gottlieb, was intended for the Jewish ministry. He engaged in Talmudic studies till he was nineteen, when a Roman Catholic father had his attention directed to the highly-intelligent youth, and gave him secular books and literary instruction.

"From this hour," Saphir himself writes afterwards, "I gradually abandoned the study of the Talmud. I saw the synagogue less frequently, and in its disputations I took but a lukewarm interest. I had plucked the first little apple from the tree of knowledge; the paradise of life slammed the door after me, a voice from paradise called after me: 'Thou shalt be an author, in sorrow thou shalt bring forth children!'"

So this young nameless author of 29 years came to Berlin to try his fortune with the pen. At first he placed this pen at the disposal of the managers of the Königstadt Theatre, and as remuneration he demanded the means to enable him to launch a critical journal. This offer was proudly refused, which was bitterly repented afterwards. Saphir, without much ado, went over to the Royal camp, and I, the most popular of the Königstadt actors, fell the first victim to his wicked, sharp-pointed pen.

When I was performing in Vienna in May, 1839, Saphir related his first literary performance in his

"Humorist" with the frankness peculiar to him, and in these words: "About this time of universal theatre-worship, I came to Berlin, and at once saw *the* great thing would be—to *speak* about theatres, to write *about* the theatre if you want to be *heard*. At that time I was a perfect stranger in Berlin, a tyro in this great theatrical epidemic; I knew no paper that desired to have my critical notices, and yet a theatrical criticism alone could pave for me the way to public recognition.

"So I paid a visit to the Royal and the Königstadt theatres, and wrote a criticism about Mdme. Stich (now Krelinger) and Mdlle. Bauer. These notices I carried to the office of the "Spenersche Zeitung," inquiring if they could be accepted. The man who sat there took the criticism out of my hands and counted the lines. I stood there quite astonished, for I thought the man estimated its value by the number of lines. But I was soon to be undeceived. The man, turning to me, phlegmatically said: 'Eight thalers 15 Silbergroschen' (25s. 6d.)

"Now, I thought this sum would be given me as a fee for my trouble; but no, I was to pay it for insertion! Frightful moment! Never shall I forget thee! Eight thalers exceeded the half of my whole fortune, including 'my estates in *la Provence*' at that time! And nevertheless the welfare of Germany depended on this criticism as I thought.

"I smiled and paid. What I felt at that moment, more over the paying than the smiling, *that*, dear reader, you are not capable of feeling if you never were in a position to be the exclusive possessor of 13 thalers and to spend eight of them for the printing of a criticism.

"The criticism appeared in the "Spenersche Zeitung," in the so-called " blotting paper," with the palest ink upon the blackest paper, and immediately below there stood, as was customary with all notices on art and literature of that period, the advertisement that at Wisotzky's there was to be good roast duck as also a duck-chase. I read the criticism with much pleasure, not without mentally calculating how much of the matter announced below I might have enjoyed had I not written the notice above!

"When the criticism appeared, it was as if an earthquake had shaken Berlin; everything was in commotion. The reader will not and cannot believe it, and only he who knew the rage for the theatre that was then prevailing in Berlin, which, indeed, almost amounted to frenzy, will not find it exaggerated. I went to Stehely's, a café near the Gensdarmen market, to hear what was being said about it. I found everything in fermentation, and a 'Referendar' (young jurist) said to his neighbour, 'He must be a perfect devil that,' which the other acknowledged with a suitable remark and smile.

"It should be known that in this criticism I had displayed my latent talent in two directions: the melting, sky-bluish, perfume-pregnant, and flower-entwined art of praise, and also the punning, wit-overcharged, motley and checkered art of fault-finding, larded with antitheses and oddities. I exhibited, at the same time, the critical *Jean qui rit* and *Jean qui pleure*, the voice of Jacob with the hands of Esau! The rest would be out of place here; thus it was Mdlle. Bauer who, so to say, first introduced me into the northern critical academy."

Of course, Saphir had displayed the second side of his latent talent towards me that time. Later, when once I belonged to the royal stage, he also displayed the first side to me, and by-and-bye we became very good friends.

Thus he wrote as early as in the beginning of 1826 about my Pauline von Thalheim in the Testament des Onkels, the only notice by Saphir I have kept, and which I shall here quote as a specimen of this critical punster's style; it appeared in his "Schnellpost," which had been founded shortly before —

". . . I cannot help distributing to Mdlle. Bauer much praise for her representation of Pauline; there was so much natural truth with true nature, so much heartiness and grace in her acting, that she moved everybody and carried one away to applause. Mdlle. Bauer may draw this lesson from it, how much she gains by a reasonable moderation of her native vivacity. Indisputably, the hat which, so to say, fettered the play of her hands, contributed greatly to this. By circumspection, she is sure to acquire more and more of systematic life, which is *the true* of art. To-day, I am certain, she, as Pauline, does not rank much below the Pauline so much cried up, and that turns so many heads!"

Afterwards Saphir published in his much-read theatrical almanac for the year 1828 my coloured portrait as Karoline in the operetta "Die Nachtwandlerin," by Karl Blum, adapted from Scribe.

It is of course natural in a man like Saphir that, for my sake, he would not omit any malicious wit of his pen. He could only stroke or scratch.

I saw the strange man and poet first, and very often afterwards, at the house of my colleagues, the Wolffs, who were far too politic not to live on terms of friendship with this dangerous pen.

Saphir, perhaps, had the ugliest face I ever saw. With his long crushed in nose, his projecting lower jaw, his sensual mouth around which played almost perpetually a diabolical smile, he looked in his shimmering spectacles like a faun.

Others have called him the man-ape. Thus Ludwig Robert writes about him —

"Saphir, this postillion of the "mail" (Schnellpost), ever riding the most superficial tinsel-wit, belongs to the genus of ground-fleas or leaf-lice who eat each other. . . . The fellow's character corresponds with his appearance; he is an imitating, malicious, haughty, conceited ape."

And on every occasion Saphir himself made sport of his ugliness. In a short attempt to write his memoirs he says—

"In my childhood and youth I had the good fortune to be a welcome guest everywhere, and especially did I enjoy the favour of the fair sex. That it was not my beauty, neither my Roman nose nor my rosy mouth, that worked this wonder you may believe. What was it then? It was my merriment, gayness, and nonchalance, combined with a perfectly discernible good-naturedness, which never fails to produce a favourable effect!"

But his high, tall, really elegant and *distingué* figure also contributed greatly to Saphir's surprising successes with the fair sex—and as for the theatrical dames, the fear of his pen and the courting of his favour were additional factors. Thus in Vienna he was the lover of the talented Therese Krones, and afterwards of Marie Gordon-Kalafati. He was father of Marie Gordon, who became known afterwards by the name of "Max Stein."

With that wit peculiar to him, which does not spare his own self, Saphir said of himself: "I and Mary Stuart have been much loved and much hated; she was hated much because she was beautiful; thank God, I have not been hated for that!"

Another comparison with Mary Stuart was true: Saphir was likewise better than his reputation ! He was good-natured, friendly, and obliging, if this did not oblige him to suppress one of his malicious puns. He was helpful and hospitable when he was possessed of some thalers or gulden himself.

At first Saphir was the life-giving element in Berlin at social and artiste festivals, till on the 1st January, 1826, there appeared his " Schnellpost für Literatur, Theater, und Geselligkeit sammt einem Beiwagen für Kritik und Antikritik" (Mail for literature, theatre, and conviviality, together with an extra coach for criticism and anti-criticism) with the motto " To merit its laurel wreath, to pretend to merit its crown of thorns; severity to the finished, indulgence to the upspringing, appreciation to modesty, contempt to conceit! " It was, no doubt, this motto chiefly which at first secured for the "Schnellpost" the interest and support of men like Hegel, Gans, and Wilibald Alexis. The journal had yet a second motto: " Just enter life boldly and quickly, though the road may be rough enough ! " on which young Moscheles at that time wrote a canon for four voices, which I, too, have helped to sing.

The "Schnellpost" burst like a bomb-shell into the harmless Berlin life, which was guarded by the severest censorship, with its never before dreamt-of witty, satirical regardlessness which always had the laughers on its side. Saphir was particularly strong in puns, which Jean Paul calls the "acoustic wit."

Even Friedrich Wilhelm III., who was usually so earnest and strict, was among the most zealous readers of the "Schnellpost." With his never-tiring interest in all the little matters in the theatrical world, his first demand when rising in the morning was the "Schnellpost," so that Prince Wittgenstein induced Saphir to have his journal published an hour earlier still. A Royal lackey stood waiting in the printing-office to receive the first number printed on vellum for His Majesty. By order of the King the censorship had to wink at the writings of the "Schnellpost," that its wit and interest might not suffer under the "red crayon," just as afterwards, under the succeeding monarch, a similar exceptional position was allowed to the "Kladderadatch."* Only when Saphir fell foul of the general favourite Henriette Sontag the King raised his forefinger warningly or even threateningly.

Saphir's prudent tactics were these: to reserve the best arrows of his fatal wit for the noblest game. Only by a paper war against celebrities, his pen, his "Schnellpost," and he himself could become celebrated likewise. And where could he have found a nobler game to chase than the beautiful Henriette and the whole Sontag mania of the then Berlin?

* The German Punch.

Just two specimens of how Saphir indulged in small wit at Sontag's expense, or quibbled at Sontag:

Once he printed an overflowing sonnet on the celebrated artiste. Henriette, delighted that her most cruel enemy had at last changed into a friend, thanked the author in a friendly letter. Only now, Saphir made known along with the letter that the sonnet was an acrostic! Eagerly the first letters were put together. They produced the word: "Ungeheure Ironie" (prodigious irony).

Worse, nay vile and low, was another joke or quibble at Sontag's expense. When for the first time she took her leave of the "Königstadt" and Berlin in order to go to Paris, when she was overwhelmed with flowers and poems on the stage, when Karl von Holtei alone flung down from the "gods" upon her and the excitedly cheering audience six different poems of homage, printed on coloured tissue paper, then Saphir mingled in this enthusiasm and among these poetical effusions of homage scattered a fluttering leaf, quite in his favourite Sontag style—an outrageous sonnet on a notorious chorus-singer of the Königstadt.

Well, then there were found in Berlin honourable men still who cut the frivolous quibbler at once.

Next to Henriette Sontag, little Louis Angely, for ever growling, the indefatigable manufacturer of farces, translator from the French, and droll comic actor of the "Königstadt," had most to suffer from Saphir's pen.

When Saphir was warned that Angely was preparing for fight, as David did against Goliath, the "postillion of the mail" answered, drily, with reference to Angely's tiny little figure: "Oh, I have already ordered high-top boots, the thrust of the dear little fellow won't go through them, and higher up he does not reach!" Well, this wicked quibbler, who was nevertheless so merry, overflowing with droll ideas which made you laugh against your will, sat, in the beginning of 1826, beside me at the tea table of gossip Krüger, waiting for the grand tragical reading of "Alexander and Darius."

On my other side sat the very reverse of Saphir, Johann Valentin Teichmann, the highly respectable and honourable "Private Secretary to the Board of the Royal Theatres at Berlin." He was then 35 years old. A letter by Zelter will give us an idea of his appearance.

Young Teichmann, descending from a modest family of the Berlin middle-class, from early youth cherished great enthusiasm for the theatre, for the stage of a Fleck, an Iffland, and an Unzelmann-Bethmann. The struggle for existence bound him fast to the chambers of the Berlin law courts from his 15th year. But the thought, "Also in thee there is concealed an Iffland, a Fleck, a Pius Alexander Wolff," pursued him day and night.

When, in 1811, Wolff performed in Berlin, and in March of 1816, together with his wife, went from Weimar to the Berlin stage, young Teichmann became the warmest admirer of the talented representer of men. He went to Wolff, opened to him his theatre-inspired heart, and recited something to him, and Wolff recommended him to his master, Goethe, in Weimar, as a pupil for the stage. Teichmann wrote to Goethe to that end in November, 1816, but received the following answer on December 3rd:—

"I am always very much chagrined if I cannot prove helpful, in the development of their talents, to young people who place confidence in me, and yet I am often obliged to have, nevertheless, to decline such requests. Our theatre has a strong cast at the present time, and I have not left leisure enough to be able to devote my attention continuously to younger members. I reluctantly inform you of this, but yet promptly, as you desire it so. I hope that you will see your wishes realised in some way. (Signed) GOETHE."

For all that, Goethe made inquiries about this candidate for the stage from his friend Zelter, who was his Berlin agent for everything. Zelter reported thus—

"Young Teichmann is of middle stature, 24 years old, fair, has blue, somewhat dim eyes, and is not badly made. I don't quite like his walk, and his manner of speaking also you will have to improve. His mouth and forehead are not bad, but the latter is better than the former. Broad upper teeth, grown straight, but have a bad colour."

Meanwhile Teichmann had expressed his desire to enter the stage also to the Berlin theatrical intendant, Count Brühl, and had been engaged by the latter to be his private secretary and librarian. Soon after Brühl gave his *protégé* the post of secretary to the Theatre Board, and here Teichmann, with his active interest in the histrionic art and his great sense of duty, was the right man in the right place. Only in his zeal as the "right hand of the intendant-general" he went, perhaps, sometimes a little too far. He was, for example, not altogether free from blame as regarded many of the sins committed and matters left undone by the management, as well as regarded the much-regretted retirement of the art-enthusiast Count Brühl.

But alas! his teeth "have a bad colour!" How many dozens of tooth-brushes and boxes of tooth-powder did good Teichmann receive anonymously every Christmas, and on the occasion of his birth-days, from the high-bred aristocrat, Count Brühl, and also from us actresses who had to suffer his sparkling oratorical effusions? But without effect. Even the gods mostly struggle in vain against the neglects of early education.*

Next at the round table was "Komödien-Schulz" (Comedy-Schulz), the most remarkable theatre-fancier whom I ever met with during my whole long stage career. He, being an eccentric, was among the best-known of the town-characters of Berlin. The very appearance of the old bachelor—he was about 65 years old—was most striking, owing to an almost incredible neglect of his person and dress. He always looked as if he had been dropped out of one of the old-clothes shops on the "Mühlendamen." His second nick-name, known over all Berlin, was "Spuck-Schulz" (spitting Schulz), because the haste with which he spoke caused a slight shower of saliva.

Friedrich Schulz was to have studied law in his far-off youth, but he had taken much more to the theatre, of which he was passionately fond, than to the *corpus juris*. Maximiliane Döbbelin, Henrietta Baxanius, and Friederike Unzelmann were his adored goddesses; Fleck, Iffland, and Unzelmann his gods. He felt perfectly wretched when he was sent as "Referendar" to Brandenburg, and was unable to revel night after night in the Berlin Theatre. He thought he would die if he was not allowed to drive from Brandenburg to Berlin to visit the theatre at least once a week, a journey which then occupied

* An adaptation of Schiller's saying: "Mit der Dummheit Kämpfen Götter selbst vergebens."

three days. If a specially interesting piece was expected our Referendar would add, perhaps, even a fourth or fifth day on his own authority, till the gentlemen of the Brandenburg law court declared that they had no use for Referendar Friedrich Schulz, who spent more than the half of his time in Berlin, and less than the half at the Court in Brandenburg, where he was doing nothing either. Thus the removal of F. Schulz, Esq., was demanded.

Fortunately the useless Referendar had in Berlin an influential college friend in the person of Friedrich August von Stägemann, well-known as poet, and afterwards as statesman. He was able to fulfil the urgent request of an early friend, and so Friedrich Schulz was transferred to the Berlin High Court of Justice (Kammergericht)! But here his passion for the theatre gave him less time still to occupy himself with law cases. Then Stägemann made a last attempt to save his friend from ruin. He took him as supernumerary into the Ministerial offices, and employed him under his own eyes. In vain! Schulz, instead of reading law records in the office, read comedies, and wrote, instead of juridical reports, theatrical notices. As "highly remarkable for incapacity" Friedrich Schulz was dismissed, but received a small pension on the recommendation of Stägemann and by the King's grace.

Who was happier than "Comedy-Schulz!" He could now devote his whole time and his free pen to the theatre without being constantly snubbed by his superiors, and without suffering pangs of conscience. He became the theatrical critic of Spener's journal (the "Spenersche Zeitung"), and found favour even before Goethe. In his little essay, "Die Berliner Dramaturgen," the Grand Master of Weimar spoke highly of this critic as having a most productive and cultivated mind, and an incorruptible fairness, coupled with the most charming humour!

Comedy-Schulz was the most ardent admirer of Friederike Unzelmann-Bethmann. She took a motherly interest in the unpractical bachelor. He was never forgotten under her Christmas tree, and always there found for himself that piece of wearing apparel or linen which he just stood most bitterly in need of. Nor did he take it ill when the charming "fairy child" made him the butt of her sometimes rather coarse criticisms.

For example, once during the carnival season the conversation turned upon the approaching masked ball in the opera house. Comedy-Schulz also wanted to go there, and asked Mdme. Bethmann's advice as to what costume he should choose so that the Berliners would not recognise him, the universally known character.

Then his friend answered with one of her irresistible merry laughs, smartly—

"Dear Schulz, put on clean linen, and nobody in all Berlin will know you."

CHAPTER VI.

OUT AND ABOUT.

Magdeburg—Heinrich Bethmann—"Blinde Gabriele" a Veritable Triumph—Hanover—The Duke and Duchess of Cambridge—Elbe—Florence—Prague—Sabine Heinefetter—Her Origin, Training, and History — Dresden—The Heinefetters Again — Kathinka Heinefetter — Her Beauty and her Successful *début* in Paris as a Singer—Her *amours*—A Tragedy—Disgrace and Death—Madness—Mannheim — Karlsruhe — Count Luxburg and his Beautiful Countess—An Emperor's Mistress—How Many Husbands?—The Dowager Grand Duchess Stephanie of Baden and her Three Lovely Daughters—Theodor Döring—Julius von Göler—*Resumé* of a Successful Tour—Prince Jerome Napoleon—A Summer Retreat at Schinznach—Theodore de la Rive—Karoline Appears as an Amateur—A Declaration of Love—A Painful Refusal.

I was expected in Magdeburg for a series of performances with much longing. I was to help good old theatrical manager Heinrich Bethmann out of his everlasting debts.

It was Bethmann who discovered me ten years before in Karlsruhe, and brought me to the Königstadt Theatre. His career had been a very downward one since. His time of successes had gone to the grave with his celebrated spouse, the great Friederike Unzelmann-Bethmann. The Berlin Court actor had changed into a wandering theatre director, who had constantly to struggle with hunger and sorrow. But for all that he was a genuine, real, plain, wandering comedian from the old romantic time of the German stage, about which Ludwig Tieck was still so enthusiastic. Often not a penny in his pocket, not a whole coat on his back, the newest theatre bill and a hundred golden hopes in his head, Heinrich Bethmann had been wandering through the German lands for years. I scarcely ever met in my comedian wanderings a more faithful and more art-inspired theatre manager; and I always experienced the greatest delight to be able to "float" Bethmann once more by my starring performances.

In December, 1834, I played my best *rôles* in Magdeburg on twelve evenings, each time before crowded houses. My highest triumph I achieved as "Blinde Gabriele."

In the second act, the blind girl goes to a side-door, calling out to the old servant Ambros to lead her. He does not answer, and Gabriele, with outstretched, groping arms, steps cautiously across the stage. Then her fingers come in contact with somebody. "Ah! there you are already, Ambros. Give me your hand." But scarcely has she touched this hand, when something like an electric current goes through her whole body, her rigid, dead eyes open still further, her bosom heaves, and she stops breathing . . . No, it is not old Ambros—but how? What if her beloved Ernest had returned from the far country and was standing before her?

In Gabriele's mien—nay, even in her empty eyes, in the stooping, trembling form, in the quiver of her groping fingers, and in the tone of her hesitating voice, the heavy struggle of heart and soul, so full of contrasts, is to be reflected: between the happiness of expectation and the fear of disappointment. . . . "For pity's sake! if you are not Ernest, do not answer!" Then, after a pause of strained listening, the whole power of blissful love breaks forth in the sweet, child-like tone of hope: "Ernest, is—it you?"

Then from the pit comes the sound of a clear, eager boy's voice crying, with evident joy, up to me: "Yes, yes, it is he—it is Ernest!"

What a thrilling effect that had upon me! Large tears burst from my eyes, and, without waiting for Ernest's confirmation, I sank sobbing on his breast.

Behind the scenes Bethmann squeezed my hand with a moist eye, saying: "You have played and conquered to-day—like my lamented Friederike." That was the highest praise from the mouth of the old comedian.

After that I played once more in Magdeburg in the following January with the most satisfactory success; even in a pecuniary sense. My share of the profits (one-third) amounted per *rôle* from 100 to 150 thalers; and many a time after that I followed Bethmann's cry for help to Magdeburg, Halle, and Lauchstädt.

Leaving Magdeburg towards the end of the same month in 1835, I proceeded to Hanover, where I appeared on eight different nights as Donna Diana, Julia, Käthchen von Heilbronn, Goldschmied's Töchterlein, etc.; here I played for the first time with the talented young character-actor, Karl Grunert. Franz von Holbein, the former husband of the Countess Lichtenau, the composer of my grateful *rôle* Fridotin, and the same who adapted Käthchen von Heilbronn for the stage, was a prudent and practical theatrical manager, but slippery like an eel, false, proud of his noble descent, and possessed of an impertinent confidence as to his successes with the fair sex; whilst his spouse, a divorced Mad. Artour, whose maiden-name was Göhring, despite her somewhat alarming years, would chiefly still play the parts of youthful lovers, so that I was not received in Hanover with over much courtesy by the wife of director von Holbein. I received 80 thalers per *rôle*.

The Duke and Duchess of Cambridge, who were then residing in Hanover, paid me many encouraging compliments regarding my acting, but the other artistes and the audience put on fashionable, reserved airs (copying genuine Old England), which used to amuse me very much at the *table d'hôte* in the British Hôtel. It was then regarded as a mark of ill-breeding to laugh heartily in the theatre, even in the merriest scene; so that, having returned from there to my old Bethmann, I exclaimed to him, jubilantly: " Thank God that I am once more with unsophisticated comedians, and a public that is not ashamed of its harmless hilarity."

* * * * * *

By the month of March I had returned to beautiful, cheerful Elbe-Florence, for a decisive series of performances. I appeared as Donna Diana, Blinde Gabriele, Junge Pathe, Goldschmied's Töchterlein, Käthchen von Heilbronn, in " Schule der Alten," " Menschenhass und Reue," and in the "Hagestolzen." This was followed up by the test-part for tragic characters, " Marie Stuart," which I had studied with Tieck after the traditions of Friederike Bethmann. The dramaturg (Tieck) was very much pleased with my performance; the people of Dresden made me happy with applause; and, accordingly, after the performance of " Marie Stuart," I signed, with a joyful heart, a contract for four years, with 2,000 thalers as salary and 200 thalers wardrobe money. Rococo and male attire were furnished to me by the management.

But, meanwhile, I hastened on to Prague, where I had agreed to play at the theatre under the management of director Stöger for fifteen evenings. In April I arrived in the many-towered city. Comfortable apartments had been reserved for us in the Schwarze "Rössel." Of course, my first business was to examine the theatre bill: "'Romeo and Juliet,' opera, by Bellini. Romeo: Mdlle. Sabine Heinefetter, prima donna at the Italian Opera of Paris." That was too enticing. I had made Sabine Heinefetter's acquaintance in Berlin as early as 1827, had admired and become fond of her when she—" Operatic singer to the Court of the Prince Elector of Hessen-Kassel"—achieved triumphs on the Berlin stage, though Henriette Sontag was singing in Berlin at the same time. I quickly dressed, and we were able to witness the performance of the second act from the box of the director.

A lovely Romeo! The well-made, lofty, and yet soft forms of a youth with noble expressive features, eloquent eyes glowing with love, fire, and truth, in the plastic acting and highly dramatic singing, a voice of the purest metal—so I found Sabine Heinefetter, after a lapse of eight years, more beautiful, more perfect in her singing, upon the boards before me, fêted by the jubilant applause of the music-loving Praguers.

I was so glad that the Heinefetters likewise resided in the "Schwarze Rössel," the old, renowned, resort of travelling actors. Next day my mother and I called upon my amiable sister-artiste. Sabine was also in the company of her mother, a good old dame, simple and of comfortable middle-class appearance, and very loquacious in her Mainz accent. Her round rosy face was ever quite resplendent with her daughters' sun of fame and happiness. Her second daughter, Clara, was starring in Vienna as " Julia," " La Dame Blanche ;" " Alice" in " Robert the Devil," &c.; and the youngest, Kathinka, I saw now for the first time in Prague. Sabine was thirty, Kathinka only fifteen years. If Sabine resembled a Juno Ludovisi, Kathinka reminded one of a Hebe by Canova. A charming child! Blooming like the Goddess of Spring, light and graceful like winged Psyche, cheerful like a sunbeam, and happy like a child of the sun, she hovered around us and sang snatches of sprightly songs with her lovely silvery voice. At the same time her light-brown gold-shimmering locks fluttered about her glowing little face, her clear roe-eyes sparkled seductively, and in the dimples in her chin and cheeks there laughed a hundred bantering rogues and cupids.

Sabine whispered to me with a sigh : " Alas, how will this lovely butterfly fare when once she must find her way through life alone, unguarded and unchecked? Kathinka is a child who is spoiled by fortune, and almost too light-hearted and of too light blood; I dread the hour when I shall have to let her leave me. Kathinka has a most pronounced talent as a colorature singer and a burning desire for the stage—or, perhaps, more correctly, for its triumphs. Until now I have trained her myself. In autumn she is to proceed to Paris, there to complete her musical and theatrical education under Cordoni. Countess Merlin and Maria Malibran will give her their protection, and introduce her into the musical world of Paris as they once did me. May God grant that everything may go well! I found the way to the stage and over it not so pleasantly smoothed for me, and strewn with roses as my young sister will. I have had to struggle hard to obtain the place which I now occupy in the opera and society. But in such a struggle one at least acquires what Kathinka completely wants—earnestness of purpose, and steadiness of character."

Yes, Sabine did have a hard struggle and heavy work to perform in the course of her life. She once related to me with sadness the tale of her joyless childhood, and of the humiliations, coarseness, and dangers through which her most blooming years of girlhood had passed. Born in poverty, growing up in poverty and ignorance, she was obliged, at a tender age, to wander through the streets and inns of Mainz and sing songs, which she accompanied on her miserable harp—songs such as the coarse multitude demanded and paid for. Hunger is painful, but it is still more painful to see mother, brothers and sisters, and an old grandmother hungering at home. Then it once happened that a noble virtuoso heard the beautiful, modest girl sing a ballad with her full silvery voice, simply and touchingly to the accompaniment of her jingling harp. He played to her the scales upon a violin, and then more and more difficult passages and ingenious figures, and the poor harpist sang them by ear with an admirable purity and precision. He undertook to educate Sabine. She soon received her first instruction in music, and an opportunity to make up much of her, till now, neglected education and social training. As early as 1824, when but nineteen years old, she was enabled to appear on the stage for the first time in Frankfurt-on-the-Maine. She sang the May song in Weber's "Euryanthe." Her splendid voice and great beauty caused a sensation. Ludwig Spohr, for some years conductor of the princely orchestra in Kassel, at once engaged Sabine for the opera of that stage, and with much kindness undertook her further musical education. He taught her his own operas—"Berggeist," "Jessonda," and "Pietro."

Her brilliant starring performances at the Royal Opera in Berlin in 1827, made the name of Sabine Heinefetter soon famous.

After she had, under Cordoni, diligently studied Italian singing, she accepted an engagement as prima donna at the Italian Opera in Paris. The French were enraptured with the beautiful German, with the unpronounceable name of "Anefettare." In the saloons of the art-loving Countess Merlin she made the acquaintance of Maria Malibran and all the artiste-stars of Paris. A starring tour brought her to Italy and now to Prague. It was her intention not to accept any more permanent engagements.

Sabine Heinefetter had almost completed her cycle of performances in Prague when I arrived. After Romeo I only saw her as magnificent Tancred. We spent together some very happy days in this most interesting old city on the Moldau, and employed every leisure hour in visiting together its many historical relics and art treasures. Kathinka fluttered alongside us as *enfant terrible*, and always manifested a greater inclination for the admiration of a gay world than for the dust of bygone ages. I hear her still laugh wantonly when we were at the famous Jewish cemetery at Prague: "I am thirsting for life, sunshine, merry laughter and bright eyes. Ugh! Here among the wild weeds of tombs and the whitened stones, and the stupid old stories about the Jews, it is terribly tiresome. And you put on such sentimental moonshine faces besides, as if you would soon apply for friendly lodgings under the nasty elder trees yourselves. Let us quickly return to the green Moldau-islet to witness the fireworks and hear the concert. I have had to promise this morning my worshipping colonel 'on my word,' the fair lieutenant 'by his moustache,' and the smart Count student 'auf Cerevis' that we will celebrate the lovely night of spring upon the islet."

Could it be that this lovely creature had no heart?

Next day we parted from each other with a hearty: "May we soon meet again all hale and hearty in Dresden!" Sabine went away to fulfil another engagement; I brought mine to a close in Prague. It turned out a very successful one. I appeared before regularly crowded houses in my most favourite *rôles* fifteen times within two-and-twenty days. My fee was the third part of the takings, which amounted to about 100 thalers per *rôle* on an average. Director Stoger held out to me very enticing terms for a contract. The public, the critics, and the artistes were anxious to bind me to Prague, but I could only promise soon to return to a more lengthy cycle of performances.

In autumn Sabine and Kathinka Heinefetter came likewise to Dresden. Frau Schröder-Devrient had gone on a leave of absence of fifteen months, and during the time Sabine was to take her place.

I was not a little surprised when both sisters introduced their betrothed to me. Sabine's intended was a handsome Dutch officer, who had quitted the service. She intended to continue starring for a few years longer, then marry her betrothed and entirely withdraw from the stage.

"What a loss for art!" I exclaimed, involuntarily.

"I love my betrothed!" she said, passionately. And her whole faithful heart lay in these words.

Kathinka's betrothed was a good-looking Frenchman, with black locks, flashing black eyes, and polished manners. I learned no particulars regarding him. Sabine avoided speaking about this, her future brother-in-law, and only once, when the charming little *fiancée* received with much glee the devotions of a fair Saxon dragoon officer, Sabine, shaking her head sorrowfully, whispered to me: "May God grant that love may at last make Kathinka sensible!"

"Look, dear, how soon the right man has come!" I said in jest to Kathinka.

"And what if after all it were not the right man?" the seductive creature said, with a ringing, merry laugh, and gaily spun through the room with her Frenchman, who, of course, knew not a word of German. Poor Kathinka, that was an evil prophetic word, and that laugh was death to you. Ay, it was not the right man. Indeed, the right man never was forthcoming for you. Eight days later Kathinka left for Paris, together with a lady and her betrothed. I have never seen her again, but heard about her only too often and too much.

Kathinka was trained as a songstress at the expense of the "Grand Opéra" in Paris. She made her *début* on that stage in 1840, with the most brilliant success. All Paris was in ecstasy about her beauty, her charming voice, brilliant vocal art, and her enrapturing acting. And then came a day when a horrible tragedy was reported in the newspapers, whose heroine was Kathinka Heinefetter.

When did Kathinka discard her betrothed, whose acquaintance I made in Dresden? In the summer of 1842 Caumartin, a young Parisian advocate, was her acknowledged admirer.

Soon after Kathinka made the acquaintance of young Mr. Steiner. Scenes of jealousy ensued between the amorous advocate and Mr. Steiner, which were not confined to words.

All these occurrences, which of course were the favourite talk of Paris, made it desirable that Kathinka should, at least for a time, quit the scene. She dissolved, in consequence, her engagement at the great opera in September, 1842, and accepted a contract in Brussels. Caumartin accompanied her thither. In the diligence the young, gay, and affectionate pair are taken for a newly-married couple on their wedding-trip. Caumartin rents a house in the Rue des Hirondelles for his mistress, and returns to Paris towards the end of October.

Soon after, Kathinka, the most popular prima donna in Brussels, makes the acquaintance of Aimé Sirey, a man of 36 years, who is fond of styling himself Count! His father was a famous Parisian advocate, and his mother a niece of Mirabeau. Aimé is highly gifted, has received an excellent education, and is possessed of a lovable and sympathetic appearance. His misfortune is vanity. As a boy he is a brilliant lion of the Boulevards and theatres; as a youth, a used-up libertine and deeply involved gambler. He is proud of having acquired at so youthful an age all the vices of his grand-uncle, Mirabeau. During the July revolution vanity impels him to play the part of the people's man, *à la* Mirabeau.

Married at the age of 26, he has spent in the course of a few years in the most profligate way his own and his wife's fortune. He is forced to retire to the country in hiding from his creditors. In the Issy, Sirey stabs his cousin in a duel, because the latter had sued him for money due to him; after that Sirey flees to Brussels. The handsome, elegant Aimé now turns into a common adventurer and protector of theatrical dames who happen to be in fashion and have plenty of cash.

Soon after the departure of Caumartin, Sirey turns to the new brilliant star of the grand opera, Kathinka Heinefetter, and the protector is not rejected.

Caumartin in Paris, meanwhile, is seriously thinking of breaking off his relationship to Kathinka. At this juncture he receives a tender, yearning love-letter from Kathinka, and on the 19th of November he arrives in Brussels in order to give his Kathinka a pleasant surprise. He alights at the café Domino, and here he is told that Mdlle. Heinefetter is just singing in a concert of the great "Harmonié." He hastens thither, and waits in a carriage in front of the door, seeing that the last number is being sung already. He sees Kathinka come out in the company of four persons, leaning on the arm of a gentleman unknown to him. Then he drives on before her to her residence, where he finds supper set for several persons. The lady's-maid is embarrassed. Soon after Kathinka enters with her company. She changes colour at thus suddenly seeing her old lover before her. In her confusion she invites him to partake of supper with them without introducing the two gentlemen to him. He refuses indignantly, and throws himself into the corner of a sofa whilst the others enjoy their supper with much heartiness. Full of wrath, he observes how the elegant gentleman by the side of his old mistress indulges in all the freedom of a declared lover. The supper is over. The ladies retire. Caumartin rises and puts on his gloves. Sirey steps up to him, saying: "Monsieur, do you not see that you are not wanted here? It is time to put an end to this." So saying, he shows the door to Caumartin. They come to blows. At this moment Kathinka opens the door, and seeing the furious rivals, she sinks down in a swoon. Mr.

Milord, Sirey's friend, carries her into her bed-chamber.

What happened in the saloon during his absence has never been quite cleared up. Caumartin relates: "I gave Sirey a box on the ear; he struck me innumerable blows with his stick till it broke in pieces. I cried: 'That is an infamy. I have the choice of arms. To-morrow morning at eight o'clock! Weapons, swords.' 'Let us fight at once!' Sirey cried, and took from off the table an object which I did not see. He rushed at me, and I received a thrust with a knife in one of my loins. For my defence I held in my hand a sword-cane. Sirey seized it, and the cane part remained in his hand. He thought I was disarmed. But I had the sword in my hand, and he in his blind rage plunged on to it. I saw the blood oozing from his white vest. That had not been my intention. I hastened away to fetch a physician. When I returned with the latter I met the landlord on the stair, who said to me: 'He is dead!' Then I hastened back to Paris and gave myself up to justice."

Enough, in the house of the songstress Kathinka Heinefetter, a man had been killed at midnight who had been regarded as her declared lover for some weeks past—killed by a man to whom the light-headed girl had addressed a most affectionate love-letter but ten days before.

Kathinka Heinefetter was judged. In Paris and Brussels she had become impossible. Nobody would pardon her for that luckless letter, full of the tenderest assurances of love, which lured the former lover (whose place had been supplied long ago) to Brussels, away from his young bride. In April, 1843, Kathinka was obliged to appear once more in public in Brussels, this time as a witness at the Court of Assizes, before which Eduard Caumartin was arraigned for manslaughter. She endeavoured to give an account of the matter that would be damaging to Caumartin. This heightened her guilt in everybody's eyes. Caumartin was acquitted, thanks to the brilliant defence of the famous Parisian advocate, Maître Chaix d'Estange, and the unanimous opinion of the physicians, which recognized the possibility that Aimé Sirey had blindly plunged on to the cane-sword held by Caumartin before his breast. Kathinka Heinefetter's fate was sealed. Gone were luck and star. It is true she appeared on several stages after that, but report always went before her, and in everybody's eyes she read the old mournful remembrance of the bloody tragedy in Brussels. And how often when she stood upon the stage in her brightest and most splendid parts a pale shadow would emerge before her inner vision! She would see the red, warm blood flow from the heart again, and hear a hollow voice from the grave: " You—you alone bear the guilt!" and her heart would stop beating and every tone in her throat would die.

Kathinka Heinefetter has heavily paid for the frivolity of her heart. Discouraged, broken, she renounced the stage in the very prime of life. On the 21st of December, 1855, she died in Freiburg in the Breisgau, of a slow disease of the heart, only five-and-thirty years old. With what sad feelings did I stand at her grave! Upon the pedestal of the monument there kneels an angel who holds a wreath of roses over her grave. Upon the mound there stood a bush of withered Catherine flowers. Your image, poor Kathinka!

In the month of February, 1857, the second sister, Frau Stöckel-Heinefetter, also died, and on the 18th November, 1872, Sabine Marquet-Heinefetter died in the madhouse of Illenau, in Baden. . . . Poor Sabine, what sufferings your faithful heart must have endured for your sweet darling Kathinka, and what painful struggles your energetic mind must have fought, before you ended in a madhouse!

* * * * * *

In May, 1835, I brought my great starring tour to an end by a series of performances in Mannheim and Karlsruhe, in my native land of Baden.

Mannheim had been the goal of my first cheering little starring excursion. How many things had changed since I played "Preciosa" with the idealistic Ferdinand Löwe at that time! My handsome, fiery Don Alonso had been laid in the cemetery of Vienna three months ago.

The old original intendant, Count Luxburg, was still in office, and just as incapable of managing a stage as formerly. When I had played Katharina II. in the "Günstlinge" by Charlotte Birch-Pfeiffer, I heard him say, in a most patriarchal, familiar way, in the Baden dialect: "Kinkele, my lass, you played pretty badly in your part of Seraphine, but you swooned very prettily!"

Also the beautiful Countess Luxburg was still enthroned night after night in her private box, presenting her classical beauty, which, to be sure, had become somewhat antique as years advanced, but was artificially preserved. She stared into vacant space with her old marble-like calmness and her old haughtiness, as if but the one thought was animating her: "Behold, I am still the beautiful woman whose charms once won the admiration of the Emperor Napoleon! Who can say that of herself?"

As wife of a French officer who had been condemned to death for some crime he had committed, she had thrown herself at Napoleon's feet, and for the price of her beauty had saved her husband. The latter was sent to join in the wars in Spain, and she became the mistress of the Emperor. She bore Napoleon a son, Count Leo, and afterwards married Count Luxburg, in the belief that her first husband had been killed in Spain and that Count Luxburg was the Count of Luxemburg. But years after, her first husband suddenly stood before her in Mannhein to claim his prior rights! He was got rid of by the payment of a sum of money. Somewhat later the beautiful Luxburg had a nasty lawsuit in Paris with her son, the Count Leo, on account of the fortune which Napoleon had settled on her and her son. She appeared in person before the Paris assizes in pompous beauty, and related with much emphasis her Imperial love story! She gained her law-suit and remained in the new Napoleonic Paris, recognised and distinguished by Napoleon III. as a sort of Napoleonite.

Even in her coffin she wished still to be "the beautiful Luxburg." She had given most minute directions as to how she was to be dressed and painted and lie on a bed of State.

How sweet, noble, and good beside the beautiful Luxburg appeared in the Mannheim Theatre the real Napoleonite—the Dowager Grand Duchess Stephanie, of Baden, a niece of Empress Josephine and an adopted daughter of Napoleon. She was no beauty, but she was enchantingly graceful and amiable. How very graciously she received me in her palace on the occasion of my two professional visits to Mannheim; her palace was open not merely to the aristocracy of birth, it stood open likewise to the nobility of the mind in art and science. Of her three lovely daughters, one became the ill-fated spouse of Prince Vasa (but was, however, soon divorced from him), and mother of the Queen Karola of Saxony; the second Princess espoused the Prince of Hohenzollern-Sigmaringen; the youngest the Duke of Hamilton. The Duchess, having lived in Baden-Baden for years, took repeated occasions to express to me her interest in my "stage reminiscences" as they came out. Her daughter became the unfortunate Hereditary Princess of Monaco, who ran away with her little son from her husband. The Grand Duchess Stephanie, for whom life brought many tears, still continues to live in the tradition of the people as the mother of the unfortunate Kaspar Hauser, who was soon to be the exchanged and kidnapped Prince of Baden. Grand Duchess Stephanie never believed the story. She ordered Kaspar Hauser's likeness to be brought to her, looked at it for a long time with evident pain, and then said firmly: "He is not my son!"

Of my meeting with Lady Ellenborough I have given an account in an earlier chapter of these memoirs.

In Mannheim I played for the first time with Theodor Döring, who was engaged here. I found him to be an original and highly talented artiste, but not an amiable colleague. Because his spouse, who was engaged along with me at the Königstadt

Theatre, in Berlin, as Auguste Sutorius, played in Mannheim the part of Polixena in "Natur und Kunst," Döring managed to obtain a decree that I was not to play this my favourite part, one of the most grateful of my *repertoire*—the same Auguste Sutorius who was once presented to Gœthe in Weimar, with these words of recommendation: "She plays also in the "Laune des Verliebten!"" whereupon good Auguste, who knew little about Gœthe, said quite seriously: "Ach geh'n S'mer mit dem grausligen Stück!" Poor Auguste, divorced from Döring, went to America, where she was lost and never heard of again.

And when I stood once more on the stage of the Karlsruhe Theatre, which I had entered for the first time as childlike, innocent Margarethe in the "Hagestolzen," thirteen years ago . . . my heart wept for the forlorn innocence of childhood, and all the triumphs of the matured and celebrated artiste could not recoup me for it.

Upon the stage I was most successful with my Donna Diana, Julie Capulet, Junge Pathe, Goldschmied's Töchterlein, Polixena, Königin von sechzehn Jahren. The "Küthchen von Heilbronn" I was not allowed to play, for the reigning Grand Duchess Sophie, the eldest daughter of the expelled King of the Swedes, told me during an introductory audience: "I consider it immoral that this madly enamoured

Käthchen follows the Count von Strahl through the length and breadth of the land and serves him as his stable boy!" This is the same lady of whom Moritz von Haber could say in public beer saloons: "My Sophie!" This word is the real cause and origin of the duels that caused so much sensation, in which, in 1843, Baron Julius von Göler, his friend Sarachaga, and the Russian von Werefkin, Haber's second, perished, whilst Moritz von Haber alone came out of them unhurt.

Julius von Göler, a most handsome and gay officer, was my early friend and most assiduous partner at the club balls in Karlsruhe; he was the first who had the courage to forsake the highly aristocratic *française* and to dance in public with the plebeian actress. Now, in May of 1835, he and the amiable, seductive Kamill von Lotzbeck and Herr von Marschall arranged a rustic ball in my honour. I met these three splendid dancers again in Baden soon after.

When my mother walked along the street of Karlsruhe together with me and my brothers, I used to hear the people say: "There goes the widow of Captain Bauer with her 'fortune!'"

The good mother did not live to see her misfortune!

* * * * * *

Thus ended the great professional tour, rich in triumphs and gold. In the course of eighteen months

I had performed in twenty-two towns on nearly 200 evenings. After such great exertions mother and I longed for a rest. In the first place we went to Baden-Baden, where I had been so happy as a child—and after that as young Court actress of Karlsruhe.

But what changes I found in Baden-Baden! The stillness, simplicity, and geniality of life in the beautiful surroundings of the Black Forest had given way to brilliant and noisy amusements. Baden-Baden had become a place of amusement for the Parisians of the *haute volée* and *demi-monde*. The bold Marchioness Bethune, a woman of colossal dimensions, was the leader in this carnival—and soon my decided enemy when she saw how I was likewise surrounded by a devoted guard, at whose head stood Prince Jérôme Napoleon, the eldest son of the ex-king of Westphalia.

Prince Jérôme Napoleon—or as he was obliged to call himself now, Prince von Montfort—was but 21 years old, officer in the Würtemberg army, and of an enchanting beauty and amiability. He had the true Napoleonic face, with the pale complexion, sharply-cut noble features, which bore a striking resemblance to his grand-uncle, intelligent, deep-blue eyes, and a charming, melancholy smile. The young Prince, the conqueror of many hearts, often showed himself unhappy and tired of life. Did he long for other conquests?

At the *table-d'hôte* the Prince was my *vis-à-vis*.

After dinner we would have an excursion together to some green coffee-garden, or a walk—and at night we met in front of the great drawing-room to listen to the splendid music. The Marchioness Bethune could have killed me with her eyes.

When we parted the Prince von Montfort said to me, with his tired, melancholy smile: "N'oubliez pas le pauvre misanthrope!" We never met again. On the 12th May, 1847, Prince Jérôme Napoleon von Montfort, a colonel in the service of Würtemberg, and a nephew to King Wilhelm of Würtemberg, died in hopeless insanity, not quite 33 years old. He had killed himself with fast living.

Also the much-coveted, very handsome Camill von Lotzbeck, with whom I gaily danced last in the great drawing-room at Baden-Baden, died young and unhappy. He loved with mad passion the wife of another, Countess O., from Paris, and followed her like her shadow from Baden-Baden to Paris—from Paris to Trouville, Nizza, and so on. . . . In this hopeless love his once so hopeful life was soon consumed.

* * * * * *

From the beginning of August we lived in summer retirement in the charming quiet watering-place of Schinznach, near Baden in Switzerland, where my mother was to take the waters on account of her rheumatic sufferings.

By the advice of my brother Louis, who had carefully studied the Swiss people during his commercial travels, and found them to be proud and reserved and full of contempt for the " dishonourable " comedians, we simply entered our names into the visitors' book as " Frau Rittmeister Bauer, and Frl., daughter, from Karlsruhe "—not hinting in the smallest degree that this " Frl., daughter," had been besides Imperial Russian Court actress, and in a few weeks would be Royal Saxon Court actress. In the quiet Schinznach there was nobody, fortunately, who had seen me on the stage. And the daughter of Captain Bauer's widow was destined here to dream the sweetest, most poetic dream of love of her life, which was not polluted by theatrical intrigues, or the used-up lustfulness of wearied gentlemen of rank.

There stayed at the time in Schinznach a very handsome young Genevan, on account of his eyes; he was called Theodore de la Rive, a *savant*, belonging to one of the most distinguished, the richest, and proudest families of the proud city on the Rhone. He was ever to be found in the company of his friend, a talented and engaging painter from Geneva, who painted the ruins of the Castle of Habsburg, some romantic spots on the wild Aar, and also—me, handing a gift to a beggar in front of the Kurhaus. The little picture is still in my possession. I am represented in the fashion of that time, with a bulky lavender-coloured dress, with very wide, wing-shaped sleeves, shoes with crossed ties and enormous fair buckles.

Theodore de la Rive soon became my shadow—the tenderest and most affectionate admirer. Whenever I showed myself in the morning in front of the the Kurhaus, during the time that my mother took the waters, my *savant* was by my side immediately, and deemed himself happy if he might accompany me upon a walk to the old Habsburg, the cradle of Kaiser Rudolph, or through the lovely green Aar-dale. At first my intercourse with the handsome professor was perfectly guileless, for he wore an engagement ring. He was engaged to a cousin, the daughter of another Geneva family as rich and proud as his own, but, as I soon learned, it was an engagement without love. The parents had betrothed them when they were children, and formally renewed the engagement when the cousin had become a professor. The whole of Geneva thought it a very suitable match. Why therefore consult their hearts?

Then de la Rive one day appeared without his engagement ring. I wanted to teaze him about it, but the word died away upon my lips when I saw his burning glance resting upon me.

I knew that he loved me passionately. I knew that it would cost me but one word—and he would have forsaken his betrothed and charged himself with the curse of his parents, and would have followed me. I felt that I loved him too, with all my heart—I felt that I might find by his side peace and happiness. But durst I rob faithful parents of their only son? Durst I couple his pure life with mine, from which my dark days of misfortune in England could never—never be again effaced? And what if he should learn that the daughter of the captain's widow was at the same time a comedienne —was acting for money on the public boards, and thus, according to traditional Swiss conceptions, carried on a disreputable trade, like travelling musicians, jugglers, mountebanks, barbers, grave-diggers, gaolers, bailiffs, beadles, night-watchmen, hangmen, and their associates—and would his love outlive that?

I was not long in having an opportunity of testing this, after I had successfully avoided his declaration of love for many days.

Once when mother, the painter, professor, and I, on a splendid evening in September, returned from a walk, we found the whole of the visitors in a bustle surrounding a caravan-waggon which stopped in front of the Kurhaus. All kinds of scenery and stage requisites peeped out under the ragged tarpaulin, and around the waggon itself stood men and women in rather bohemian costumes, whom I recognized at first glance as brother and sister artistes.

"Ah! travelling actors!" I cried with much glee. "That *is* a surprise, a delightful surprise!

A theatrical performance in Schinznach! What a pleasant prospect! Mother—I wish I could play with them! I have longed to play with plain, live, travelling actors," I said.

The professor looked at me in perfect horror—then he said with circumspection: "You are joking, mein Fräulein. You only know the wretched comedians under the glare and shimmer of the dazzling stage, and with lofty lies upon their lips. You should just cast a glance behind the wings—or worse than that, into the domestic life of these disreputable people, of whom it is said even in Schmid's Commentary of the old Bavarian law: "Mimes are funmakers, who fight over their meals, and carry on all sorts of nonsense."

I could not help laughing in the good fellow's face, and hastened to meet the travelling brethren, with whom the stout landlord was having a violent altercation. And I heard their story; they said: 'We are on the way to Berne, and on the waggon lies prostrate the daughter of our director, who was suddenly taken ill; she plays the lover parts, and now the hard landlord refuses us a shelter and his hall for a few performances, our exchequer being exhausted."

I spoke to the landlord with some energy, became bail for the bill of the comedians, threatened him with an immediate departure—and he received the wanderers into his hostelry, and gave up to them his large hall for a performance on the following evening.

After supper I made the round of the table together with the Geneva painter, hat and booking-sheet in hand, and I had great satisfaction in inducing all the guests to take seats, and, indeed, some of them made very considerable over-payments. Even my professor, who had become pensive and silent, gave a considerable sum, though shaking his head. I was able to hand to the beaming director 250 francs. Such a sum he had not handled for a long time.

Kotzebue's "Braut und Bräutigam in einer Person" was to be performed. The director's pretty daughter had recovered far enough to be able to play the title *rôle* . . . when, shortly before the commencement of the play, she had a relapse—a swoon, and could not appear. . . . The director came hurrying up to me in great distress, "What's to be done? It is impossible to put another piece in place of this one at a moment's notice, without a 'first walking lady.' What will the people here think of me? As an honest man I must give back again the money I have received for the places booked, and after that I shall be unable even to pay the landlord's bill, nor will there be any money left to defray our expenses on the way to the next town and to nurse my poor sick daughter." So saying, the old man shed copious tears. . . .

Then I said, with prompt resolution, "*Herr Director*, I shall play the part of your daughter. I have played it before on an amateur theatre not altogether without success. You advance before the curtain, saying that a lady amateur has undertaken at the eleventh hour to play the part of your daughter who was suddenly taken sick, and would desire their kind indulgence. Quickly let me have the officer's uniform of your daughter; I shall meanwhile dress for the first act.

I still see before me the astonished faces of a respectable audience when the curtain rose, and I stood before them in a white dress, *à la* "Linon," ornamented with ivy leaves, taking some pains to appear as dilettante-like as possible.

But my poor Geneva professor especially sat there perfectly nonplussed and pale as if an evil phantasmagoria tormented him. Although I loved the good fellow heartily, I felt some malicious joy.

At first I played my part as an amateur with great success. I advanced nervously, spoke slowly, and without any elocutionary effort, like a good school-girl who has committed her piece beautifully. The rest of the caste did their best to "haul me through." They pushed me from side to side unnoticed, winked to me with their eyes, and whispered to me their advice. The good director emerged with his prompter's book behind every wing beside which I had to act. And in this manner the first act passed over rather tediously, although my stout colleague was a splendid old coquette, and the representer of characters was a remarkably fine coxcomb-lover, and also the rest of the company did their best.

But soon I said to myself, with Mephistopheles, "Enough of that!" When I saw scene after scene gliding on in this languid way my proud artiste blood rebelled. I commenced to play away with unrestrained vivacity. And when I made my appearance on the stage in the smart uniform of a swaggering lieutenant of hussars, over the clattering of the sabre and chinking of the spurs, the tickling of the little mustache on the lip, I quite forgot the valued amateur performer. I played with a zeal, a sparkling humour, a rollicking hilarity such as I had perhaps never yet displayed in this *rôle* upon the proudest Court theatre, with the most famous artistes, and before the most brilliant audience. To please the many French people who were present I interlarded my lieutenant's jargon with as many *parbleus* and other French slang as possible. At first the other actors looked at me puzzled, but soon they allowed themselves to be carried away by my humour and fire. The much-respected audience sat there with large wondering eyes; but after they had just laughed for once right heartily they were carried away too into the general giddiness. Thus "Braut und Bräutigam in einer Person" came to an end amidst merry laughter and great clapping of hands. Only the poor professor sat there the whole evening as if labouring under a severe nightmare.

When the curtain had fallen all the actors surrounded me as if by preconcerted arrangement. They gazed at me with beaming eyes, and the director said—

"Kind deliverer, enchantress, you have betrayed yourself. No dilettante plays like that. You are an artiste, you belong to us!"

"Yes, to us," joined in the rest in a jubilant chorus.

Deeply moved, I gave one hand to the director and the other to the stout sister artiste, saying—

"Yes, ye good people, I belong to you from my very heart and soul. It is my pride to be able to call myself a comedienne. Long life to our art, the noble, elevating, cheering art of representing men."

Then I heard, proceeding from the wings, a stifled "je comprends!" Before me stood Theodore de la Rive, ghost-like, pale. The actors withdrew with much tact.

"Pardon the cruel game to the comedienne," I said, much moved. "Now you know why our ways must for ever diverge. You belong to a rich and proud family, I, from my own choice and inclination, to the disreputable people."

"And still I love you! In this most bitter hour it has become to me clearer than ever that I shall never be happy without you. Be mine, and I will brave all the prejudice of the world, the being disinherited by my family, and . . ."

"Also the curse of your parents? No, I could not bear that because I love you from my heart."

And I remained steadfast and unmoved to all his entreaties and vows. At least, this time I heard the voice of duty, and that I find, even this day, when I must look back upon so many errors of the heart, a sweet remembrance.

I kissed him with tears when we took farewell of each other. We did not see each other again. I returned to the stage. He broke off the engagement with his unloved cousin and entered upon a voyage of exploration around the world for several years. I have since frequently thought of him with ardent longing. A few years ago I read the announcement of his death in a newspaper. He had become a celebrated naturalist. Was he happy?

CHAPTER VII.

LAST APPEARANCES.

Dresden—Tieck again—His Family Circle—Kleist—
First Performance of "Glöckner von Notre Dame"
—A Failure—Tieck and Schiller—Eduard von
Bülow—Lola Montez—A Scene—Reminiscences of
Lola—Baron von Brunnow—Karl von Holtei—
Countess Ida Hahn-Hahn—Her Novel, "Faustine"
—Another Authoress, Henriette Paalzow—Julius
Mosen—Hofrath Hanfstängl—Prince Ernst—The
Grand Duchess Cäcilie of Oldenburg—Oldenburg—
Death of the Grand Duchess—Dresden—Richard
Wagner—Dorothea Tieck—Death of Karoline's
Mother—Karoline Wearies of the Stage—Coco Dies
—Threatening Letters—Attempt at Black Mail—
Grasping Critics—An Intellectual Lover—Also a
Gambler—Love-Letters in Pawn—Redeemed—Prince
Felix Lichnowsky—Is it Peace?

After having paid, from Schinznach, a visit to the Neuchatel lake and the places and friends of my joyous and guiltless youth, I repaired with my mother to the "Olympian Dresden," as Herder writes, towards the end of August, in 1835, to commence my last engagement.

Tieck, whom I revered with the greatest enthusiasm, and the stage became the centre of my life. The aged dramaturg became my teacher and friend. He went over every new part with me, and after each new performance I went to hear his critical opinion on it. The gloomy old house at the corner of the Alt Market became a dear home to me. Up there in the book-girded, homely study of the master I have spent never-to-be-forgotten momentous hours, have been taught, advised, praised, and blamed by him quite as a good daughter would be by a good father. The gentle Hofräthin, who bore her illness with quiet resignation, the daughters, the intellectual and feeling Dorothea, to whom we are indebted for many an excellent translation of Shakespeare, and the cheerful, fair Agnes with her splendid contralto voice, were kind and affectionate to me, and even Countess Finkenstein scattered over me the cornucopia of her favour abundantly, as long as the sun of grace of her idolized friend Tieck was smiling over me.

The people of Dresden said: "The old dramaturg has another favourite for a change; he wants to show that Julie Rettich's place has been completely filled up on the stage and in his heart, and that her departure for Vienna does not pain him. . . . But how long will it last?" Well, it lasted for many a happy, long year, and up to this day I feel grateful from the bottom of my heart to the great dead, who was much praised and much abused.

I shall never forget the rare evenings which I had the privilege of spending in Tieck's family circle.

On such homely evenings the poet kept on his very becoming gown-like frock of black velvet, and in his whole bearing and conversation he was simpler, more human, more amiable than on the official reading evenings. How cheerfully he would speak of his indigent childhood, his stormy youth, his motley experiences as man, and of his most favourite comedians!

Often he would read out to us his charming tales, such as "Blaubart," "die Haimonskinder," "Magelone," the "blonde Eckbert," and how he understood to read them, so wonderfully fairylike, sweet, and enchanting, and again thrilling and causing horror! Besides, he was fond of coupling with these early products happy reminiscences, as, for instance, how these very tales had won for him the friendship of August Wilhelm Schlegel, and united the two poets afterwards for a combined translation of Shakespeare's works.

As much as he admired Shakespeare and Goethe, as little he liked Schiller. He used to call him "a Spanish Seneca."

He had also been in contact with poor Kleist. Owing to the great diversity of their human and poetical dispositions, they could not become intimate. Tieck, while distinctly recognising Kleist's great dramatic talent, spoke of the unhappy poet's fixed ideas, which would increase so alarmingly now and then that he once tried in all seriousness to push

Adam Müller from the Elbe-bridge, in Dresden, because he fancied that he loved Müller's wife to madness and that he could not live without possessing her. That Kleist hated cats was likewise a cause of offence in Tieck's eyes, who was very fond of cats. And that Kleist once charged a kitten with having tasted his preserved pine-apples in order to bring about a catastrophe, greatly inspirited Tieck, who knew well the nature of cats, to sharpen his sarcasm.

Rahel, Bettina, and other coquettish blue-stockings, were not rarely the butt of his biting satire. He called them "monkeys escaped from paradise," and liked to repeat the story how the rather grown-up "child," Bettina, was riding upon the back of his sofa, and said to him, in ridicule of his affected Goethe devotion, and in her Frankfurt dialect: "I say, Tieck, I must have a child by Goethe at any cost; that will be a perfect demigod!"

His parodies on the "windy" Klemens Brentano were exquisite; the latter was especially fond of sighing out to tender women his physical sufferings and winning them to tears of compassion and pity by his weary-of-the-world distraction and forlornness. "When Brentano was trying on these hellish arts in my house too, I said to him, seriously: 'You may lie to my womankind as much as you like, only one condition I must impose upon you, dear friend, let your lies be cheerful!' and my poetical onion promised everything possible and desirable. But one day when I returned home, what do I find? My wife and Countess Finkenstein, and my Dorothea and my Agnes, all swimming in tears, and in their midst, my sighing, distracted fox, Brentano. But I cured my womankind and gave a lesson to the rogue in the tearful dress: 'Does the devil ride you? Did you not solemnly promise me that you would tell nothing but merry lies to my women?'"

"My women!" It makes me smile to-day when I think of how naïvely patriarch-like these words sounded on Tieck's lips, and how sharply, how derisively, the naughty tongues of the Dresdeners pronounced them. They called Tieck the "Count von Gleichen."

Tieck, like his favourite heroes, had led a wandering artiste's life for a long time, partly with wife and child. The high-flowing adventurer-like time of his youth continued to ferment in him, and would not let him be content with a settled life and a settled place of abode. Besides, his pecuniary circumstances never being of the most brilliant kind, he lived now here, now there, and often for years as the guest of friends; in Ziebingen particularly he stayed oftenest and longest, at first at the estate of his friend von Burgsdorff and afterwards in the house of the "Oberpræsident," Count Finkenstein. When the Count died, in 1818, his daughter Henriette went with the Tieck family to Dresden, and with her abundant means she founded for her idolized poet a comfortable home free from care. She conducted and paid for the household, she did the honours on the occasions of his readings and *soirées*, she unweariedly nursed him when he suffered greatly from gout, she accompanied him, who was a lover of the theatre and afterwards a teacher of the dramatic art, to the theatre ... and Tieck's transcendent, early love, his spouse Amalie, approved of these strange relations with wonderful gentleness and a most delicate tact, and the old romanticist seemed to feel very comfortable as Count Gleichen II.

When I made the acquaintance of Countess Finkenstein she had with a touching fidelity revered and honoured her friend for over thirty years, accommodated herself to each of his many humours, fulfilled with the sacrifice of fortune every wish of his expensive love of travelling and books and—oh wonder!—had heard him read certainly ten thousand times—nay, what is much more remarkable still, with the same rapture, with transfigured countenance, and a most lively enthusiasm—the various plays of Shakespeare and the Spaniards! Love overcometh everything, even the nerves.

Every acquaintance, every educated stranger, found admission to these semi-public readings. A word of recommendation, nay, a simple self-introduction, were sufficient to be graciously received by Tieck. And no savant, virtuoso, collector of curiosities, or inquisitive tourist who passed through Dresden, neglected to spend an evening in hearing Ludwig Tieck read. The old romanticist was partly regarded as a sight himself. Eventually, the hired lackeys and guides of the hotels called in the morning quite unceremoniously at Tieck's house inquiring from Tieck's old domestic, Friederike, if there were readings that night, adding that they had to announce such and such a number of strangers. And Tieck's dear vanity was flattered to see himself thus run after.

Besides, he was inexorably punctual as to the commencement of his readings. Even though he might be engaged in the most interesting conversation with the most distinguished and fashionable guests, at 7 o'clock precisely he gave the signal to his old Friederike, and the famous little table with the two wax tapers suddenly stood in the centre of the room; Tieck sat behind it in an arm chair. Breathless, anxious silence in the room. What is he going to read to-day? One of Shakespeare's nerve-shaking Henrys, or the terrible Richard III., or one of his beloved Spaniards: "The open secret," or "The Judge of Zalamea"? These anxious queries could be read on the faces of all the natives, and generally beside it a hearty mark of exclamation: Would that it were a short comedy to-day! And then, when Tieck said with his splendid sonorous voice: "The Judge of Zalamea, a drama from the Spanish, by Calderon!" we, the initiated, fell with quiet sighs and most resigned faces into the cosiest possible position. But if the sound that came from between the two tapers was: "Der zerbrochene Krug," or, "Minna von Barnhelm," then a breath of relief went through the saloon.

When Tieck was in a particularly good humour he would ask of those immediately about him: "What do my honourable guests wish to hear to-day?" And on all sides I, the spoiled favourite, received stealthy, imploring looks and soft entreaties to give words to the general humming, which I did, saying: "If you please, goldigster Herr Hofrath, a comedy, whether it be Holberg's 'Wochenstube,' or 'Geschäftige,' or Goldoni's 'Lügner,' or a merry piece by Gozzi. I have not laughed heartily for ever so long." Then he would sometimes threaten with his finger, smiling at the same time in a most roguish manner, saying: "Who would believe that, you wantonness! Well, you shall laugh to-night, merrily and heartily. Do I not myself like to hear it?" Thus we were saved from the Henrys and the Spaniards.

Holberg's "Wochenstube" is a splendid picture of life in a small town. A lying-in woman receives her first visits, and is forced to welcome all cordially, to entertain and treat them; for such is the established *bon ton* of the little town. The first arrival is a very bashful dame who can scarcely pronounce a word; then follows a gossip with irresistible volubility of tongue; a *pleureuse* (weeper) allows free course to her soft, soft feelings and salt, salt tears; a steady printer's wife only has in view, and on her tongue, the practical side of life; a schoolmaster's better half enlarges on the philosophy of life, and at last, as sensational climax, three sisters enter at the same time, who always address the lying-in woman all three at the same moment. How Tieck managed to read so that one really thought one heard three different voices at the same time is still a puzzle to me. Here the vocal artiste almost became a vocal magician. But the effect was brilliant indeed. We did not laugh, we literally shrieked like wanton, happy children, and even the invalid Hofräthin joined in heartily. But the little, withered face of the Countess Finkenstein beamed forth from her tulle puffs like sunshine. With splendid spirit the "master" also read the old monastic farce: "Die Sindfluth."

When Tieck intended to read from his own compositions, all the regular frequenters were formally invited to the reading a few days before, and about 50 persons would generally assemble in the saloon, the side and ante-chambers. It was taken very much amiss if anybody sent an excuse. We were received with a certain solemnity, and treated to tea and more festive cake than ordinarily. The wax tapers were thicker. Tieck wore his best dress-coat and most solemn knot in his high, white cravat, and in honour of the occasion the Countess had a few more dozens of tulle-frills trembling round her ancient little face.

In quite an enrapturing manner Tieck read his "Fortunat," "Octavian," "Genoveva," the "gestiefelte Kater," and, above all, his "Blaubart." The latter was a special favourite with Countess Finkenstein, and she looked forward like a child to the pleasure of the chief effect which Tieck managed to produce with a single word. At the commencement of the scene in the blue room she would lift her green shade and look at the unsuspecting strangers with the eyes of a falcon sure of his prey. No ear, no heart could resist Agnes' awful scream by Tieck, "Blutig?" As if shaken by a dead man's hand the novices were startled, and a chill even went through the ranks of his veteran listeners.

More and more afflicted by gout, the aged romanticist rarely left his poet castle. Only when he was obliged to attend rehearsals or performances at the theatre in his quality of dramaturg—this post he had held since 1825, and received for it the modest sum of 800 thalers—or when he was commanded to read to the Court, he descended the stair with difficulty and employed a sedan-chair to carry him to his destination. He rarely went into society; twice a year he visited the intendant, Herr von Lüttichau, whose wife was an enthusiastic admirer of the old romanticist. Only his passion for books often made him forget his gout, and also his slender purse. If it came to his knowledge that somewhere a rare book, especially a very old edition of Shakespeare, was to be sold, he abandoned visitors, study, theatrical rehearsals, everything, hastened downstairs with youthful vivacity, promised the sedan-chair porters an extra gratuity if they stepped along at a brisk pace, and paid for the beloved book, in the unconcerned style peculiar to him in money matters, whatever price was required of him. He took home his treasure triumphantly, and should the Hofräthin sigh at the big price he had paid, he would caress her like a child. And the Countess had to raise sum after sum to make good the big deficit occasioned by the book-purchase.

One Sunday the first performance of the "Glöckner von Notre-dame" came off before a bumper house. At the outset the thing looked very well, my dance as Esmeralda was received with applause . . . but soon after, when the unfortunate Gervaise began to moan from the depth of her dungeon, hurling up her wild malediction to the light of the lamps, our torture began; the audience *laughed*! And so it went on to the end. The famous group when Esmeralda hands to Quasimodo the jug, aroused hilarity on account of Pauli's regulation-mask—one eye and two humps; Frollo's lamentations in the dungeon-scene were laughed down. Moreover, Quasimodo-Pauli was unlucky. During the rehearsals he carried his Esmeralda with becoming gracefulness from the funeral-pile into the "sanctuary" upon the steps of Notre-Dame. But during the performance the tight costume of Quasimodo, and the fear that his two humps might shift, impeded him, and after three steps he let me glide out of his arms. Thus, of course, the calling of "sanctuary" was bound to produce a comic effect.

The recognition of the mother passed without producing the least effect, and previous to the fall of the curtain the dragging of the huge money-bag across the small stage produced the most unbounded hilarity among the gentle audience.

Next morning I found Tieck wearing a red dressing-gown, and in an anything but rosy humour sitting in his library. He began a conversation on an indifferent topic, evidently desirous of evading a discussion about the luckless "Glöckner." But I said undauntedly: "Do you not think, Herr Hofrath, that our playing was not to blame for the fiasco of last night?"

Then he started and said: "Doch, doch! (certainly, most certainly!) You, as well as all the rest, did not play with sufficient romantic grandiosity. Nobody succeeded in captivating, in overwhelming the audience."

"Herr Hofrath!" I exclaimed, with warm indignation, "the audience did not laugh down us actors, but the wretched ridiculous piece. But you—you are unjust. And you know that I sacrificed something when I agreed to undertake the part of Esmeralda to accommodate myself to your and the intendant's wish . . . and this is my reward!" I burst into tears.

Dorothea had entered the library. She took me into her arms and said feelingly: "Do look at my father, do." And to be sure, Tieck smiled benignly: "Well done, child! How the true comedienne blood boils up! That is the way I like my comediennes. But let us make peace now, 'Brause kopfchen'" (little hot-head).

Indeed, Tieck was irresistible when he adopted such tones.

But the greatest sacrifice I brought the old dramaturg was when, at his urgent request, I undertook to play Lady Macbeth—I, with my comedy-face, with my merry voice, with my conversational tone of speech, was to play the dreadful Lady Macbeth!

On making known to him my doubts, Tieck said lightly: "A comedienne must be able to conjure up from her inner heart according to want the true tones of her character; and as for the comedy-face, you put on a black wig, blacken your eye-brows, paint yourself a greyish-white, and be not sparing with the 'lines of energy' about the corners of the mouth and the eye-brows."

But then I said resolutely: "No, Herr Hofrath, Dresden shall not see me as a caricature, believe me. I will undertake the part to please you, and will not be idle in the study of the part; but I know too well that I have not got the stuff of a Lady Macbeth in me—I am sure to make a fiasco."

And although I did not exactly make a fiasco, the audience nevertheless remained pretty callous despite my utmost zeal to infuse awe and terror into their souls. Even to this day I appreciate the verdict which the learned Prince Johann, afterwards King of Saxony, pronounced to Tieck regarding my Lady Macbeth: "I acknowledge Fräulein Bauer's great diligence and her intelligent appreciation of this most dreadful of Shakespeare's female types, but— one was unable to *credit* her Lady Macbeth with being able to do all the terrible, gruesome, bloody things she said and performed!"

When I asked Tieck why he did not have Macbeth performed according to Schiller's adaptation instead of after his daughter's translation, he said haughtily: "The good fellow has taken too many liberties with Shakespeare's play! I will not be his accomplice."

Tieck, with his extensive theatrical knowledge and ability, would assuredly have been the greatest dramaturg of his time had he not been at the same time the old romanticist, and so obstinate and full of humours and whims.

His most mournful experience as to his Spaniards Tieck had with Calderon's "Dame Kobold," in Dresden—fortunately before my time. The play was received very unfavourably at its first representation at the beginning of January, 1826. But when, against the advice of the stage-managers and his friends, Tieck announced Dame Kobold again a few days afterwards, and when it became known among the people that Tieck had declared haughtily that the Dresden people ought to be educated to the height of a Calderon and his Dame Kobold, a threatening multitude crowded the theatre that night, which answered the rising of the curtain, and the first words by Julius and Pauli, by hissing so that the two artistes bowed and withdrew. A second attempt to start the play was prevented more demonstratively still. The audience got their money returned and went home laughing.

How did Tieck revenge himself? Next morning he had the play " Erziehung macht den Menschen " (Education and good breeding make a man), by Ayrenhof, put on the stage.

* * * * * *

And what numbers of interesting and amiable men I became acquainted with during Tieck's reading-nights!

One of the most zealous of Tieck's disciples was Eduard von Bülow, who sat unweariedly at the feet of the master, and under his direction translated plays and novels from the English, French, Italian, Latin, and Spanish. He was then somewhat over thirty years old, and was the father of the musical prodigy, Hans Guido von Bülow, who became such a great pianoforte virtuoso afterwards. In Eduard von Bülow's whole appearance there was something enigmatical, mysterious, gloomy; and when one evening at Tieck's house he read out to us his gruesome novel, "Das Gewissen," the thought forced itself upon my mind: those are dark pictures taken from his own life!

I was to come into quite peculiar and somewhat more intimate contact with Eduard von Bülow through Lola Montez. That Spanish dancer, who was not very celebrated, still less notorious, then, suddenly emerged in Dresden, in order to dance on the royal stage. She was said to have weighty recommendations to the Court, to be descended from an aristocratic family, to be wonderfully beautiful, and to have charmed already the Court in Pillnitz by her singing of Spanish national songs to the accompaniment of a guitar. No wonder that this interesting dancer greatly engaged the Dresden theatrical public even before her appearance on the stage. I had not yet seen the heroine, but the theatre porter one morning came running up to me quite out of breath and heated, giving thus vent to his feelings : " To-day the Spanish lady is up again, and but yesterday she has upset all our heads. No, you cannot believe what whims she has in her head ! She demands quite for her ownself special drapery, light, and scenery ; she intends to have herself admired first of all in the background on the stage amidst red drapery, and light reflected from many extra lamps from above, as *tableau vivant*, in a fantastic position, before she sallies forth. Nobody pleases her, and even our ballet master often does not understand her funny French. Then her eyes flash, and she stamps with her foot like a naughty boy. I was to tell you, by the bye, miss, that you need not come to the rehearsal at nine, but only at ten o'clock ; for till then the Spanish lady alone will occupy the stage."

Hardly had the old porter, who was greatly put about, left me, when Herr von Bülow, who lived in the same house with me, sent his compliments to inquire if he might, in spite of the early morning-hour, be permitted to call on me, on an important matter that admitted of no delay. It must indeed be something important which could bring the learned gentleman so soon out of his dressing-gown. He who ordinarily spoke and walked so softly, and slowly, and deliberately, entered my room in the greatest excitement, his cheeks flushed, and his first winged word was : " Lola Montez ! "

"You too, sir!" I interrupted him, laughing. "Where do I find a clue to this inconstancy?"

"Lola Montez would like to make your nearer acquaintance. Yesterday as Donna Diana you took the fiery child of Spain by storm. Beautiful Lolita sat beside me, clapping her hands like a child, and called out again and again, almost somewhat too loud for our Dresden habits: 'Oh, la bella Donna! Je voudrais la connaître!'"

"Very flattering! But who and what is this maiden from abroad, I am curious to know?"

"The most lovely, charming, and amiable creature."

"And you say that to my face, the face of the *bella Donna?*" I said jestingly, interrupting the enthusiast.

"Beg pardon! I wanted to add: that saw life under a Spanish sun! She is the daughter of a gallant general who fell for Don Carlos. She was obliged to flee her country—without means, without protection. But she is possessed of courage, energy, and great talents. Her innate, graceful talents for dancing were wonderfully developed under a French ballet-master; besides she sings charming Spanish national songs, which she accompanies on the guitar. Free and glittering like a butterfly the enchanting creature flutters through the world and . . ."

"Enchants our most serious scholars and poets!" I again interrupted with a laugh. "But so quite alone, without protection, does this dangerous butterfly flutter through the lands?"

"Oh, she is virtuous—virtuous and proud and brave, like Jeanne d'Arc. When my wife, who is also charmed and enchanted by Lolita, as all are who see her, gently hinted at the danger of her want of protection, Lolita, with flaming eyes, drew a small pointed dagger as sharp as a needle, made a charming gesture, saying proudly: 'Voilà mon protecteur!' Is not that charming? And how honest, how naïvely open-hearted she is! When I conducted her through our picture-galleries yesterday she said that Raphael and Coreggio wearied her with their everlasting red-haired Madonnas; on the other hand, she stopped with shining eyes in front of a very middling painting of a Spanish bull-fight and a fandango, clapping her hands with delight—and the evening before yesterday she yawned aloud over the glorious tenor-air by Moriani and said that Lucie was enough to put one to sleep."

"And that, you, the poet, admire?"

"Yes, I admire the pure unadulterated nature in this girl. She has not yet been affected by the sickliness of our æsthetic teas. I think her original, striking, bold."

"But Dresden!"

"Yes, in the lukewarm view we take of life, the standing alone, the independence, the whole of the frank and bold originality of the beautiful Lola, might not be judged quite so favourably, and therefore I have come to ask you to take the charming creature a little under your protection on the stage."

"In other words, I am to chaperon the beautiful Spaniard? I, who am still Dresden's leading actress? Well, I must say that it is a peculiar new part which you allot to me."

But eventually I promised to take a kindly interest in Lolita.

At ten o'clock I went to the rehearsal of the comedy "Die Wasserkur." But I arrived much too soon. Lola Montez had not done yet with her new arrangements, draperies, and attitudes. At last the lightning from above fell with sufficient brilliancy upon her "living picture," and she could sally forth to perform her Spanish national dance. Her manner of dancing was peculiar. She danced neither very ingeniously nor gracefully. Her *pas* came out by starts, quicksilver-like. But her bounds were bold, fiery, striking, and she looked wonderfully beautiful. I had time to look at her from one of the wings. Her figure was too thin to be perfectly beautiful, but her delicate, girlish head, with the jet-black glossy hair, the transparent delicate paleness of her youthful face, the regular aristocratic features, and, above all, her eyes, her large, deep-blue, shining eyes, and her lovely smile, were intoxicatingly beautiful. And this strange mixture of child-like ways, wantonness, flashing glow, and unrestrained defiance in her whole appearance, had a kind of weird captivating power. Now I understood the momentary frenzy of Herr von Bülow, who was ordinarily so sedate. Was I not myself already irresistibly captivated by the beautiful spoiled child?

When the dance was finished, I advanced from the side-scenes. Scarcely had Lola perceived me, when she threw herself upon my neck with shouts of joy, and cried: "Enfin! ma bella Donna. The vous thaime, nous nous préthenterons the thoir enthemble! moi, the dantherai, vous parlerez, the thera tharmant." And so she went on in her lisping accent, quite bewildering. "I love beauty and the dance. I also want to be celebrated like you—but as a dancer. I am passionately fond of dancing. We are both beautiful—I like the south, you like the north. I love you, and you must love me too." And hopping away, she called out to me with her clear merry voice and her child-like laugh: "Au revoir, ma bella Donna—à the thoir, à the thoir!"

But strangely enough, the audience remained pretty cold over the attitude of the beautiful Spaniard and her quicksilvery bounds that evening. Where in the world were her admirers? Had I not seen that afternoon wreaths and bouquets that were intended for Lola Montez. Were their lordships the married men not permitted to do public homage to the dancer? I was told that the flowers had been reserved for the second dance. But Lola would not dance any more before such ungrateful barbarians! So the intendant, von Lüttichau, told me rather excitedly. I was on the way to the parlour, carrying my two little spaniels on my arm, with which Fräulein Berg was to appear in the second act as an enthusiastic dog-fancier. "You must help me to bring round the obstinate little thing!" the intendant continued. "My resources are finished, and as for you, the little hobgoblin is quite infatuated with you. I had to promise her to put another comedy on the stage to-morrow in which you appear. No such an illbred young damsel have I ever yet before encountered on the stage. There, see yourself!" So saying, Herr von Lüttichau opened the door of the dancer's dressing-room.

What presented itself to our eyes was, indeed, an exceedingly comical picture in the frame of the door. Lola Montez stood in the middle of the room dressed in her tiny Spanish ballet costume; her hands supported on the toilet table, she hopped like a little school-girl, and struck out savagely with both her heels worse than the most spirited little foal. And in a semi-circle around her at a most respectable distance—owing to her kicking—there stood, with downcast, helpless mien, the bandmasters Lipinki and Reissiger, the theatrical secretary Winkler, Hofrath Carus, Herr von Bülow, and another half-dozen of glowing enthusiasts, whilst Lola shrieked, during her gymnastics: "Non! the ne dance plus! on n'a pas applaudi quand the faithais tha" (indicating kissing hands) "the ne dance plus devant un tel publique."

I with difficulty restrained myself from joining in this scene with ringing laughter, especially when her admirers, with nonplussed faces, requested me by signs to come to their assistance. I entered the dressing-room. Scarcely had Lola noticed me and my little dogs when she stopped in her wild jumps, and with a daring "salto mortale," she came up to me, singing out jubilantly: "Oh, ma bella Donna! Oh, thes tholis thiens! Oh! thes hithoux ... mais, the ne dance plus devant un tel publique méconnaissant," and she was about resuming her former operations.

"And what is to become of the many beautiful flowers which are intended for you, and whose fragrance already fills the house?" I said, in French.

"Flowers! Flowers in the theatre? I have seen none; no one has thrown me any, although I threw my prettiest kiss."

"Don't you know you are to get the flowers only after the second dance? Such is the custom in Dresden."

" Pas possible ? "

" And there are wreaths among them with streamers of satin and poetry printed on them."

" The dantherai! The dantherai! Quel bonheur! de tholis bouquets, des rubans, des vers—the dantherai! the dantherai! . . ." and snatching a dog from my hands, and throwing it up high into the air and catching it again, Lola Montez danced about the small room like a twirling-stick, so that her admirers timidly sought the corners.

The defiant child had changed into a gay, jubilant one. Thus she danced her second dance, was applauded and called out by her admirers, and wreaths and bouquets and poems were thrown at her feet. Beaming with happiness, she gathered them up, and after the dropping of the curtain she could find no end of showing us her treasures, and to cry: "Oh, que the thuis heureuse! voyez donc thes fleurs, thes rubans et thes vers!"

And this rapture was so child-like, sincere, and natural that no one grudged her this little triumph, and no sneering smile spoiled it.

Lola Montez appeared only once more as ballerina in Dresden, in 1842, for the public did not appreciate her quicksilver *pas*. But the number of her personal admirers grew from day to day, and the beautiful Lolita swam for the period of a fortnight from one festival given in her honour to another; the proudest ladies in Dresden did not disdain to pay their respects to the beautiful daughter of the Carlist general. On the occasion of such an enchanting feast, Lola was desired to appear in her complete costume as dancer. From the Court the Spanish songstress received a beautiful bracelet as a keepsake. Enough, Lola might be well satisfied with her *début* in Dresden, and she played her *rôle* as Carlist general's daughter with much tact and good luck to a successful end.

But when Lola Montez came back to Dresden the following year, her halo of virtue had faded away. The dreadful Prince Reuss had just turned her away, an unfaithful mistress. Also, the belief in her claim to be the daughter of a Carlist general had exploded. She was not received at Court now. Even her former patronesses and admirers shunned her, and did not know what to do with embarrassment when even her name was mentioned. The young adventuress continued to be seen in the company of a few bold young gentlemen, among them Gottfried Semper, the architect.

Nevertheless her star was to rise again shortly after in Berlin—just as a brilliant shooting star. She danced in the Opera House, and the golden youth of Berlin lay at her feet. Also the handsome, melancholy, pale-looking Prince Waldemar, named after his travels in the Indies, the Indian Prince, who was destined to die so young, temporarily forsook Bettina's beautiful daughter and paid his passionate homage to the Spanish dancer, and the bold Amazon visited him in his tent during a military bivouac in the neighbourhood of Berlin.

On the stage Lola manifested the same caprices as in Dresden. Once when she was to appear with a guitar which did not please her, she threw it on the ground between the wings, broke it to pieces with her feet, and, in full costume, hastened out of the house. She was already seated in a cab—at that moment Intendant von Küstner got sight of her, and said to her very gravely: "If you do not fulfil your engagements on the stage this evening, I shall be obliged to make it publicly known—and you will never again appear on this stage, *mademoiselle, jamais!*"

Then she bethought herself, left the cab—and danced with another guitar.

But when the handsome, pale "Indian Prince" no longer sufficed her—when she raised her fiery eyes to a brilliant Emperor—Lola experienced that one does not in Berlin chastise gendarmes with impunity!

Emperor Nicolas was in Berlin on a visit. In his honour a grand military review was held on the Kreuzberg. Among the thousands and thousands of spectators was also Lola Montez, beautifully mounted on horseback; but she did not merely wish to see, she also wanted to be seen. Already her spirited horse and her audacious whip had made a path to nearly where the Russian Emperor was— a few more tricks and kicks, and she would have succeeded in directing upon her seductive person the rather susceptible eyes of the autocrat of all the Russias—when a Prussian gendarme seized the reins of her horse, calling out to her a threatening "Zurück!" but the next moment her horsewhip came smacking down upon his grim visage. Lola was arrested, and that she was only expelled from Berlin was owing to an autograph secret order of King Friedrich Wilhelm III.

Lola's successful career at Munich, where she ruled over King Ludwig, overthrew the Cabinet Abel, which opposed her elevation to the rank of Countess von Mansfeld, and became the cause of the revolution in Munich, and of the abdication of her royal patron . . . and her melancholy death in misery and despair in a hospital of New York, in 1861, are known.

Also her enthusiastic admirer, Eduard von Bülow, died early after an adventurous, obscure life. Soon after Lola's departure and Tieck's going to live in Berlin, Bülow likewise left Dresden, living without rest, now here, now there. Afterwards I heard that he had been divorced from his wife, and having got entangled in revolutionary intrigues, had been obliged to quit Germany. Soon he married a cousin of his, a mysterious Countess Bülow, and took up his abode with her in the old Castle of Oetlishausen, in the Canton Thurgau, not far from my Broelberg, which I must call my "Qualberg." There Eduard von Bülow died as early as 1853.

Another enthusiastic disciple and admirer of Master Tieck was the poet Ernst Baron von Brunnow, a brother of the distinguished Russian Ambassador in London. The widowed Frau von Brunnow, with her son and daughter, had one of the most agreeable houses in Dresden, and the most select company of townspeople and strangers assembled regularly at her house on Sunday evenings. Both her son and daughter were unfortunate enough to be terribly deformed and shockingly ugly—perfect dwarfs, with gigantic heads, and hunches and humps in front and back. Naughty scorners said of Ernst von Brunnow, the poet of "Ulrich von Hutten": "He carries his Parnassus upon his back!" But in these ugly shells there lived noble souls and a wealth of genius. They bore their ugliness and asthmatic troubles with great resignation and cheerfulness. Fräulein von Brunnow, moreover, was a passionate dancer—and, owing to her amiability, she never wanted partners who did not even fear the appearance of ridicule; but why this dancing gnome was so fond of marking her humps in front and back with gigantic pink bows, I have never been able to understand.

Well, if good Ernst von Brunnow, of whom his excellent mother used to say with tears in her eyes, "My noble Ernst makes me the happiest of mothers!" —if only this noble Ernst had not had two small weaknesses, the first to wish to read like Tieck, the second to love me passionately.

I see to this day in my remembrance, the ugly, gnome-like figure, squatting in an easy-chair of red velvet, his shocking giant head popping up between the two candles, and the two greenish watery eyes glittering, burning with love, and hear the giant mouth declaim with pathos the poet's favourite sentimental romance, in which a sweet girl sucks the poisoned wound of her lover. And all around me I hear elderly young ladies with sympathetic sighs and moans, saying: "How ethereal—full of feeling—graceful—ingenious—original—highly poetical."

When soon after I brought a beautiful bouquet to the unhappy poet on the occasion of his birthday, his tearful eyes looked at me so very amorously, and the good Baroness said with emotion: "Beloved Karoline, give my noble Ernst a kiss—he loves you so warmly, you know—and if he were well . . ."

My blood curdled—but I controlled myself, made the amorous gnome, who reached up to my elbow stand upon a stool—fearlessly seized the ugly head—shut both eyes—and kissed him on brow and eyes.

In the autumn of 1836, Karl von Holtei appeared at Tieck's readings, together with his second wife,

Julie Holzbecher, with whom I had played on the Königstadt stage in Berlin twelve years ago. Both had meanwhile become rather reduced in circumstances, their principal engagements having been with small wandering troupes for a long time past. Poor Julie appeared especially discouraged and broken-hearted. They were going to try if they could not rehabilitate themselves for a greater theatre by a series of performances on a leading Court-stage. With this object in view, Herr von Holtei read at Tieck's his own theatrical compositions, in which he was going to appear with his wife. I heard him read out with much humour, " Drei und dreiszig Minuten in Grünberg," at which performance his singing Silesian accent stood him in good stead, but, on the other hand, it stood very much in the way of his Shakespeare-readings.

But Herr von Lüttichau roundly refused the request of the travelling artistes to be allowed to perform on the Dresden stage—till Holtei succeeded in winning over Princess Amalie. Then the Intendant had to obey. Holtei, in private life so nimble, appeared on the stage very stiff—and his poor Julie was a shy little bird, with broken wings. Matters were aggravated, because the couple did not understand how to put themselves on a friendly footing with the other artistes of the royal stage in Dresden.

Holtei always had a grudge against me, because I succeeded better on the stage than his two spouses.

At the very outset of my engagement at the royal theatre in Berlin, I was paid a much higher salary than Luise von Holtei, and had I not been there, perhaps Julie Holzbecher, a pupil of Mad. Stich's, might have been engaged. And now the pair met me again in the envied position of leading actress in Dresden while they themselves could not get a footing on a large stage, and had to wander on, without home, without rest.

But only two years later, Julie von Holtei was to find the rest she had longed for so ardently—under Riga's fields of ice and snow! But what hot, wild struggles of the heart preceded it! Only in Riga the unhappy woman had felt what Goethe calls "Glück ohne Ruhe—Liebe bist du!" (A happiness without repose—that is love!) She loved for the first time in her life, but she loved another man. And what storms, what torments, then broke over that poor heart of hers! Even her husband could not give back to her her peace, when he—in the consciousness of his own weakness—permitted the unlawful intercourse.

Julie died whilst being confined of twins. The shocking tragedy was played out.

The particulars of this sad story I learned in Breslau from my friend Professor August Kahlert, to whom Holtei had told everything in his strange frankness.

Two authoresses I met in Dresden who were then

world-renowned and much read—but to-day about forgotten. The first was Countess Ida Hahn-Hahn, who made her appearance in Dresden in the winter of 1842, with the Courlander Herr von Bistram, who was said to be her husband.

Her novel, "Faustine," had appeared quite lately, and attracted the greatest attention in society. Was it not generally known that the Countess was proud of having herself depicted herself as Faustine, and that, like her heroine, she boasted "to live the second part of Faust"; and that, in this novel, she unveiled her relations to Herr von Bistram as boldly as, a few years ago, she had, in other novels, revealed her love to the beautiful, highly-gifted Heinrich Simon, a Government assessor at Greifswald.

The chief-priestess of the worship of Hahn-Hahn and Faustine was Frau von Bardeleben. She gave several æsthetic Hahn-Hahn teas. I, too, was invited. I had to play in the "Majoratserbe" till nine o'clock; after which, to lose no time, I drove in the elegant toilet that had bewitched the heart of the "Majoratserbe" (heir to an entailed estate), Emil Devrient, to Frau von Bardeleben. All the ladies were put into merry excitement by the sight of the pompous stage-toilet at the tea-table—only Countess Ida Hahn-Hahn silently sniffed with her little nose the aromatic steam of tea, as if she wanted to say: "Neighbour, your smelling-bottle. Pooh!

pooh! I smell the smoke of lamps! How shocking to invite me to meet a comedienne!"

And from this high horse the Countess did not come down for the rest of the evening. When Frau von Lüttichau asked her if she had seen the "Majoratserbe" by Princess Amalie on the stage in Dresden, where the play was acknowledged to be given in the most perfect *ensemble*, over her narrow, red lips lightly and coolly glided the words: "Yes, I have seen it!" Not another word, and yet Emil Devrient and I counted our *rôles* in the play among our best.

No, I did not take vengeance by telling the "Frau Gräfin" of her *cher père*, the travelling, eccentric "theatre Count" in reduced circumstances, with whose troupe I had played in Lübeck three years ago, and who had offered with so much kindness to paint me with his own much-loved aristocratic paw, and how admirably he was versed in preparing with his own distinguished hands the thunder and lightning of the stage.

I knew that her papa, the theatrical Count, was the most awkward reminiscence in the "immense soul" of Countess Ida, and that she strove honestly and most successfully to think of him as little as possible.

I watched. Countess Ida was 37 years old then, and in spite of all the storms that had beaten through her life her appearance was still interesting and attractive. By no means beautiful, but *only just* beautiful, as may be read in her novels. She might have been the model of all her heroines of blue blood in the dress of white and azure cashmere, with the little pink satin hands under a cover of white mull. Even the painter alters colours, and the sculptor the form.

Her figure tall, almost haggard, her deportment aristocratically elegant; her features firm and regular; her complexion pure and delicate. Red lips smile gracefully, and when speaking exhibit white teeth that are just a little too large and prominent. Beautiful fair locks ingeniously cover the eye that had been operated upon so unsuccessfully by the famous Dieffenbach in Berlin, a year before. The remaining eye, however, sparkled so much with wit and vivacity that one hardly noticed the absence of the other.

An opportunity was afforded me to see that the authoress Hahn-Hahn had endowed all her heroines likewise with the most genuine hands and fingers *à la* Countess Hahn-Hahn. The Countess related with much glee a very droll caricature upon the authoress of "Faustine:"—a crowing cock (*Hahn*) with a curly female head!—and condescended to illustrate to us the spread-out, common cock-feet by her own hands upon the table cover. Truly the smallest, whitest hands, and most delicate little fingers

I ever saw. One almost feared that these tiny little things would snap under the burden of a tea-cup.

The Countess talked, with an agreeable voice, in the purest North German dialect, with grace and wit, of her many travels and her distinguished and celebrated acquaintances. She even confided to us that in Dresden she had at last succeeded in obtaining good, pure cow's milk, which was so beneficial to her delicate frame, and that on account of her health she only used the best and most expensive beech-wood for heating her rooms. In short, her dearly beloved, precious, highly aristocratic *I* hovered over the æsthetic tea-table as goddess of fashion, wisdom, and coxcombry the whole evening.

Herr von Bistram was then a man of 40, of elegant and aristocratic appearance, tall and well-made, and upon all the promenades, in the theatre, and in company, the shadow and the echo of Countess Ida—*her serviteur très-humble.* However, he was held not to be a wit. In a dedication of one of her novels the authoress thanks him, saying: "When everybody forsook the sufferer you remained faithful to me, and nursed me while sacrificing your own comfort." But would she sacrifice to him her celebrated and piquant authoress name: Ida, Gräfin Hahn-Hahn? No, the Countess' thoughts could never be so plebeian as that.

And but seven years after that, the *rôle* of Faustine and of *Madame la Comtesse blasée* in society was played out. Herr von Bistram-Andlau was dead. The Countess Ida, who had once sung:

> " Ich lass ihn ewig nicht!
> Im Himmel selbst ohn' ihn kein Glück!
> Das ist mein Trost, mein Hoffnungs blick!"

now wrote with much resignation: "It is all the same to me whether I speak to a jack starling or to a man." The aging priestess of free love became a Roman Catholic, and entered a cloister.

What a contrast to Countess Hahn-Hahn was Henriette Paalzow, the authoress of "Godwie Castle and St. Roche!" I made her acquaintance during my starring-engagement at Warmbrunn, in 1841. Count Enno Schaffgotsch, the amiable brother of the possessor of Warmbrunn, introduced us to each other upon the promenade.

Henriette Paalzow was even then a complete invalid, and altogether paralysed. Her brother, royal limner, Professor Wach, pushed her forward in a rolling chair. A touching, self-sacrificing affection united brother and sister, which death alone could sever.

They were noble and pleasing, and truly aristocratic in their appearance—Wach still a handsome man, with a well-made figure and a highly spiritual, genial face, and in his whole bearing exhibiting a noble character. He had gone through the campaign by the side of Prince Wilhelm, who had continued his friend for the rest of his life.

Henriette, quite spiritualized and transfigured by her severe bodily suffering, appeared more like an ethereal being from the other world. When, at her request, I visited her and read out to her Hebel's "Haberchörnli":

"Und I merk, mi zit isch us!" (And I feel my time is up.) she tenderly pressed her brother's hand with a genial smile.

Henriette Paalzow had the finest manners—but she was somewhat solemn. She was the intimate friend of Princess Wilhelm, who had long been taken for the authoress of "Godwie Castle."

I met the brother and sister again in Dresden on their return journey from Warmbrunn.

In spite of all her geniality, Henriette Paalzow wrote about the novels of Countess Hahn-Hahn: "Well, I do declare, those books are lewd! The authoress has wit, but no character! Experience, observation on the filthiest ground; volubility and smartness of style, but want of thoroughness of thought, half truths and imperfect views."

Among the younger authors in Dresden Julius Mosen was my favourite. I made his acquaintance at a ball given by the amiable lithographer, Hofrath Franz Hanfstängl, in winter, 1838. The latter was just then publishing my picture as "Donna Diana," painted by the most famous portrait-painter of Dresden, Professor l'Allemand, and was making a name and fortune for himself at the time by the publication of his much admired lithographs of the masterpieces of the Dresden Gallery.

Hofrath Hanfstängl and his wife, who was beautiful, young, and graceful, had one of the most pleasing and hospitable houses in Dresden. All that the Elbe-Florence possessed of brilliant youth and beauty, of amiable wits and artists, and of interesting strangers was sure to be present at these most pleasant Dresden balls. With what delight did not I dance there—also with the young Prince Ernst of Koburg, the now reigning Duke. The Prince was making a somewhat lengthy stay in Dresden at that time for the sake of his education. He was of handsome and engaging appearance; he did not merely move in the circles of the Court and aristocracy, but with an amiable tact and affability also in the society of the higher middle-class. Prince Ernst was my most frequent partner at the balls in Hanfstängl's house. We talked about our first meeting in the Rosenau, where I had romped about in the park with little Princes Ernst and Albert, and where . . . no, of my portentous meeting there with his uncle, Prince Leopold, we spoke not, but I read it in Prince Ernst's eyes, which were even then very susceptible to female beauty, that he knew about it, and was now, while he danced with me, thinking of it.

When the reigning Duke Ernst, the Prince's father, came to Dresden on a visit to the Royal

Court he never omitted to ask for a piece at the theatre in which I played. After the excellent representation of the "Chévalier St. George" the Duke even came to the stage to express to me his admiration and to talk of the old time in Koburg. How much was there that each of us did not care to talk about!

But let us return to that gay ball in the winter of 1838 at Hanfstängl's. Emil Devrient and I were the last guests to arrive, for we had previously to play comedy in "Noch ist es Zeit." When the handsome, seductive "first lover" of the stage entered the ball-room a whisper of gratified expectation passed through the ranks of the ladies. Emil Devrient has been much loved in his life, but I scarcely believe that his vain, selfish heart was capable of returning the affection even once.

My interest was immediately awakened by a dancer with an expressive face of a darkish southern complexion, flashing eyes, and very active creole features, who whirled the graceful hostess about the room with so much fire that his dark locks stood on end. It was the author of "Nussbaum," of the "Blaue Blume," and of the song of "Ritter Wahn," Julius Mosen, at that time 35 years old, and practising as an advocate in Dresden.

He got himself introduced to me, and we danced much, but talked still more together. I soon felt uncommonly drawn towards the poet on account of his rare combination of wit, mind, and enthusiasm for his poetical tasks, as well as his touching modesty. Mosen told me that he would presently send in a new tragedy to the intendant, entitled " Die Bräute von Florenz," in which he had written the hero for Emil Devrient and the " brides " (Bräute) for Fräulein Berg and me. " But you," he added, smiling, " will unfortunately have to die of poison!" I promised gaily that I should execute that in the most touching and acceptable way. We parted that evening like two good old acquaintances, for, in spite of all the restlessness and passionateness of his character, the poet had something in him that awakened confidence, and from his words and features there shone forth a noble, childlike, cheerful heart.

Mosen had given up attending Tieck's reading evenings long ago. He was one more of those who had forfeited Tieck's favour. Once he said to me: " Tieck is a great poet, but he has no heart. Name to me a single instance of a young poetical talent to whom he has reached a helping hand; nay, whom he would even suffer beside himself! He is the greatest egotist I know, surrounded by his prejudices, as one might say, in a net. I, too, have honestly tried to sit at his feet as his disciple, to learn from him and to look up to him with admiration. But I am not blind, and not a heartless speaking-machine, no automaton like Countess Finkenstein, who, just as Tieck desires to make her go, dances and weeps and laughs, and says 'yes' and 'no.' I can and will not speak against my conviction; therefore I have avoided the corner-house at the Altmarkt, richer by a bitter experience."

The bond of friendship between Julius Mosen and me was tied more tightly still by our mutual admiration for the Grand Duchess Cäcilie of Oldenburg. I had often to relate to the poet my reminiscences of the beautiful and lovable princess, with whom I, when a child, had danced so gaily in Karlsruhe, when she was still Princess Cäcilie of Sweden.

Julius Mosen had come into nearer contact with Grand Duchess Cäcilie during a sojourn in a sea-bathing place; he had done homage to her in lofty songs and dictated his poems to her. The Princess had promised him an appointment as dramaturg in Oldenburg as soon as it could be arranged.

Soon after that ball at Hanfstängl's I was to see Cäcilie of Sweden again after an interval of 14 years. When I performed in Bremen in April, 1838, her lady-in-waiting, Frau von Scharnhorst, invited me, in the Princess' name, to a series of performances in Oldenburg, writing at the same time: "Our theatre is but small and cannot offer brilliant fees for starring performances; but the Grand Duchess hopes that the artiste would like to come to her old early partner Cäcilie."

And did not I like it! What a meeting was that

between Princess and artiste! The Grand Duchess Cäcilie was a lady of nobly beautiful, royal appearance, but hearty and friendly as in the bygone bright days of our childhood. Of these she plainly told the Grand Duke, whom she called, in the style of the middle-class, simply "mein Mann," and who was considerably older than she. He spoke to me with much discernment and wit concerning my "Donna Diana."

Two years after this I gladly accepted a new invitation for a somewhat more lengthy engagement in Oldenburg. "Marie Stuart" was performed before a bumper house, even the orchestra being seated for the audience, something quite unheard of in the small residential town. Both living and acting were pleasant in Oldenburg. I was delighted by a good nicely-rounded *ensemble*. The actors held together in harmony like a great family. Herr von Starkloff was an intellectual and feeling intendant, well acquainted with men and art. He was, however, still more a kind patron of men and art. He was sincerely devoted to the Court and his theatre; for the actors he cared like a father. He had but very limited means at his disposal, but as no costly opera and no ballet consumed the greatest part, he was able to do very much for the drama. What especially charmed me with the intendant was his superb humour; and, nevertheless, but a few years later he was destined to be the victim of a gloomy hour. He drowned himself. First, so fond of life, he suddenly became tired of existence like Raimund.

A lady playing the parts of "first lovers" was required in 1840, because the beautiful and talented Mad. Moltke had suddenly died. Half-joking, I had said to mother, more than once, "When my contract in Dresden is up we will transfer our residence to Oldenburg. I believe the Grand Duchess would be glad to have me here!"

And one day the Grand Duchess herself began to speak of it. It was after my "Marie Stuart" had been received with so much favour. The Grand Duchess spoke in a truly womanlike way about my conception of the part. Then she suddenly said —

"Could the Queen of Scots resolve to rule over the hearts of little Oldenburg, including mine, permanently?"

I replied, with emotion, that it had been a favourite cherished wish of mine for a long time to become a faithful subject of Cäcilie of Oldenburg.

"But our stage is small and not rich," she said, softly, as if embarrassed.

"The longer leave-of-absence, the cheaper rates of living here, will, I am sure, restore the equilibrium!" I said, firmly; and smiling under tears, I continued, "and if there should, indeed, be still a deficit in the weight of gold, the little Karlsruhe wood-nymph in the ivy wreath will lay into the balance her revering heart and the most cherished early recollections."

The Princess reached me her beautiful hand with heartiness. I kissed it, and promised to come at the end of four years when my contract in Dresden would have run out.

The Grand Duchess had taken a charming brooch from a casket. A bee, ingeniously worked in precious stones, sits on flowers with drops of diamonds. She handed it to me with the words, "May this little bee remind the artiste of this hour, and of the flowers that are awaiting her in Oldenburg!"

When, after my sixth performance, I called at the Castle at Oldenburg to take leave, I found the beautiful Princess downcast, weary, and sad. "I could almost envy you your gay, fresh artiste heart and your ever active life with its variegated stirring incidents!" she said, with a melancholy smile. And when I looked in astonishment at Cäcilie of Oldenburg, who was loved and doted upon by her husband and her people, she continued, more sadly still, to say: "I was reminded, as I am often, of my two dear little boys a little while ago, who were taken away from me. Then I feel, among all the splendour, so dreadfully poor and solitary. My husband, too, would so much like to have children."

Her farewell and "Auf Wiedersehn!" awaken a sad echo in my heart even to-day. . . .

. . . This was a favourite theme of conversation

between Julius Mosen, his young, witty wife, and myself. And we lived in the joyful hope of soon meeting again in Oldenburg, and working together in the cause of art under Cäcilie's eyes, for the poet had already received the call as dramaturg.

Then, at the end of January, 1884, Mosen comes to see me; he is deeply pale, and sobbing aloud, he says: "Our Grand Duchess Cäcilie has suddenly died."

Soon after Mosen went to Oldenburg as "dramaturg" with his young wife. I never played on that stage again. Cäcilie was no longer there to await me.

Julius Mosen was carried to the grave in Oldenburg after he had been fettered to the couch of pain for twenty years. But the spirit and the heart lived, glowed, worked divinely, free and pure in the chained Prometheus.

A few months before his death he sent me hearty greetings in remembrance of happy days in Dresden, through his faithful spouse and loving nurse. In October, 1867, Minna Mosen intimated to me the deliverance of her sufferer; and three years later the poor mother wept for her blooming heroic son, Erich Mosen, who had fallen in the battle of Mars la Tour!

In spite of the difference of age their wedlock turned out a happy one. In the meantime they remained in Dresden. The saloon of Ungher-Sabatier became the centre of the musical—indeed of the whole artiste life in Elbe-Florence, and the

Eldorado of all journeying virtuosos. Their large fortune permitted the amiable couple to display an absolutely astounding hospitality, to keep open house and open table as I had hitherto only found so constantly done in St. Petersburg.

I heard at the time that Karoline Ungher had been the object of the most passionate love of the unhappy poet Lenau, and that they did not get married, because another lady, although married, stepped between them and laid claim to prior rights on the heart of the poet. This was certainly fortunate for the gay, happy songstress. But whether it was not a misfortune for the poor poet, who can tell? Whether Karoline Ungher, if she, as the spouse of the restless man, could have prepared for him a sunny home, free from cares, have become his guardian angel and have saved the excited poet from the gloomy demons of his own heart who can tell? Who would presume to answer this question.

Since the spring of 1877 Karoline Ungher-Sabatier has slept in the beautiful little cemetery of San Miniato, the favourite little marble church of Michael Angelo, near Florence, where the great songstress spent the last years of her earthly existence.

One more artiste I have to mention before I bid adieu to Dresden, Richard Wagner. I had made his acquaintance during my first starring engagement in Magdeburg, where he held the post of bandmaster in the modest wandering troupe of Heinrich Bethmann—himself but modest then.

In the year 1841, Wagner came to Dresden to have his " Rienzi " performed. He had composed the opera in Paris, and for Paris—but the Parisians had rejected him and his work. Then the gifted Schröder-Devrient took an interest in the homeless " Rienzi," and she managed so that the opera of the unknown composer was first performed in Dresden. And it was indeed a brilliant evening. Madame Schröder-Devrient and Tischatschek, the most lovely tenor of his time, in the title-*rôles* did their utmost—and Richard Wagner's reputation was established. The composer was appointed second conductor at the Dresden opera, the chief post being held by Reissiger, successor to Karl Maria von Weber, and Richard Wagner was still modest enough at that period to accept a second post. Altogether, his whole conduct at that time gave no indication that in him there lay dormant a haughty conceit which, in the course of years, could rise to word-upsetting mania and senseless folly.

Years after, I found Richard Wagner again at the lake of Zürich, a conceited, arrogant swaggerer, who rewarded the most generous hospitality of a noble man by endeavouring to destroy the peace of his house.

* * * * * *

And thus the years came and went, and I liked them less and less, in daily life and on the stage. Only the first three years of my engagement in Dresden are among the happy—ay, the happiest years of my life. That was the sunny time in which my relations with the dramaturgical grand master and paternal friend, Ludwig Tieck, were still quite cloudless. But only too soon were there more and more chilling shadows between us.

I was no longer a child on the stage, and in life. I could not, and durst not, constantly sacrifice myself to the caprices of the dramaturg, and undertake parts, such as Lady Macbeth, that were unsuitable for me. I took up a more independent attitude towards Tieck, as well as in my opinion about the artistes that were in his black books. I seized more and more frequent opportunities to shirk his reading-desk, so that, many a week, I could only be once marked as one of the audience. In the corner house at the Altmarket, the sun of favour went down duller and duller every day. Tieck grew colder, more reserved, and the Countess more irritable and ready for the fray. And then, one day, a young female made her appearance from Grätz, and Tieck, Countess Finkenstein, and the host of her admirers never tired of singing the praises of this young, brilliant histrionic talent every day more loudly, in order to arouse in me the fear that the *débutante* would put me in the shade. Tieck taught her my most favourite parts with much zeal. The people began already to talk of this new favourite of the dramaturg, and that the old favourite had at last also fallen into disgrace. And then the Grätzer lady made her *début*, and made a miserable fiasco! She did not even speak correct German. This abortive plan to pain me, and to oust me from the favour of the Dresden people, only still more embittered the capricious Tieck against me. He who had been so much delighted when my gaiety brought a little sunshine into his melancholy study, when I called on several occasions, sent word that he was not in. Of course, I stopped my calls after that, and saw the "master" only during reading rehearsals. And thus the shades between us grew darker and longer. A scene, an altercation, never took place, nor indeed an open, honest rupture. I simply swelled the number of the many, many others that had fallen into disgrace.

I fear that Ludwig Tieck never was capable of a true, disinterested, unselfish friendship and love. When in February, 1837, he had lost his spouse, his glowing early love, and long-continued faithful and genial mate (she died of dropsy), and I placed a wreath on her coffin, speaking with tears in my eyes of the great loss he and we had suffered, Tieck indeed looked paler and graver, but he answered me with the greatest composure, and said —

"Her disease was incurable. She has suffered

much, and was glad to die. That makes *me* feel easy."

But this selfish heart was to be tried still more painfully. In the spring of 1841, there also died suddenly, after a short attack of measles, his eldest daughter, Dorothea, who had been at the same time his most faithful friend in life, and his ablest assistant in his labours. With her sank into the grave a deeply spiritual manifold existence. She had only lived for her father and his art-creations. With an acute understanding, and great diligence, she furnished many excellent translations for the Shakespeare of Tieck-Schlegel. She was at the same time deeply religious, true and open. She suffered privately from the mist of incense in which Countess Finkenstein and other blind admirers were wont to wrap the great romanticist, and to which the vain man only too readily submitted, till, even before his own otherwise so clear eyes, a mist would hang. She could venture with a firm hand to divide this mist from time to time, and to show to her beloved father the world and its forms, and many of his own weaknesses, in the clear light of day. Dorothea has guarded her father from many an act of folly and injustice.

Still but too often she experienced the grief of seeing the misty spirit of Countess Finkenstein prevail.

Years before this period, Dorothea Tieck, her

mother and sister Agnes, had become Roman Catholics, and it was said that when her engagement to Baron Malsburg, the Minister resident at Dresden to the Court of Hesse Kassel, had come to nought, she had intended to take the veil, but, for the sake of her father, had renounced the idea. Tieck himself is said to have joined the Church of Rome when in Italy. His whole religious and political nature was of a Catholic kind.

Dorothea, in spite of her great, penetrating understanding, did not feel happy. She too was glad to die. Theodor Hell described to me a touching scene at her death-bed. Her young sister Agnes sank down by the side of her bed during the last hour crying with sobs: "Dorothea, you must not leave me! how shall I live without you?" and Dorothea had, with a genial smile and radiant face, softly whispered to her: "Child, learn of me how to die!"

Under this blow Tieck nearly broke down. It afforded him little consolation this time that Dorothea likewise was glad to die. He locked himself up in his library, and would see nobody. There he sat musing, dumb, without tears.

And the cares of life also threatened to invade him. The fortune of the Countess was gone, and the old romanticist was tired of writing, of working, of earning money. The Countess complained of bad health, and grew almost totally blind. The circle of enthusiastic friends had become precariously thin during late years, and in front of the beloved reading-desk there were more empty than occupied seats now. Agnes thought of also taking her departure, in order to follow a beloved man, an architect, Gustav Alberti, to Silesia, as his spouse. It became even lonelier around the two old inhabitants of the enchanted castle.

Then fell like a sunbeam into their gloomy shadows a call from Friedrich Wilhelm IV. of Prussia to the romanticist: to come to Berlin at a salary of 3,000 thalers, to live during the summer months in the park of Sanssouci, and to gladden the King by his talent as reader.

Tieck's true friends in Dresden breathed freely once more. This royal favour was the best balm for the wounded heart of the father. And the old dramaturg himself was to experience a great delight in Berlin: the King had him prepare for the stage his Antigone, with Mendelssohn's music— and even his "Gestiefelter Kater" was performed. That had been a favourite wish of Tieck's for years.

What the old dramaturg had been for Dresden we only felt when he was gone. Dresden had lost in Tieck an attractive centre for her spiritual life. The interesting strangers and the most important pillars of native art and science no longer found in him the alluring will o' the wisp, who was so clever in making the different wits explode against each other in a brilliant display. And Dresden's stage, did it ever have a more brilliant time than under the reign of Ludwig Tieck? Though this sovereign often was capricious, obstinate, unjust, the life-spending rays of his genius and amiability were, nevertheless, predominant. And who ruled on the Dresden stage after Tieck's departure? At first an æsthetic tea-club of delicately strung, so-called lady-virtuosos, whose influence the intendant von Lüttichau could not evade.

Countess Finkenstein died in November, 1847, in Berlin, after having undergone a painful and dangerous operation of her eyes. It was said that she had brought on blindness by weeping. The old romanticist now stood there a lonely man in the bustling life of his native town. In 1850 he occupied the summer-residence in the park of Sanssouci, in the immediate neighbourhood of his royal friend, for the last time. There my dear old colleague from the gay time of my artistic activity in Dresden, Herr Porth, paid him a visit, and wrote to me about it: "I found our old dramaturg remarkably fresh in mind and as enchantingly amiable as he had been in his very best days in Dresden. He had become milder and juster in his judgment. I shall always keep the rare man in affectionate remembrance despite his many weaknesses and peculiarities. As often as I pass by the corner-house of the Altmarkt a kind of longing comes over me, a longing for the beautiful, enjoyable, and instructive hours I spent in it. At the time of the old dramaturg Dresden undoubtedly had its most glorious art-epoch."

This longing I fully endorse!

On the 28th of April, 1853, Ludwig Tieck died in Berlin, exactly eighty years old, weary and tired of life. "Lonely he stood in his time!"—as the poet sang once.

* * * * * *

Around me, too, it became more lonely, drearier, and sadder. My dear mother began to complain. She all of a sudden aged strikingly, and her mind became dull and weak. In Dresden I was unable to devote to her the necessary care and nursing, wherefore I found myself compelled to take the sufferer to Mannheim, into the house of my brother Karl. There, where the good soul had, so full of hopes and joy, witnessed my first starring tour nineteen years before, she sank rapidly. On the 10th March, 1842, a few hours before her departing this life, when she could no longer speak, she beckoned to us that she wanted to write, and, with her hand trembling, she wrote into her old little note-book in scarcely legible letters:

"Louis, you have never grieved me. . . . Lina, God cannot pardon England's sin—I pardon you everything and love you!"

And then the best, most self-sacrificing of mothers

had breathed her last. She was laid in the same cemetery where the murdered Kotzebue reposes. We placed at the head of her grave an antique tombstone, worked after a design from her own hand in her early years.

Entirely orphaned—a weak reed in the blast of life—I returned to Dresden to the boards of delusion to play comedy again. With what anxiety in my heart!

Together with me grieved the old parrot of Princess Charlotte, whom mother had so faithfully nursed for twelve years. As soon as the door opened, he looked round to see if the missed one would not enter. Disappointed he hung his head in sadness. He talked and whistled no more and did not find pleasure in dainties now.

Suddenly, one morning, when the warm sun of summer shone so brightly into the open window, he again whistled his favourite air, which he had learned from a shoemaker, who lived in our courtyard—Raimunds: "So leb' denn wohl, du stiller Haus!" (Farewell, farewell, thou quiet house!) When I returned home from the rehearsal Coco was dead. I missed the sagacious, faithful bird, too, in my loneliness.

Matters were made worse by all kinds of troubles, for which I felt all the less a match, as I now wanted the advice and assistance of my good mother, who knew the world, and was possessed of experience and energy.

A certain Mannstein, formerly a chorus-singer on our stage, but able with the pen, was going to write a brochure about his colleagues, but as payment in advance for his eulogy he asked for money through a Mr. Meyer, a little Jew of literary propensities, who sneaked in everywhere. I gave him ten Frd'ors. But soon after I received from Mannstein a very threatening letter, demanding more money, and making allusion to my English "still-life." I sent no more money. Thereupon appeared Mannstein's "gelbes Büchlein," in which my talent for the stage was flatly negatived, and where he had nothing else to eulogize in me than my "not ungraciously formed back of the neck"—on the other hand, he made many malicious allusions to Countess Montgomery and her two invisible English sons. I said something in a passionate way about extortion. This was reported to Mannstein, and he wanted to make use of it for a new act of extortion, in that he threatened he would bring an action for slander against me. I defied him, and undertook to prove the truth of my assertion, mentioning my colleagues, Emil Devrient and Koch, as witnesses that Mannstein had tried to extort money from them likewise! Emil Devrient declined to bear witness, not to compromise himself. Koch and I had to appear before the Court in the

Town Hall and give evidence. I gained the law-suit—but it caused me much annoyance.

The most modest of the money-demanding critics was Eduard Maria Oettinger. He only once borrowed from me thirty-six thalers, which, of course, I never saw again. On the other hand, Franz Wiest, a Viennese, who was editor of the "Rheinland," in Mainz, managed to relieve me of twelve Frd'ors during my starring performances there in December, 1841, for which sum I was well treated in the "Rheinland." Of course, the principal of the then theatrical extortionary press was Saphir, who demanded, however, not merely gold, but also love.

Now, neither on the stage nor in my profession had I much pleasure. I had to hear many a fine or rude hint that I was no longer young enough for this or that part. The place of "youthful lover" was given to the beautiful, fair, and talented Fräulein Bayer, afterwards Frau Brück, from Prague. I had to cede to her many of my most favourite parts, and all Dresden welcomed the new, brilliant star with the same jubilant joy with which they had once welcomed me.

That is the bitterest experience for a woman accustomed to adoration—twice bitter for an artiste of the boards once celebrated, now *passée*.

Then there appeared a comforter and spoke to my lonely aging heart of love, and I believed him but too readily.

Mr. Wilmoth was an elegant and clever man, with a beautiful head of brown curls like Lord Byron, and the most beautiful magnetic eyes. He, as the tutor (or governor) of a young rich lord, lived on a great footing in Dresden. He visited me every day, and wrote to me the most intellectual love letters. Already all Dresden, which then was a small, petty, gossiping town of 70,000 inhabitants, regarded us as an affianced pair . . . when I learned from a reliable source that Wilmoth was an unworthy man—a gambler by profession, who passed every night at the gaming club. " Last night he lost 100 Frd'ors there to the young Prussian Prince Kurakin, and as pledge of his debt of honour he has delivered to him your love-letters."

I thought that I should die with woe and shame. But I gathered up strength and courage enough to redeem those compromising love-letters by paying the debt of dishonour—and I never saw Wilmoth again.

But Dresden and the stage lost their charms for me still more by this latest and bitterest experience. Like one drowning I seized the first straw held out to me to save myself in a new life.

It was Prince Felix Lichnowsky who held out that straw to me! Could it be one that would save me?

CHAPTER VIII.

THE CURTAIN FALLS.

Prague—Festivities in Honour of Coronation of Kaiser Ferdinand I. as King of Bohemia—Prince Lichnowsky—A Well-merited Rebuff—A Princely Boor—The Festivities—The Cholera—Schweidnitz—Henriette Hanke—Ratibor—Adventures—Seven Years Later—Prince Lichnowsky Again—Hunted by the Mob—How are the Mighty Fallen—Landrath Wichura—A Proposal of Marriage—The Engagement Broken Off—Count Ladislas Plater—An Old Lover and a New Bond—The Countess Plater.

In August, 1836, director Stöger came to Dresden, being commissioned in Prague by the Bohemian States to invite Frau Schröder-Devrient, Emil Devrient, and me to co-operate in the festivities which the town of Prague was preparing for the coronation of Kaiser Ferdinand I. as King of Bohemia. Emil Devrient and I were to appear together six times, and to receive for each evening 150 florins. So we rolled along on our way to the many-towered coronation town on the Moldau, where I had finished a brilliant and gay engagement at the theatre but a twelvemonth ago.

But how unpleasant it was now in the noisy town that was crowded with men, and in the "Schwarze Rossle" that was crammed full to the roof, and in which for mother and myself only an uncomfortable room in the third storey had been reserved. And at the endless *table d'hote* there prevailed an uncomfortable crowding, and a deafening confusion. We were badly seated, and still worse served with meals. At dessert the gentlemen, mostly officers, began even to smoke their cigars.

Opposite me there sat Wilhelmine Schröder-Devrient between two famous composers—Spontini and Meyerbeer—in whose operas she was going to sing. Both were accompanied by their spouses. My cavalier was the one-eyed General Count Schlick, whose acquaintance I had made during my starring engagement in Brünn.

At the table there was a hum like in a beehive. Above all other voices, however, there was heard a remarkably shrill one, that of a young, exceedingly handsome officer. He was a genuine hero of a novel, with a beautiful head of dark, well-dressed hair, and dark eyes that whirled and glowed like fire-wheels; a pale, delicately-cut face with noble features, which were enhanced by a pert little moustache and a pretty Henri-quatre beard, though it had a somewhat coquettish appearance. And this Adonis in two-coloured cloth was strikingly free and easy in his manners. He fluttered up and down the whole table, talked here and laughed there, and before I could yet inquire about his name he was standing behind Frau Schröder-Devrient's chair with a cup of champagne in his hand. He laid his left hand unceremoniously on her beautiful bare shoulder and touched glasses with her, saying aloud : " Wilhelminchen, what we love! It was nice though, was it not?" At the same time his burning eyes were steadily fixed upon me whilst he whispered something in the ear of Schröder, whose cheeks were colouring with an angry blush. Reluctantly from her lips, accompanied by a movement of her hand, came the words over to where I sat : " Dear colleague, Prince Lichnowsky desires to be introduced to you." A nod on both sides, and the Prince stood behind my chair and whispered into my ears. He spoke so fast as to make one feel giddy—clever, *baroque,* ingenious, trivial, audacious, nay frivolous things in motley mixture, and always in a mocking tone—so that I cast reproachful looks over to Schröder-Devrient, implying: Why must you in this hum and buzz send me this will-o'-the-wisp into the bargain ? She shrugged her shoulders with undisguised displeasure. The Prince quickly took that up, and whispered into my ear so wicked a thing that I can here merely hint at it. " Wilhelminchen and I have had our little romance together too, but she is too old for me—is at least a dozen years older than I am, so that I was soon tired of her. I say, Wilhelminchen, you love me like your son, don't you?"

Frau Schröder sat there with white lips, shaking with wrath. I said: "My Prince, permit me to withdraw. I am not accustomed to such language."

Then he laughed scornfully, saying softly: "How—the artiste would master me—le preux chevalier? You reject me, Prince Felix Lichnowsky? What if I made you suffer for that? But no, be without fear, my angel. You please me. Au revoir, ma belle blonde." And onward he whirled.

I sat there quite stupefied. General von Schlick said, grumbling: "I wish I could warm the lout's ears! But such is the 'ton' among the aristocratic boobies of our days, who before they are twenty have ruined their health and fortune in profligate orgies."

I was, however, somewhat ill at ease to know whether the *preux chevalier* would make the *artiste* suffer for the rebuke which the *lady* was obliged to administer to him. All the more surprised was I therefore when, on the following day, Prince Felix Lichnowsky in all formality requested the honour to be allowed to pay his respects to mother and me.

We durst not refuse him. If so, I should for a certainty have been hissed off the stage. We therefore received the Prince with cold civility. But he appeared not to notice our reserve. On the contrary he, from the first, made himself quite at home with us by taking possession of *two* chairs, one upon which he sat, and a second upon which he placed his two feet. This, too, was the prevailing *bon ton* among the young fashionable lions of the day, because the fashionable ladies in their drawing-rooms permitted such manners. Thus Prince Felix Lichnowsky might be seen afterwards in the same boorish position on two chairs in the room of Countess Ida Hahn-Hahn. And I, a public actress, should have combated such familiarities? Impossible!

Thus the Prince *lay* opposite me *on a visit*, smoked his cigar, and in his benumbing, frivolous manner he talked on all sorts of subjects. The presence of my mother soon proved inconvenient to him, so he whispered to me very audibly: "Tell me, does she always sit here as your chaperon? Very unpleasant! I should have wished so much to have begun a little romantic intrigue with you as with Wilhelminchen. Oh, you should go raving with love, as so many, many have done before you!"

And in spite of our cold reserve he returned often and even oftener. It even proved futile for us to send word that we were engaged. The Prince simply pushed aside our man-servant and entered the room unannounced and laughing. Thus he once met at our apartments General von Schlick, when a nasty quarrel ensued between the two, which nearly led to a duel. The general said to me: "I wish that you had allowed me to fling this lout down the stairs."

Also, during the public festivities which we strangers attended, seated in reserved places, Lichnowsky always forced his way up to me, and paid his court to me in a very conspicuous, nay, compromising, manner.

The festivities passed over in a rather melancholy fashion, despite all the splendour displayed, for the unhappy King Ferdinand, with his huge head, and small imbecile eyes, and his boyish shyness, could not possibly arouse any sympathy; and poor angelic Queen Maria Anna was universally pitied for having by a wicked policy been fettered to this epileptic "Trottel."

During the coronation ceremony in the cathedral of St. Veit upon the Hradschin, King Ferdinand played a positively ridiculous *rôle*. Like a puppet, he was pushed and led by courtiers and his own spouse, and under the huge crown of Wenzel his thick head appeared still more shapeless. Lichnowsky was never tired of making his remarks, especially about the noble knights of Wenzel, who, in their silly costumes, looked indeed rather *baroque*.

In a trellised private pew of the dome the dethroned King Charles X., then eighty years old, and the Duchess d'Angoulême, and young Count de Bordeaux, called Henry V., looked at the coronation of the King of Bohemia, the same proud Bourbons whom I had seen in all their power and splendour but seven years before. What must have been their feelings?

Neither was serious disturbance wanting, which cast its bloody shadows upon the coronation ceremony. The butchers of Prague wanted to avail themselves of their old privilege to attend the coronation in their ancient suits of arms. Now when the guard of the Hradschin, who had no exceptional instructions for the butchers, would not allow these armed men to pass, and the butchers wanted to force an entrance, there arose a conflict, in which both sides had killed and wounded.

The most beautiful and interesting of all the feasts was the grand pageant of the peasantry outside the town upon the "Invaliden wiese," which gave the new King a many-coloured picture of his Bohemian land in its various national garbs and products.

Each of the sixteen districts of Bohemia had, moreover, fitted out its smartest rustic couple of sweethearts, who now executed dances on the common before their Majesties. They were supposed to be different national dances; but in their affectedness they reminded one more of the ballet in the opera. Indeed, I was told that they had been taught these dances for weeks previously by a master of the ballet in a room of the Hradschin.

The mob in the town celebrated its coronation orgies by the most revolting gluttony. Through the length of whole streets stood tables and benches decked with food for the hungry and thirsty. In different places the cooking and roasting was done, especially of geese, the favourite national dish of the Bohemians. But the thousands of roasted geese rarely reached a table. As soon as they were lifted off the fire, when but half-done, they were torn to pieces and swallowed by the fighting mob. The generous Bohemian beer flowed in pools. With ten thousand newly-burned earthenware coronation-pots in their hands, the noisy multitude, who were soon enough intoxicated, besieged the numberless drays, knocked out the bottom of the casks and rolled about in the pools of beer. Full of disgust we turned away.

And the grand performances in the theatre were for us actors literally a torment. Nobody took any interest in what was done on the stage. The audience, in festive dress, mingled and jabbered in a confused crowd. Much annoyed at this, Emil Devrient and I spun off our *rôles* in " Donna Diana," " Stille Wasser sind tief," " Entführung," by Jünger, in the " Letztes Mittel," " Strudelköpfchen," and " Verräther," by Holbein, as fast as we could. Wilhelmine Schröder was literally furious at this want of respect and consideration; and at many other things beside. She sang the part of Armand d'Orville in Meyerbeer's opera: " Die Kreuzritter in Egypten," and had beside her on the stage the beautiful young Jenny Lutzer, who afterwards became Franz Dingelstedt's wife; and before these fresh, sweet sympathetic tones the ruins of her voice must of necessity pale. And to see that Felix Lichnowsky neglected her, and paid conspicuous court to me, gnawed at her passionate heart.

So Lichnowsky once said at the open *table d'hôte* quite loudly : " The three most beautiful ladies at the coronation-festivities are undoubtedly the Empress-Queen Maria Anna, the Princess Schwarzenberg, and Karoline Bauer. Don't you think so too, Wilhelminchen ? "

Then one day the dismal cry of alarm rang through Prague : " The cholera has broken out! " Everybody fled; foremost among the fugitives were the Court. Also the hoary King Charles X. took flight with his family—to succumb soon after in Goertz to the same shocking disease that had driven them away from Prague. Emil Devrient and I wanted to abandon our last performance; but I was unable to resist the desperate prayers of Stöger. Thus I remained for two days more.

When Lichnowsky came to bid us good-bye he proposed to me, *à bout portant*, to correspond with him.

" What for ? " I inquired, astonished.

" To turn your head ! " he said, with the naïve arrogance peculiar to him. " I write in an enrapturing style, and am in correspondence with George Sand."

"And have you turned her head, too?" I laughed out, much amused. "No, my Prince, I require what little understanding I have very much indeed, and dare not allow my head to be turned."

So we parted amid the expiring noisy coronation festivities, and the first terror of the cholera-stricken Prague, to meet again seven years later.

It was in the blooming spring of 1843 that I followed the urgent invitations of the wandering theatrical "directrice," Emilie Faller, for a short engagement in Schweidnitz, not thinking that it would be my last tour.

Emilie Faller, in spite of her small decrepit figure, was possessed of much enterprise. Thus she presented herself to the people of Schweidnitz not merely as "Donna Diana" and "Maria Stuart" but also as the "Jungfrau von Orleans." My "Johanna," in the glittering armour of silver, even earned for me a torch-light procession. Burgomaster Berlin solemnly presented me with a laurel-wreath, and upon a cushion of white satin a printed address: "Dedicated with the highest esteem to the lofty dramatic artiste, Fräulein Karoline Bauer, on the occasion of her professional visit to Schweidnitz, as a token of our highest admiration and recognition, 22nd April, 1843."

On the day after the torch-procession I received a visit from "Frau Pastorin," Henriette Hanke from Jauer—the authoress of the "Perlen" and innumerable other novels. The good soul, I am sure, did not dream what torments I had suffered, fourteen years before, during the reading of her good honest stories, whilst "mein hoher Herr," as Käthchen says, sat opposite me and—drizzled.

Henriette Hanke, moreover, was an amiable, pleasant little woman of 58 years, the very picture of a country pastor's wife, with faithful eyes, a lively little tongue, and the most faultless tidiness in her own person. Just as bright and tidy was her house in Jauer, with its high front-gable, where I had to visit her on my return journey.

Regarding her literary activity she said to me: "I do not over-estimate my feeble powers; but it makes me happy to write for other people's pleasure and my own!" Afterwards, on her journey to her publisher in Hanover, she visited me in Dresden. She was certainly an excellent and enviably happy woman.

Now, whilst I chatted gaily with Henriette Hanke in the hotel at the market in Schweidnitz, a a very showily-dressed, self-sufficient, stately dame was ushered into the room, who introduced herself to me with the drollest volubility of tongue as Frau Nachtigall, the theatrical directrice from Ratibor, with a request that I would accept a short engagement there.

The whole—especially the names, Nachtigall and *Rrratiborrz*, trumpeted forth by the sweet "nightingale" with a genuine lieutenant's burr—awakened in me an irresistible laughter. To make amends for that I promised to come to Ratibor for a few performances, and joyfully the nightingale fluttered away. Thus I have played in Ratibor too, and have been present there at truly gigantic ladies' coffees, in charming gardens which were just then exhibiting their sweetest verdure of spring.

The stage, which had been erected in a very long, narrow hall, caused me at first to start a little. It was, indeed, a miserable piece of patchwork, and almost on the same level with the space for the audience. Add that upon this genuine gipsy stage I was to sing and dance Preciosa, but had to go a-begging first for the music, for Ratibor had no band, but an excellent orchestra of dilettanti.

Indeed, the whole arrangements of the wandering comedian craft attracted me, so that I gaily set out, together with director Nachtigall, to gracefully invite Justizrath Jonas, directrice of the orchestra of dilettanti, and himself a distinguished composer, and some other eminent violins and flutes and basses, to lend us their help at the performance of Preciosa. And they did so with much pleasure, so that they made this performance of Preciosa in Ratibor an especially memorable one for me. At the rehearsal, to which the wives and daughters of my musical dilettanti were admitted, there prevailed a very jolly tone, and I could not help smiling when I requested the Herr Justizrath to play the solo just a little more slowly or: "Herr Doctor, please make the flute join in a little faster!"—or: "Most honoured first fiddle"—("Herr Baron!"—somebody whipered to me)—"*pardon*! Herr Baron, please do not play the tremolo for the recitation quite so softly!"

And for the performance itself the delighted Nachtigall-pair had prepared quite brilliant surprises. Whilst Preciosa passed before the spectators upon a beautifully decked litter born on the shoulders of the gipsies, Viarda followed proudly mounted on a donkey, after whom two goats, two sheep, two large white poodles, which gipsy-boys led by red ribbons. "Where all love, Karl alone may not hate!" I said to myself, and quickly took upon my arm my charming little spaniel Kora . . . and Ratibor was much edified by it.

The following morning I received a very strange visit. A dame, somewhat elderly, long and thin like a May-pole, with long sandy cork-screw locks, a tiny little face covered with freckles, a gigantic nose, with a sky-blue shawl and green pompadour, glided in softly, curtseys, takes a deep breath, sighs, and says —

"Mein Fräulein, I saw last night your Preciosa, and I hope to see it again. You who play sweet love so beautifully, may be able to help me, save me from the tantalizing torments of my heart. I, too, love, but am unhappy in my love. I love your Ferdinand Heckscher, from Dresden. I have seen him play in Breslau sweet Hamlet and dear Mortimer; and since that time Ferdinand has been my only thought by day, and my dream by night."

"But do you not know that Heckscher has long been married?"

"Here exactly lies my ill luck. But seeing that I cannot marry him, I would, at least, love him—of course in all honour. I will join the stage, and at least be his Ophelia and his Maria; and you, mein Fräulein, must help me to achieve this, since you play so beautifully the most noble love."

I almost fear that in that hour I did not less beautifully practise the most noble plain speaking.

Another little adventure in Ratibor is prettier. I had played that evening young, smart Armand Richelieu in a coat of red velvet, embroidered with gold, and pretty breeches of white silk, and shoes with buckles. Well, next morning a very pretty little girl of about fourteen years of age enters my room, and blushing, stammering, sobbing, she manages to utter: "I should like to be an actress —your pupil—follow you everywhere, and be always with you. Your Armand Richelieu was too charming, and wherever I am I hear him sigh: 'Diana, I love thee!'"

Then a light dawned upon me. The poor child in the simplicity of her heart had, for the first time in her life, fallen deeply in love with my shining, amorous Armand Richelieu. Whether I cured the little one at that time of her mad love, I don't know. But should she read these lines, she, now perhaps herself a mother, a grandmother, will smile at a sweet delusion of her youthful heart, and remember kindly the seductive Armand who will then rest under the green turf.

I had heard a great deal in Ratibor of the mad Prince Felix Lichnowsky, who lived on his neighbouring country-seat, and furnished an abundant daily supply for the scandalmongers of the town. Six years before that time the Prince had quitted the Prussian service owing to debts and other irregularities, and had gone to Spain to evade his unhappy creditors, and to offer his sword to the pretender, Don Carlos; three years afterwards he had returned from Spain with the rank of Carlist Brigadier-General, and now he lived on his hermitage, near Ratibor, by no means as a pious hermit.

And then, one evening, shortly before the commencement of the "Letzter Waffengang," when I was already dressed in my costume, the Prince stood before me behind the scanty wings of the Ratibor stage, to renew his acquaintance with me.

He had aged, his chequered life not having passed over him without leaving a trace; but he was still the same elegant, arrogant libertine he was at Prague, of whom a contemporary says: " Prince Felix

Lichnowsky, like Prince Pückler, belongs to those dandies, roués, lions who attract the attention of the multitude at any cost by their contempt of men, their triviality, impudence, liaisons, horses, and duels ... a kind of modern Alcibiades, every day cutting the tail of another dog. ..."

Within the first five minutes I had learned from the Prince's mouth: "My friend Liszt has lately been living with me at my hermitage for several weeks, and we have led a very agreeable life together." Yes, indeed, in Ratibor people related the wildest stories of this pasha-life!

"My friend George Sand has sent me a famous Parisian cook, for the Silesian cookery kills body and mind. With my friend, the highly-intellectual Countess Hahn-Hahn, I am in very active correspondence."

"And it has turned the unhappy woman's head?" I interrupted, with a laugh.

Lichnowsky looked at me fixedly; then he said, with an aristocratic air of offended dignity —

"A—h! the artiste from Prague would like to give me a lesson!"

"Why does the Prince from Prague provoke it?" I replied, laughing.

The play, which was just then beginning, put a stop to this dangerous play of words.

During the *entr'acte* Lichnowsky, as if nothing whatever had happened between us, came to see me on the stage, and introduced to me his friend, "Landrath" Wichura, a portly gentleman. We chatted and laughed, I not dreaming then how portentous this new acquaintanceship would be for me, and that the Landrath would be for me the proverbial straw to save me from drowning.

After the performance I had to sup with the two gentlemen. Champagne went round. My good mother, my guardian angel, was, alas, gone!

For the following forenoon the Prince invited us to a *déjeûner á la fourchette* at his "hermitage," as he liked to call it. The Prince's law agent in Ratibor, a worthy old gentleman, and his spouse were to chaperon me; and in this company, to the amazement of Ratibor, we set out for the charming, princely country seat. Lichnowsky did the honours of the host in the most amiable way; Landrath Wichura courted me very conspicuously. We inspected the park which contained many fine trees; I tried the glorious 'grand' which Liszt had consecrated. George Sand's Parisian cook had done his work in a masterly style; but, unfortunately, served us with dishes as small as if for Liliputians, so that I, who always had a good appetite, asked for a German pancake as dessert only to satisfy my hunger.

But I was not to rise from table without having had a new skirmish with my Prince from Prague— the *preux chevalier*. The conversation turned about director Nachtigall, and suddenly Lichnowsky said, roughly —

"Just fancy, this Nachtigall had the impudence to call here and to invite my friend Liszt to play upon his miserable Ratibor stage. A Liszt, and my guest, to play in Ratibor, and with a Nachtigall —unheard of! You may imagine that I gave this Nachtigall a becoming answer."

The bite stuck in my mouth, and, trembling with indignation, I said, sharply —

"My Prince, am not I your guest, too? and do not I play in Ratibor, and with a Nachtigall? If your friend Liszt had done nothing worse here than play the piano in Ratibor, he would not have degraded himself in any way."

"Ah! the town-gossip of Ratibor has reached your ear, too, I see!" Lichnowsky said, with a scornful smile. "But, of course, we are not going to quarrel, but to see my smoking and dreaming cabinet."

The room was furnished quite in a Turkish style, with thick carpets, and swelling divans along the walls. Outside the windows nodded green branches. It really was a room for dreaming.

Only a number of pictures which adorned the walls did not altogether match the Turkish furniture; but, perhaps, were all the more suited to the Turkish dreams.

"All I once loved!" the Prince said, with an affected sigh.

In this gallery of beauties I recognized Lola Montez, Wilhelmine Schröder-Devrient, Charlotte von Hagn, Madame Pleyel, the Parisian pianoforte virtuoso . . .

"I only regret that your picture is wanting here, which L'Allemand is said to have painted so beautifully."

"You would augment this gallery by it? I must distinctly protest against it, my Prince. Have you the smallest title to do so?"

"Alas, no! Perhaps you would like *this* place?"

So saying, he conducted me into the library, where I found the portraits of Mars, Dorval, Rettich, and Sophie Schröder.

"Yes, my Prince; this place would honour me."

Laughing, the Prince related how he had once mystified the whole of the high nobility in the neighbourhood by inviting them "to the chase," but had not treated them to anything but the living hares and roes of his fields, no luncheon in the wood, no dinner in the castle; and how he had enjoyed seeing the ever-longing faces of his hungry guests. "At least, that was something new, and it continued to be the talk of the people for the whole winter!" the narrator concluded, triumphantly.

During the conversation, the thought recurred to me again and again: What a strange mixture of brilliant and trivial qualities, of chivalry and foppery, of a nobly grand and a frivolous character is united in this handsome man who is so richly endowed by nature! Two demons were constantly struggling for his possession. Which will conquer eventually—the good or the evil?

On our drive home, the Prince and Wichura accompanied us on horseback for a few miles, and the Landrath did not leave my side. But I had eyes only for the Prince, who, in enchanting beauty, and with most perfect horsemanship, like a genuine hero of romance, pranced along by the side of our carriage, and understood cheerfully and amiably how to talk of another happy meeting in *Silesia*. Why did he emphasize the word Silesia so peculiarly casting a knowing look and smile at the Landrath at the same time? On bidding me good-bye, he pressed my hand, and said, with the charm so peculiar to him : " Forget the *preux chevalier* and remember kindly the poor Silesian hermit!"

Even to-day I see the handsome man, audacious and haughty, in the freshness of frolicsome youth, galloping away, and at the bend of the road beckoning to me the last graceful farewell. . . . But another picture follows close in the wake of this. . . . It represents Prince Felix Lichnowsky, but five years later, now a member of the Frankfurt Parliament, on the 18th September, 1848, with the hoary General von Auerswald, fleeing and chased like a poor, frightened, pursued roe, prancing through the Bornheim heath, pelted with stones, and cursed by an inhuman mob whom the *preux chevalier* had so often provoked by his icy scorn and his most pronounced contempt from the tribune of the Paulskirche and from his horse. How timidly and fearfully the horsemen look behind them, having lost their way in the narrow alleys between the gardens, and are now unable to find an exit. But what keeps the *preux chevalier?* He *must* not leave his horse, and, like a cowardly spy, hide from the howling mob in the nook of a cellar. The proud knight *must* seek safety upon his horse, and he will find it; or, if the worst comes to the worst, he must defend his life to the last drop of his blood.

But the proud knight has, in this hour of danger, completely lost his head and heart. He hides in the dark cellar of a gardener's house, whilst General Auerswald, in the gown and cap of the gardener, seeks refuge in an attic.

But only a few minutes later the inhuman mob has spied out the hoary General, and dragged him down into the garden. He receives blows with sticks, sabres, rifles, and scythes.

"Have mercy! Is there no father of a family among you whom his innocent children await at home? I, too, have at home five young children, whose mother died but lately. Do not rob them of their father likewise."

In vain! Does the bloodthirsty hyæna know

mercy? Two bullets from the guns of the assassins lay low the unhappy man.

Past his lifeless form they drag the Prince Felix Lichnowsky. . . . Pale with terror, he implores them, saying: "Grant me my life, and I will do everything for the German people!"

"Too late! You should have thought of that sooner! . . . Look, your comrade has had his dessert already with the rifle. It is your turn now."

In the Bornheim Alley they tear his coat to shreds. Then his proud blood once more boils up, and, with the courage of despair, the Prince seeks to snatch the gun from his nearest assailant. That is the signal! Pierced by bullets he drops down. . . .

His friend, Prince Felix Hohenlohe, appears too late on the scene to save him. He may only prepare for him a quiet resting-place. In the rich country house of the banker, von Bethmann, Lichnowsky's bloody head reposes in the arms of a fair woman who had often held the winning seducer in loving embrace, whilst his arm, hacked and bruised by scythes, writes a last loving adieu to another lady, who, although fifteen years older than he, nevertheless understood how to attach him to her person—through her wit and her great . . . wealth. . . . He thanks the Duchess of Sagan for her love, and begs her to pay his debts of honour. . . A few hours later his brilliant, adventurous life is finished.

What confused, anxious thoughts, complaining

and accusing, must have passed through the head and heart of Felix Lichnowsky in that portentous hour!

When I read of his awful death in Switzerland, it reminded me with thrilling emotion of that cheerful parting scene in Silesia, five short years before.

* * * * * *

Landrath Wichura called on me in Ratibor next day, and soon in Dresden, in order to ask formally for my hand.

I did not love him, but I did not refuse him. I was longing for a deliverer from the Dresden engagement, which I felt daily more intolerable. Moreover, I liked the idea well enough, of being a Frau Landräthin, and a Gnädige Frau (my lady), in a country-seat of beautiful Silesia. So it came to pass that our wedding-day was fixed for March, 1844.

King Friedrich Wilhelm IV. had given a written permit to Landrath Wichura to marry an actress. The Landrath told me marvellous stories of the brilliant preparatious for our wedding, and for my festive reception upon our estate. Four-and-twenty countrymen had been newly clothed to meet me on horseback, in solemn procession before entering the policy. An experienced lady's maid had been engaged for the Gnädige Frau Landräthin (her ladyship). For the little dog Cora, the attentive bridegroom had had made a little tester-bed of green silk. The wedding was to take place in a fortnight, and Prince Felix Lichnowsky offered to be my best man. The latter had already successfully employed his influence with King Leopold of the Belgians, that the English pension that was allowed me should be capitalized and paid over to me.

Then all of a sudden I received a letter from the worthy hand of the Burgomaster of Ratibor, and proofs that my affianced was a wretch, who, moreover, was in constant dread of his creditors, and now hoped to save himself with my money. And I immediately broke off the engagement.

Landrath Wichura lost his place, the right to wear the Prussian cockade, and afterwards shot himself dead.

But what now? Was I humbly to petition the intendant for the renewal of my contract amidst the derisive laughter of my younger sister-artistes, and perhaps even under degrading conditions?

Never! Rather . . .

And a saving hand was held out to me. At that time there lived in Dresden Count Ladislas Plater, a Polish fugitive, who had loved me as early as fifteen years ago in Berlin. . . . It was an evil hour when I seized that hand confidingly and followed it out into life.

I have had to pay for it bitterly all my life. . . .

END OF THE MEMOIRS OF KAROLINE BAUER.

CHAPTER IX.

L'ENVOI.

The Countess Plater—History of the Count—Their Marriage—In Switzerland—The Count and Countess Settle at Kilchberg—The Villa Broelberg—An Ill-suited Pair—Meanness and Avarice—Thirty-three Years' Suffering—The Countess Takes Steps to Return to the Stage—No Vacancy—A "Polish Hell"—The Countess goes to Paris to Bury her Brother—A Drearier and a Gloomier Life—Influence of the Count over his Wife—A Fall Indeed—Death by Chloral—The End.

In the spring of 1844, Karoline Bauer broke off her engagement with the Silesian Landrath Wichura, and immediately tied a new bond with Count Ladislas Plater, who was just then living in Dresden, under police surveillance, he being a Polish refugee. The unfortunate woman let go the one deceitful straw, seizing the first ray of safety that came in sight, not dreaming that it was again a straw which condemned her to struggle on against drowning, without a chance of deliverance for a period of many cruel years.

Count Ladislas Plater was born in the year 1808, in Russian Lithuania, where his wealthy family held much landed property. During the years of 1827 and 1828, he stayed in Berlin, where he attended the college; here he paid his court to the young and beautiful actress, Karoline Bauer, with Polish passionateness. She, a year older than he, did not pay special attention to the green admirer, and indulged in fun together with her mother at his expense; because he always adored with empty hands, emphasized with so much self-love his *Moi*! *Moi*! and had outrageously red hair. She and her mother used to call the Polish *adorateur*: Our " Papelmätzken " (Our red *moi*).

Count Ladislas Plater experienced in Berlin the bitter disappointment of seeing his adored one giving the preference to the Russian Count Samoilow, who, as we have seen before, turned out to be an adventurer, *a valet de chambre*, of the name of Grimm, and of her eventually following the golden allurement of Prince Leopold of Koburg to come to England.

The poor forsaken red-haired *moi* now plunged into the Polish revolution, and, without having achieved special deeds of renown, after the fall of Warsaw, fled with his brother Cæsar to Paris. Their estates were confiscated by Russia, and only by stealth was their mother, who had remained behind in Lithuania, able to bring, little by little, a portion of her fortune across the border for her sons.

Count Cæsar Plater lived the life of a *bon vivant* in Paris; Ladislas, impelled by a burning ambition, rather chose the part of a Polish agitator, patriot, and martyr, and managed to trumpet about the Polish cause, not without a certain amount of skill and pertinacity, but always at other people's expense. Thus rich Polish emigrants gave the money for the journal "Le Polonais," which appeared in Paris under Count Ladislas Plater's name in 1833-36, and for a journey to England for the purpose of political agitation, on which occasion he gathered names for an address in favour of the restoration of the kingdom of Poland. Nay, in weak moments, he even dreamt he saw this Polish Royal Crown upon his own red head!

In France Count Ladislas Plater tied a tender bond with young Countess Felez. Then he saw in Dresden, in the beginning of 1844, after a separation of fifteen years, his early Berlin flame, Karoline Bauer; she still had the same bewitching influence as of old over him, and ousted from his heart Countess Felez.

And the seductive German actress, after her latest experiences with Landrath Wichura and her weariness of the theatre, was just in the most favourable mood for hearing him.

Did he promise to wed her? One morning Karoline Bauer and Count Ladislas Plater had disappeared from Dresden.

As he would have had difficulties with regard to his passport, being a Polish agitator and under police surveillance, Count Ladislas Plater travelled under the name and with the French passport of the Parisian merchant, Louis Bauer, together with Karoline, *viâ* Mannheim, where Captain Karl Bauer lived, to Paris, to her brother Louis. "The brothers raised no objection to it," Karoline writes. . . . Soon after, in the spring of 1844, the pair emerge in Switzerland, under the name of "Count and Countess Plater." There, according to an assertion of Count Plater, they were legally married somewhere, on the 17th April, 1844. Karoline Bauer has never dared to assert the same.

Madame la Comtesse de Felez lives this very day in Bordeaux, in great indigence, and writes to Count Ladislas Plater at Broëlberg one jeremiad epistle after the other: reminding him of his obligations towards his early love and their son. . . . In vain! Ladislas, once so loving, now often simply returns these inconvenient lamentations to Madame de Felez—though not without having read them. *Monsieur le Comte*, beside other secret arts, also practices the art of opening letters over steam, reading them, and if their contents do not please him, of sending them back to the post "to be returned," after having, of course, carefully closed them up again. I do not know what the criminal law in Switzerland says to that. If, in this wicked world, the Polish Royal Crown should come to nought, Monsieur le Comte Plater would be specially adapted for the post of a director of a

Doret post-office. May it be that Madame de Felez is the innocent cause why Karoline Bauer could not become a legitimate Countess Plater? Hints on the part of the departed make us suspect it.

After a short stay in Lucerne, and after the projected purchase of the Napoleonic Castle Arenenberg having come to nothing, Count and Countess Plater settled in Kilchberg, on the Lake of Zürich, permanently, in a villa charmingly situated on the slope of the hill. The villa received a white-red Polish flag and the name of "Broëlberg," because the family of the Platers which hailed from Westphalia was originally known by the name of "von dem Broële."

This beautiful green Broëlberg, with its delightful view over the lake of Zürich, and the glittering Alps of Glarus in the distance, was destined in the course of many dreary years to become more and more a "Qualberg" (mount of torment) to Karoline, as she never ceases mournfully to repeat.

Count Plater soon turned out a true Polish dictator, an obstinate, haughty tyrant, and a jealous Othello. Besides this, he endeavoured to establish in Switzerland a genuine Polish rule, and to treat the free Swiss as he once treated his Polish serfs: with horsewhip and kicks. As the Swiss did not stand that, the "tyrant of Broëlberg" never got altogether out of his rage. But he, the bigoted Catholic, especially hated the people of Zürich, who are Protestants and speak German; he hated them almost as much as his hereditary enemies, the Russians and the Germans, whom he liked to call *Messieurs pommes de terre.*

And Karoline Bauer was a German—a Protestant —and continued to be so till her end. But her master compelled her to always speak French with him, and to attend with him Catholic mass in Zürich. Count Plater did not learn—nor in his Polish arrogance, wish to learn—to speak German, in spite of a sojourn of nearly forty years in German Switzerland.

Karoline Bauer continued an artiste who clung with body and soul to the stage and its triumphs . . . but there must be no mention of that on the Broëlberg. If at any time her thirsty comedienne heart overflowed with recollections and longings for the stage, and for those old happy days of freedom and renown, she ever received the severe answer of the haughty aristocrat: " Karoline Bauer—la comedienne est morte."

What a melancholy existence: to be no longer the admired actress Karoline Bauer, nor to be able to call herself in honour *Madame la Comtesse de Broël-Plater,* and to have to carry on this distressful life for more than a generation in spiritual and bodily chains and fetters!

Nevertheless, Karoline Bauer's fate was to suffer more still from another curse which her master imposed upon her—under his literally incredible Polish avarice! It always cost her a terrible struggle when the Count was to furnish the necessary money for household expenses or when he was called upon to pay an account. . . . " He always wishes to thrash the people who want money from him—and whipping won't do in Switzerland as it does in Poland!" What torments are not expressed in this complaint of his unfortunate companion for life?

Once, when a Zürich lawyer presented to the Count an inconvenient bill-of-exchange, the petty tyrant of Broëlberg threatened him with a loaded revolver.

Under this awful stinginess Karoline Bauer suffered for thirty-three years most fearfully. As long as she herself was possessed of a centime she always paid for her lord, in order to keep the Count's establishment upon a tolerably decent footing and the name which she bore before the world free from petty debt summonses. During all those years she privately augmented the wages of the servants, because Broëlberg would otherwise have been without them. If a cow, a horse, or anything else was required in their household, and the " Herr Graf" insisted on paying only Polish prices, then Frau Graf secretly gave to the dealers the difference of the sum demanded. If the Count had to sell a calf, and had invited by letter all the butchers about the lake of Zürich to attend, and bargained with them for hours, then the Countess secretly put into the hands of the dealers the number of francs which her lord had extorted, and the unaristocratic bargain was finished. This cowardly management revenged itself dreadfully on the mistress of the Broëlberg—when her cash was finished. How often did Karoline Bauer, during the long years of her stay on the "hill of torment," seriously think of fleeing from it and her tyrant? As early as autumn of 1853 she takes serious steps to return to the stage. She writes to the Intendant von Lüttichau, cautiously inquiring whether a good friend of hers, an able actress, between forty and fifty, could find an engagement at the Royal Theatre in Dresden, to play the parts of matrons, in the line of Werdy.

Did Herr von Lüttichau see through this inquiry? He answers by return of post from Pillnitz, October 4th, 1853:—

"Honoured Countess!—It makes me very happy, after such a long interval, to receive the proof that you still think of me with affectionate attachment, and you may rest assured that I think of you very often indeed, and that the amiability which was so particularly your characteristic will never be forgotten by anyone who knows you. I still represent you in my mind with the same charms that encircled your whole interesting person—and, to speak candidly, you have as yet found no adequate successor with us! If the lady about whom you address me, were suited for the same line in which you excelled so greatly—if besides, she possesses at least in a measure your personal merits—I should at once engage her. But since it concerns the line of Werdy, in which Fräulein Berg is so excellent, there would be no vacancy here in that case. But I should wish to meet with a second Fräulein Bauer. I wish that you could help me in finding one! But unfortunately the chances are small!

"I am more than happy to hear of your proposed visit to Dresden during the winter. Indeed, I believe it would please you to assist at some of our performances. The tone of the opera has been greatly raised by Fräulein Jenny Ney. She is, without dispute, the greatest songstress of the world at the present day. She is, by a long way, superior to what Schröder-Devrient was in her best time, and also leaves Lind and Sontag far behind her. Tichatschek is unchanged as yet in vigour and voice, so that we are able to produce very creditable performances! In the drama Emil Devrient and Mad. Bayer-Bürk are our chief pillars. If Dawison should come our stage would, without doubt, occupy the foremost rank; as you may convince yourself personally if we have the great pleasure of seeing you among us. . . ."

Had the desired line been vacant in Dresden for

Karoline Bauer at that time, with what delight would " Frau Gräfin Plater " have left her tyrant and returned to the stage as Karoline Bauer—and probably not have died so wretchedly as she did upon her mount of torment. She did not see Dresden again, but for years she cherished the fond dream of re-entering the beloved boards—at last even in the line of "grandmothers."

Her sole consolation in her " Polish hell," that was growing even hotter, was her brother Louis, who came to see her in Switzerland every summer and supported his sister morally and pecuniarily in her hard task and heavy expenses. She writes : " As long as my brother lived I was not separated from Germany ; *he was genially German.* . . . Since his death I am forsaken in the spiritual domain— and have grown dull in mind. . . ." He managed her fortune, and as often as she required it he sent her money, articles of toilet—indeed, everything. It was her hope and consolation that she could find a refuge with him at any time if her misery should prove unbearable—and her lord knew it. He was afraid of the energetic Parisian " brother-in-law," and on his account he restrained himself considerably.

Once, in the spring of 1862, Karoline had packed all her trunks to leave Broëlberg for ever during the absence of her lord and to flee to her brother in Paris. . . . Then Louis telegraphed to her : " I have to go from home at present. Don't act rashly. Wait till I come!"

The following summer he had intended to visit his sister in Switzerland, and, if need be, take her away with him. Then on the 29th of July she receives a telegram from Paris. She opens it in the joyful expectation that it contains the announcement of the day of her brother's arrival, and, breaking down, she reads: "Votre frère n'est plus! Venez au plus vite!" An operation necessitated by the presence of stone had caused his death a few hours after the operation.

For the last time she leaves her mount of torment and hastens to Paris to bury her brother—and to sink her own last hopes for freedom and happiness into the same grave. Now, completely bowed down, she follows her lord back to her Swiss prison, the gates of which close more firmly than ever behind her. She was almost a prisoner, like that mysterious Countess in the castle at Eishausen, of which these memoirs give an account.

Louis Bauer had bequeathed all his fortune to his sister Karoline, and completely disinherited his brother Karl, now a half-pay Major, and his two daughters, not dreaming that this heritage would not turn out a blessing for his unhappy sister, but rather the contrary.

For now Count Ladislas Plater exercised an almost demoniacal influence over his mate for life, and he was not satisfied until Karoline Bauer had made over to him by a legal act her whole fortune on the 29th July, 1864.

And in what did this demoniacal power of this unloved, dreaded man consist, to whom fate had chained Karoline Bauer in an evil hour?

In the cruel little word: "Go, if you wish the world to know that you never were my legitimate wife!" Yes, indeed, a cruel, heartless word to address to a woman who once had been his hot, early flame, and who had sacrificed to him everything.

Through this word and the handing over to him of her whole fortune Karoline Bauer was now completely in the hands of Count Plater down to her grave. Though in her despair she often pulled her chain ever so often, she was unable to break this "unassailable bond." Indeed, whither could the aging woman, whom the hopeless struggle of years against her "tyrant" had completely bowed down, have turned her fleeing feet, nameless, dishonoured as she was, without a centime in her possession? Even a return to the stage was impossible. In after-years she would sometimes make up her mind to wander through the world reading her "Stage Reminiscences" in the style of Charles Dickens, and thus be free once more. More frequently still the thought came to her to put an end to her existence by suicide. But to accomplish even this she wanted the strength.

So the struggle for existence went on—and life on the mount of torment became drearier and gloomier from year to year. The avarice of the Count grew daily, and the financial distress of the mistress of Broëlberg became more and more burdensome, as she now wanted the plentiful assistance of her brother Louis. In her eternal trembling fear she had neither the courage nor the strength to explain to her lord that the prices for all means of living had trebled during the last 20 or 30 years, that coachman, footman, cook, groom expected higher wages in 1874 than what they received in 1844; and Count Plater found it much more convenient to carry on his Polish management as before, and not to have to double or treble the allowance for household expenses.

And this Polish avarice ruined poor Karoline Bauer unmercifully—physically and morally—*verdorben und gestorben.* . . .

As long as she had left a trinket or jewel that could be sold it went to Zürich to the jeweller or broker. At last she had left neither watch, nor ring, nor bracelet, and her toilet grew poorer and poorer. The only article of value she still possessed was a necklace of genuine pearls, a present from Prince Leopold of Coburg, but it the Count kept in safe custody.

And when she had nothing left belonging to her that she could sell, the unhappy woman sunk so low that she secretly, with the connivance of her servants, sold the property of her lord—the hay from off the loft, the home-grown wine from out of the cellar, the fruit from the garden, &c., &c. Even on her death-bed, a few days before her demise, she clandestinely sold wine for several hundred francs. . . . Moreover, she never got quit of the most pressing debts. She borrowed of her neighbours—nay, even from her charwoman—at high interest. After her death there were found to exist 2,500 francs of such debts. Did Count Plater pay them, I wonder?

Can a woman sink deeper still? Ay, alas! When all her resources for raising money were dried up Karoline Bauer, in her despair, had recourse to even worse means. She paid with promises, and gave assignations for payment after her death by her testament, although she knew but too well that she had no fortune now, and could therefore not bequeath anything. Such promissory notes she gave, "in God's name," for 500 francs to her coachman, her faithful female cook of many years' service, and others, thereby to bind them to her service year after year, despite the small wages they received. In this manner the unfortunate woman became a swindler.

On the 14th July, 1870, Karoline Bauer writes to Martin Perels, the editor of the "Deutsche Schaubühne," who took much pains to advance her interest by means of his own journal and other papers. . . . "I have yet a little secret for you in store. This morning I carried to the register-office of this parish a designation, a simple codicil: 'After my death my executors shall have to pay to Herr Martin Perels, Literateur, Berlin . . . francs. . . .' This move may prove to you how sorry I am to be unable to present anything to you *at present*, but how much I acknowledge your sympathy, your intellectual aid. . . . How ever truly and affectionately yours. . . ."

No such codicil was found.

* * * * * *

But—let us come to an end—to the most cheerless end of a human existence, once so richly adorned by God, greatly gifted, much celebrated and much envied—which was wrecked in vanity and selfishness from want of moral basis and moral strength, and under the harsh oppression of a Polish tyrant.

On the evening of the 18th of October, 1877, Karoline Bauer takes the little phial with chloral which stands in front of her bed, and which contains many a dose yet for sleepless nights, and empties it to the dregs. . . . She awoke no more. . . .

No loving heart said a prayer with her!—no loving hand closed her dim eyes! The Count's cow-boy made her funeral toilet for her.

Karoline Bauer, the Protestant, was buried with Roman Catholic rites in Rapperswyl. She, the bitterest hater of Poles, is entombed in the burial-vaults of the Counts of Plater, and her portrait hangs in the Polish museum. . . . As what?

Upon her tombstone stands: "Madame la Comtesse de Broël-Plater!"

FINIS.

www.ingramcontent.com/pod-product-compliance
Lightning Source LLC
Chambersburg PA
CBHW021207230426
43667CB00006B/592